Privatizing the Public University

Privatizing the Public University

Perspectives from across the Academy

Edited by
CHRISTOPHER C. MORPHEW
and
PETER D. ECKEL

The Johns Hopkins University Press
Baltimore

© 2009 The Johns Hopkins University Press
All rights reserved. Published 2009
Printed in the United States of America on acid-free paper

2   4   6   8   9   7   5   3   1

The Johns Hopkins University Press
2715 North Charles Street
Baltimore, Maryland 21218-4363
www.press.jhu.edu

Library of Congress Cataloging-in-Publication Data

Privatizing the public university : perspectives from across the academy / edited by
Christopher C. Morphew and Peter D. Eckel.
p. cm.
Includes bibliographical references and index.
ISBN 978-0-8018-9164-9 (hardcover : alk. paper)
1. Privatization in education—United States. 2. Public universities and colleges—United
States. I. Morphew, Christopher C. II. Eckel, Peter D.
LB2806.36.P756 2009
379.1′180973—dc22   2008035748

A catalog record for this book is available from the British Library.

*Special discounts are available for bulk purchases of this book. For more information, please
contact Special Sales at 410-516-6936 or specialsales@press.jhu.edu.*

The Johns Hopkins University Press uses environmentally friendly book materials,
including recycled text paper that is composed of at least 30 percent post-consumer
waste, whenever possible. All of our book papers are acid-free, and our
jackets and covers are printed on paper with recycled content.

CONTENTS

In the United States, the first decade of the twenty-first century is fast becoming notable for its promarket, antitax, small-government sentiment. As a result, public higher education faces turbulent times, marked by privatization. Through privatization, private funds replace public dollars, governance and oversight are loosened in favor of market forces, and competition among institutions reigns. It is a trend that is shaping higher education and garnering significant attention from policymakers, campus leaders, academics, and the media. Discussion about policy includes the extent to which and the rapidity with which public universities are becoming "privatized" (Eckel, Couturier, and Luu, 2005; Lyall and Sell, 2006; Yudof, 2002) even if some see the word as overly dramatic and, as a result, problematic (Breneman, 2005). Nevertheless, the term now has a firm place in the higher education lexicon.

In most contexts, privatization is defined as the retreat of public dollars from public universities and a corresponding increased reliance on private money and diverse revenue streams, increased competition for resources, and freedom from excessive public regulation (Eckel, Couturier, and Luu, 2005). Examining privatization from this vantage point, the contributors to this volume agree that revenue and governance factors privatize the institution, replacing historic public policy controls (and revenue streams) with those of the market. According to this rationale, institutions must compete vigorously in the economic marketplace (as well as in the marketplace of ideas) and are viewed by policymakers and university leaders alike as quasi-state agencies, if state related at all. These trends affect public-sector organizations broadly, often constituting new public management, or NPM. According to an NPM approach, the economic market becomes the dominant policy model. Deregulation, the creation of (quasi-)markets for public services, performance-based contracting, policies that foster competition among social agencies, the use of market incentives and levers, and the rise of performance indicators and auditing systems become the tools of public policy (Middlehurst, 2004; Mok and Lo, 2002;

Sporn, 2006). The NPM approach is not limited to the United States or other economically developed countries but is appearing worldwide. Broadly generating profound effects on the public sector, it has special connotations for higher education. Mala Singh, UNESCO vice president of the Regional Scientific Committee for Africa, summarizes the effects of NPM on higher education in South Africa and beyond:

- The requirement of higher education to demonstrate efficiency, effectiveness and value for money through business re-engineering drives: integration into public finance and accounting systems, external quality assurance, and other accountability frameworks.
- Declining investments of public funds, costs passed to students, and the requirement to "do more with less" (e.g., massification of access at existing or reduced levels of funding); pressure higher education to diversify funding, thus reducing the primary responsibility of the state for public higher education and allowing other funders to exert pressures.
- The dominance of managerial and entrepreneurial approaches results in running higher education institutions like income-generating business.
- The privatization of higher education encourages competition.
- The increasing development curriculum reforms intend to appeal to employers and students as "customers" and "clients."
- Shift of public and private funding from basic to applied research, increased emphasis on academic/industry links, and greater concern with issues of intellectual property rights and the prioritization of research for product development and commercialization (2001).

Although some experts decry the privatization of public higher education, the reaction has not been uniformly negative. Some accept the new ground rules and view their independence from the state as a way to gain the necessary flexibility to advance their institutions through financial competition and in ways they were unable to do before. This is the argument promoted by the presidents of the University of Virginia, Virginia Tech, and the College of William and Mary (Couturier, 2006), even as they attempt to leverage their institutions' positions within a state system that demonstrates many of the trends of privatization. Many university leaders, it would seem, see privatization as a logical and positive response to the reality of declining state funding.

Thus, no clear sentiments exist about privatization and what it might mean for higher education in the short and long term. Unfortunately, most of the debate about the issue is not deeply informed by theory. While privatization often finds its way into discussions of such matters in both the public policy arenas and on college campuses, it is the common, if not flippant, use of the term that demands a deeper understanding of how privatization (or the elements grouped under its label) shapes and reshapes higher education.

Drawing on Diverse Perspectives

This book seeks to address the complexity of privatization and the uncertain questions it raises. To understand this phenomenon with adequate detail and nuance, we call on diverse conceptual perspectives and theoretical frameworks from a range of fields and disciplines, including economics, public policy, political science, sociology, and organizational theory. Using the tools and lenses of their respective disciplines, the contributors independently examine what privatization might entail and theorize about what privatization might (or might not) mean for the higher education community. The strength of the book as a whole, therefore, is the sum of these parts: the diversity of disciplinary vantage points.

We emphasize that the contributors were chosen not because they represent a point of view on the subject of privatization but because each is a prominent higher education scholar with distinct disciplinary perspectives. Our goal is not a "fair and balanced" look at privatization but rather to examine, from these diverse perspectives, fundamental questions about the privatization of public higher education, including its assumptions and likely outcomes. The contributors were encouraged to be provocative, with several chapters pushing the envelope quite effectively. In the end, each contribution provides a justifiably critical view of privatization without advocating for or arguing against privatization.

No current book objectively examines the subject of privatization. Many authors on the subject stake out an ideological position early on (often that privatization is threatening public higher education) and then advocate from this position to its correlate conclusions. Other books on privatization provide an uncritical examination and offer readers road maps for the privatized future. Each of these approaches represents a normative perspective and a wan approach that often dilutes the authors' ability to ask (and to answer) critical questions about the phenomenon.

This edited volume is the result of a three-day conference called "The Privatization of the Public Research University," which took place at the Institute of Higher Education in Athens, Georgia, in September 2006. Organized by Christopher Morphew and the Institute of Higher Education and funded by the Office of the Provost at the University of Georgia, conference participants wrote about privatization from their disciplinary perspectives.

Organization of the Book

Eight chapters of this book address privatization of public higher education. The final chapter weaves together the diverse perspectives. As editors, we intentionally allowed contributors leeway in how to approach and write about the topic. We posed these broad questions:

- What is important about the privatization of the public research university?
- What does your discipline or field tell us about privatizing public universities?
- What do we already know about this phenomenon? What do we need to know?

In chapter 1, Stanley O. Ikenberry constructs a solid foundation for understanding privatization and where it came from, including a recent history of the privatization of the American public research university. Ikenberry's experience as a higher education scholar and as president both of the University of Illinois and the American Council on Education offers a unique perspective about privatization. As he points out, the era of his university presidency was also the time privatization trends prevalent at public research universities today were introduced. His commentary also introduces several topics covered in later chapters. For example, he asks what will be the effect on access and affordability and whether the "new bargain" between institutions and state governments that has resulted in privatization demands new governance schemes. In addition, he raises important questions about whether privatization represents a de facto or deliberate trend on the part of state governments.

In chapter 2, Michael K. McLendon and Christine G. Mokher provide a broader look at the formation of public policy that incorporates concepts grounded in political science, focusing on the origins of privatization. They argue that privatization can be seen as a product of multiple policy antecedents. In this sense, the privatization of public research universities can be understood as one part of a changing relationship between the states and public agencies and as outgrowths of the political and social contexts of the state and its corresponding political processes.

The privatization of research universities is not singularly a U.S. phenomenon, and much can be learned through a comparative lens. Many similar trends are under way in Europe, as illustrated by Carlo Salerno in chapter 8, although Europe has arguably moved more slowly toward privatizing its higher education systems. Salerno shows how European countries—owing to a shared sense that they have fallen behind American higher education—have been increasingly willing to implement market-based mechanisms that are now playing a considerable role in Europe's future plans for its higher education system. Salerno rightly points out the significant advantage the United States has long enjoyed as a result of its structure and how privatization is more congruent with the American approach and organization than with the historical model of higher education in Europe.

In chapter 3, political scientist Robert C. Lowry asks why we have public universities. Seeking an answer to this fundamental question through an analysis of the costs and benefits of such institutions, Lowry discusses the notion of public universities as "equilibrium institutions" and questions whether they still play the same role in balancing public and private concerns for how higher education should and can be delivered. His chapter provides an innovative means of examining questions that are at the core of the privatization debate but often ignored as decision makers focus on the symptoms, rather than the causes, of privatization.

Robert Toutkoushian (chapter 4) provides a dispassionate investigation into state support for public higher education. From his perspective as an economist, Toutkoushian highlights how privatization is perceived differently in universities, depending on the elasticity or inelasticity of their supply curve (i.e., their level of selectivity). He demonstrates why privatization might be embraced by some public universities while feared by others and explains how an economist might answer some of the key questions associated with privatization. Much of the complexity he identifies exists because higher education does not follow traditional economic models. Virtually all universities—unlike businesses or most other service providers —charge *less* than their product costs and provide a subsidy for those who enroll. This financial reality has an enormous effect on the privatization debate.

In chapter 5, the editors adapt an organizational framework of "garbage can" decision-making theory to explore the prospective implications of privatization. Garbage can theory proposes that decision making in organizations such as colleges and universities is most likely influenced by mechanisms that appear haphazard on the surface but follow a logical pattern, rather than relying on an arranged marriage between problem and solution. We predict how privatization is likely to affect decision making at privatized public research universities, and the analysis suggests that privatization is likely to produce more, rather than less, of the kind of organizational behavior that already causes skittishness in higher education's critics.

If public universities are to be privatized in some form, their governance may require different structures and policies. In chapter 6, Gabriel Kaplan draws on a range of disciplines to explore the need for new governance structures in a privatized higher education environment and reiterates that we know very little about what privatized institutions may need in terms of leadership. Kaplan walks the reader through several different governance scenarios and discusses the benefits of both substantial and light state oversight.

Public universities are not the only public institutions that are privatizing. As

Mark Stater notes in chapter 7, many lessons can be learned about privatizating formerly public agencies through research about the experiences and outcomes associated with privatization in the United States and abroad. Some lessons are clear, while others are more nuanced. For example, Stater's analysis indicates that privatization has produced greater service and outcome inequities in formerly public agencies. However, although competition in several privatized sectors has produced greater efficiencies and correspondingly lower prices, it is not clear that these results are found in higher education.

In chapter 9, we draw insights and lessons from across the text and identify common insights, alternative arguments, and common ground. On the basis of the previous rich discussions, we speculate on implications for higher education and outline a set of questions for the next generation of scholars to address.

These thoughtful contributions yield a comprehensive, robust, and very different look at privatization in higher education that brings larger policy and organizational realities to life.

As editors, we would like to thank the contributors to this volume. Without their willingness to share their ways of thinking with others and their willingness to answer questions from outside their fields (and, more important, from the editors), this volume would not have been possible. In the end, this book and its original conference was an exercise in translating different languages, each talking about the same topic. A thank-you goes to Ashleigh McKown of the Johns Hopkins University Press for her support and encouragement. Thanks also to Micki Waldrop at the Institute for Higher Education at the University of Georgia for her help in preparing the manuscript and for her willingness to advocate for *The Chicago Manual of Style*. A final note of thanks must go to the Office of the Provost at the University of Georgia for supporting the original conference and to the American Council on Education for its interest in the changing relationship between states and their institutions.

REFERENCES

Breneman, David. 2005. Entrepreneurship in Higher Education. In *Arenas of Entrepreneurship: Where Nonprofit and For-Profit Institutions Compete*, ed. Brian Pusser, 3–10. New Directions for Higher Education Report 129. San Francisco: Jossey-Bass.

Couturier, Lara. 2006. *Checks and Balances at Work: The Restructuring of Virginia's Public Higher Education System*. San Jose, CA: National Center for Public Policy and Higher Education.

Eckel, Peter D., Lara Couturier, and Dao T. Luu. 2005. Peering around the Bend: The

Leadership Challenges of Privatization, Accountability, and Market-Based State Policy. Paper 4 in The Changing Relationship between States and Their Institutions Series. American Council on Education, Washington, DC.

Lyall, Katherine C., and Kathleen R. Sell. 2005. *The True Genius of America at Risk: Are We Losing Our Public Universities to de Facto Privatization?* Westport, CT: Praeger.

Middlehurst, Robin. 2004. Changing International Governance: A Discussion of Leadership Roles and Management Structures in U.K. Universities. *Higher Education Quarterly* 58 (4): 258–79.

Mok, Joshua K. H., and Eric H. C. Lo. 2002. Marketization and the Changing Governance in Higher Education: A Comparative Study. *Higher Education Management and Policy* 14 (1): 51–82.

Singh, Mala. 2001. Reinserting the Public Good in Higher Education Transformation. *Kagisano*, CHE Higher Education Discussion Series No. 1.

Sporn, Barbara. 2006. Governance and Administration: Organizational and Structural Trends. In *International Handbook of Higher Education*, ed. James J. F. Forest and Philip G. Altbach, 141–58. Dordrecht, the Netherlands: Springer.

Yudof, M. Janary 11, 2002. Is the Public Research University Dead? *Chronicle of Higher Education*, B24.

Privatizing the Public University

CHAPTER ONE

Privatizing the Public Research University

• ℰℐ •

STANLEY O. IKENBERRY

As many ponder the future of public research universities, the link between higher education and prospects for individual and societal success has never been clearer. For the individual, higher learning means a brighter personal future: greater lifetime earnings, better career opportunities, higher quality of life, and less vulnerability to unemployment, disease, imprisonment, marginalization, and worse.

For societies—governments, communities, and regions around the world—the twenty-first-century benefits of higher education are equally compelling: economic competitiveness, adaptability, social stability, reduced dependency, a strengthened tax base, even improved national security and defense. For both individuals and societies, the gap between those who have and those who do not grows each day and is defined largely in terms of education.

It should come as no surprise that demand for higher education is escalating in the United States and around the world. That the will and capacity of governments —particularly in the United States—to support higher education appears to have weakened at precisely this moment is a gnawing, annoying frustration.

The consequences of this weakened will are felt most by public higher education and give rise to a number of questions: What is the future of the public research university and public higher education in general, including the community college? Precisely how is the relationship between the states and higher education changing and how should it change? De facto or deliberate, are we moving toward the privatization of public higher education in the United States as some suggest, and if so, what does this portend?

When did the shift toward privatization begin? Aims McGuinness, senior associate at the National Center for Higher Education Management Systems, has argued that the changed relationship between public universities and the states actually began in the 1980s (McGuinness, 1999, 198–225). It was during this period that higher education's revenue stream diversified with increased federal and corporate support and greater reliance on tuition revenue while state funding of the core capacity of universities (undergraduate and graduate education, for example) weakened. The historic mission of public research universities—teaching, research, and public service—has grown to include economic development, major health care operations, athletic and entertainment programs, and many other interests. As the revenue stream has become varied and as the relative role of the state has diminished, the relationship of public universities with state governments and the public at large has became more problematic. Cuts in state support in times of economic recession have come quicker and deeper, and recovery has been slower and more challenging.

Tuition revenues have moved from a small fraction of public university budgets to a significant revenue source over which most public universities have a modicum of control. Beyond tuition, revenue from gifts, grants, and contracts is greater, along with income from patents and copyrights. The culture of the public research university has become more entrepreneurial, causing Derek Bok to ask, "Is everything in a university for sale if the price is right?" (Bok, 2003, x).

The combined effect of these forces has been to move the character of public research universities in the direction of what some have called privatization, although the precise definition of the term remains elusive—as demonstrated to some extent in the chapters that follow. At times, the language of privatization sounds like a yelp of pain and protest from university presidents struggling with weakening support from state government. At other times, talk of privatization sounds less like a threat than an opportunity, the aim of smart negotiations, striking the ultimate bargain in which the inevitability of less state support is traded for a promise of greater autonomy.

Whatever the definition, at issue is the future of public higher education and the future of America. Jim Duderstadt put it well when he mused, "Today one might even conclude that America's great experiment of building world-class public universities supported primarily by tax dollars has come to an end. It could be that the concept of a world-class, comprehensive state university might not be viable over the longer term" (Duderstadt, 2000, 313).

The public's voice about privatization has been largely silent, except for anguished outrage over spiraling tuition at public universities. Policy professionals such as Pat Callan at the National Center for Public Policy and Higher Education have talked of the "privatization" of public higher education as a threat to access, a betrayal of the public trust, and on its face suggestive of weak leadership by presidents and boards. Still, in state after state, the drift toward disinvestment in public higher education continues unabated.

In their insightful book *Academic Capitalism and the New Economy,* Sheila Slaughter and Gary Rhoades discuss the displacement of academic values and the public good by commercialization and academic capitalism—patents, copyrights, athletics, and an altered campus culture. "In the new economy," they argue, "market and market-like activities are foreground, while the state and the many subsidies it provides are background" (Slaughter and Rhoades, 2004, 4).

In an essay on the modern research university, Don Langenberg, former chancellor of the University of Maryland, quoted Goethe: "Genius develops in quiet places, character out in the full current of human life." Langenberg observed that "genius creates wondrous things. Yet genius alone is not enough." Rather, Langenberg argued, it is in "*the full current of human life*" (emphasis added) that the research university's character is formed (Langenberg, 2006, 3).

The modern public university is well into the full current of human life. Its character is changing, but whether society should find that shift reassuring or worrisome is far from clear. The taproot of privatization in the minds of many is states' declining role in funding public higher education. Given the diminished will and capacity of states, what are the ramifications? Is there a better way for states, for example, to fund public research universities? Or as David Breneman has suggested, "Are the states and public higher education striking a new bargain?" (Breneman, 2004, 1–15).

An avenue that needs more exploration is transparency, or ways to make the link between state investment and societal outcomes more apparent. Traditionally, "block grants" have provided relatively unrestricted funding from states to public universities and have been regarded as the hallmark of good public policy. The downside to lump-sum state appropriations, however, is that, as the university becomes more complex in its mission and program, and funding sources become more varied, policymakers (and the public) find it difficult to connect decisions on state funding with the practical consequences for access, quality, affordability, and accountability on campus. At times, it seems that both universities and policymakers are not only comfortable with the ambiguity but welcome it. Institutions want the freedom to set priorities, and policymakers faced with tough decisions welcome protection from the voters. Still, those worried about privatization might ask, Is there a better way?

A quarter-century ago the worry in higher education circles was about the future of private higher education in the United States. Two policy answers emerged: (1) a vast increase in federal student aid and (2) a system of federal and state contracting for specific functions and services from private institutions. Increased federal funding for undergraduate education came indirectly through students, rather than directly to institutions. Today, as tuition in public universities rises and as missions and clients proliferate, should we expect to see a comparable policy shift in funding public universities?

Beyond funding policy, the pressures of privatization invite a fresh look at how public research universities are governed. One specific governance proposition deserves testing: Do public research universities require more diversified and decentralized governing boards?

Why diversification? Access by governing boards to a broader range of talent and perspective on the governing board is one obvious benefit. Most public university boards face an enormous range of issues, from hospitals to farms, from athletics to the arts, from undergraduate education to patent policy. Many public university governing boards tend to be relatively small and tend to have material "capacity gaps." A broader range of expertise, diversification of talent, and more variation in origin of appointment to the board could greatly strengthen governance and decision making at the upper levels of public research universities.

The changed funding base also invites a fresh look at university governance and control. States are no longer the sole or even the majority stakeholder. The interests of the "state"—governors, state legislators, and taxpayers—are now joined by those of students and parents who pay a much higher fraction of the costs, by alumni and donors who are wooed to play a larger role, and by federal agencies that pursue national interests and priorities at public research universities. The modern public university has no "single public interest"; instead, it has a host of interests and publics that range far beyond the traditional reach of state government.

A final governance issue requiring dialogue is the link between the governing board and the campus. Is it time for governance of major public research universities to move closer to the campus? For the last half of the twentieth century, statewide or mega-governing boards grew as higher education grew larger. California, New York, North Carolina, and Wisconsin serve as useful examples of huge state governance systems designed to guide massive state investment and enrollment growth during the 1960s.

Today's governance challenge has changed. Rather than adding revenues, states are fiscally constrained. The mega-boards that managed expansion reasonably well are now often impotent to guide retrenchment and set tuition and student aid policy in large heterogeneous systems. The connection between what goes on at the campus and what happens at the board table has become more tenuous. If the interests and priorities of the "public" are to have a stronger voice at public research universities, then ways need to be found to bring governance closer to the campus.

Beyond governance, and throughout the privatization dialogue, attention turns to the question of access. How important is it to sustain and enhance access to higher education, especially access to the public research university? Doug Bennett, the president of Earlham College, argues, "The single most important issue facing higher education today is the problem of access. Not enough Americans are completing a college education—often for financial reasons" (Bennett, 2006, B7). Among the access priorities, few are more threatened by the prospect of privatization than access for low-income, middle-income, and minority students. To what extent is access to public universities diminished by escalating tuition? What are the implications if the trends in tuition increases of the past twenty years continue for the next twenty? And what comfort can we find to suggest this is not likely to happen?

From the American public's standpoint, the issue may not be the future of the public research university but the future of access to it. The implications for individuals and for the society, for communities, for economic competitiveness, and for the American Dream, are profound. If privatization is a fact of life in twenty-first-century America—and it may be—what adaptation in public policy is needed?

To return to the beginning, what, precisely, do we mean by *privatization*, and what are the ramifications? Is privatization simply a shorthand description of the diminished will and capacity of state government, or does the concept suggest a broader, deeper transformation in the culture of public research universities and the society in which they function? Whatever the answer, to paraphrase John W. Gardner, what we have before us are breathtaking opportunities disguised as insoluble problems (Gardner, 1965).

Turning back the clock—restoring state support to earlier levels and pushing commercialization and academic capitalism outside the campus gate—is not likely to happen. If we better understand the world in which the contemporary public research university functions, the implications for individuals and society will become clearer and the policy options and alternatives will become more obvious. The ultimate question may be, How can the public research university swim in Goethe's "full current of human life," yet retain its true public essence?

REFERENCES

Bennett, Douglas C. 2006. Underinvesting in the Future. *Chronicle of Higher Education* 55 (2): B7.

Bok, Derek. 2003. *Universities in the Marketplace: The Commercialization of Higher Education.* Princeton, NJ: Princeton University Press.

Breneman, David W. 2004. Are the States and Public Higher Education Striking a New

Bargain? Public Policy Paper Series No. 04-02. Association of Governing Boards, Washington, DC.

Duderstadt, James J. 2000. *A University for the 21st Century*. Ann Arbor: University of Michigan Press.

Gardner, John W. Secretary of Health, Education, and Welfare Swearing in Speech, Washington, DC, July 27, 1965, www.pbs.org/johngardner/chapters/4.html.

Langenberg, Donald N. 2006. Research Universities in the Third Millennium: Genius with Character. In *Defining Values for Research and Technology: The Universities' Changing Role*, ed. William T. Greenough, Phillip J. McConnaughay, and Jay P. Kesan, 3–10. Lanham, MD: Rowman & Littlefield.

McGuinness, Aims C., Jr. 1999. The States and Higher Education. In *American Higher Education in the Twenty-First Century*, ed. Philip G. Altbach, Robert O. Berdahl, and Patricia J. Gumport, 198–225. Baltimore: Johns Hopkins University Press.

Slaughter, Sheila, and Gary Rhoades. 2004. *Academic Capitalism and the New Economy: Markets, State, and Higher Education*. Baltimore: Johns Hopkins University Press.

CHAPTER TWO

The Origins and Growth of State Policies That Privatize Public Higher Education

• ℰↃ •

MICHAEL K. MCLENDON AND CHRISTINE G. MOKHER

Privatization emerged as a major focus and a deep concern of many leading analysts and observers of public higher education at the turn of the twenty-first century (e.g., Ehrenberg 2005; Geiger, 2002; Hearn, 2003; Lyall and Sell, 2005; Morphew, 2007). Although little agreement exists over the parameters, scope, or magnitude of the privatization phenomenon in higher education, most treatments—whether analytical, anecdotal, or hortatory—have approached the topic through a fairly narrow lens, examining privatization at the level of the individual institution and focusing primarily on privatization's effects. These effects include those on campus mission, campus operations, patterns of revenue generation and expenditure, stratification among institutions, faculty work and professionalism, college access and affordability, or college student success. Rarely, however, have accounts focused comprehensively on privatization as a form of policy choice by state governments or on the factors underlying that choice.

In the context of state policy for higher education, what might privatization entail? Should it include public-private ownership distinctions, distinctions between public and private financing, monopoly versus competition distinctions, or the increasingly common provision of publicly funded services and activities by nongovernmental entities? We understand privatizing efforts in state policy for higher education as encompassing potentially a broad range of approaches, including (1) growing dependence on private sources of revenue to finance public higher education; (2) increasing reliance on market mechanisms with which to promote competition and through which to allocate higher education goods and services; and (3) diminishing direct control over the governance and management of campuses, both substantively and procedurally.

In this chapter, we employ a conceptual framework originating in political science and used increasingly in higher education studies to argue that state policies privatizing public higher education have grown in popularity, that they have taken a variety of forms consistent with the threefold approaches noted, and that they have been driven by a host of social, economic, and political factors occurring within individual states and arising between and among them. First, we discuss the context for state-policy privatization in postsecondary education by examining factors that we believe have helped shape policy climates conducive to privatization. Next, we identify and describe five policy trends in the states over the past 30 years that may be characterized as privatization initiatives. Finally, we review the accumulating empirical research on the origins and spread of each of the five policy initiatives. Because much of what has been written about state privatization is largely anecdotal, our purpose in this final section of the chapter is to distill what is known empirically about the antecedents of state-policy privatization.

The Contemporary Climate for State Policy Privatization in Postsecondary Education

Over the past three decades, the political and fiscal landscapes of American state government have undergone change in a number of important respects. These changes have created distinctively new policy climates for postsecondary education and helped lay the groundwork for many of the policy-privatizing measures we will discuss. We have identified five factors: (1) new structural constraints on the capacity of states to raise and spend public tax dollars, (2) shifts in the partisan complexion of state legislatures, (3) the advent of legally mandated term limits on state elected officials, (4) the rise of "education governors," and (5) the broader "reinventing government" movement.

A profound change in state government over the past three decades has been the limited growth in state revenues and new restrictions on taxing authority. State tax revenues have not kept pace with the increases in total personal income, particularly in states without a personal income tax, as consumption has shifted toward services and e-commerce. These types of expenditures are subject to few or no taxes, which reduces the level of resources available to the state (Boyd, 2002; Hovey, 1999). Since the wave of state tax revolts that began in the 1970s, states have had little success in boosting tax revenues, as the public has increasingly pressured elected officials to reduce or hold the line on taxes, and many states have introduced formal voter-imposed tax restrictions or limitations (Breneman and Finney, 1997; Hearn, Griswold, and Marine, 1996). Amid citizen interest in reducing the size of government, many states, such as California and Colorado, have adopted tax and expenditure limitations (TELs), which limit the growth of state expenditures relative to other indicators, such as the growth of state personal income. By 2005, 23 states had adopted TELs—many of these constitutionally imposed (Archibald and Feldman, 2006). In states where they exist, TELs have restricted state spending on all budget areas, which has had important implications for public universities, since higher education tends to be disproportionately cut during periods of fiscal duress (Archibald and Feldman, 2006; Delaney and Doyle, 2006). While state appropriations to higher education have become a smaller proportion of institutional revenues, public colleges and universities have faced increasing competition for scarce governmental funding, particularly among other budgetary areas such as K–12 education and health care.

During the same time, state legislatures witnessed considerable changes in their partisan composition. For example, in 1985 Republicans held the majority of seats in both chambers of the state legislature in only 11 states, but by 2005, the number of states with unified Republican control had nearly doubled to include 20 states. The share of statehouse seats controlled by Republicans also increased over this period. Analysts have thus begun to question whether the different perspectives that Democratic and Republican members have on many issues, such as the role and relative size of state government (Alt and Lowry, 2000; Barrilleaux, Holbrook, and Langer, 2002), might also influence legislators' behavior in the policy domain of higher education (Doyle, 2005; McLendon, Heller, and Young, 2005).

The advent of term limits for state elected officials also has produced a distinctively new set of challenges for America's legislative institutions. In 1990, voters approved citizen initiatives limiting the terms of legislators in California, Colorado, and Oklahoma, and by 2005, 15 states had limited legislators' terms. Term limits first took effect in 1996 when 26 House members and 4 senators became ineligible to run for reelection in Maine, and 22 members of the Assembly became ineligible for reelection in California (National Conference of State Legislatures, 2007). Legislative turnover rapidly multiplied over the years as legislators' terms were limited in more states. In 2006, 268 legislators reached their term limits, including 109 standing committee chairs (National Conference of State Legislatures, 2006). Although proponents believed that term limits would decrease political careerism and promote diversity within legislatures, evidence suggests that term limits have not accomplished many of these aims. Instead, they have produced greater numbers of inexperienced lawmakers, diminished organizational capacity, and polarized legislatures. Term limits appear also to have helped swing the balance of power in many states away from legislatures and toward governors' offices and the executive branch, particularly in the budget-making process (Carey, Niemi, and Powell, 2001; National Conference of State Legislatures, 2007). Although evidence of the effect of these institutional changes on state postsecondary education policy is sparse, some observers maintain that term limits may have helped suppress state higher education spending by facilitating the election of legislators who favor limited government and by removing legislative "patron saints" from office who had long championed higher education (Leubsdorf, 2006; Peterson and McLendon, 1998; Richardson et al., 1999).

Another significant change in state governments over the past several decades has been the rise of "education governors" who have played an increasingly important role in promoting education reform efforts. During the 1980s, the National Commission on Excellence in Education's report *A Nation at Risk* heightened concerns about the quality of public education. In an effort to address these concerns, Moe (2003, 177) notes that "every governor now wants to be the education governor." Relative to individual state legislators, governors have larger constituent bases and greater political responsibility for the state economy, which made them natural leaders for educational reform in the early 1980s. In the following decade, governors became even more powerful in the educational arena by increasing coalitions with the business community and important interest groups (Gittell and McKenna, 1999). With the help of these coalitions, governors focused on issues of standards, choice, and efficiency and played a pivotal role in introducing legislation on issues such as vouchers and state standards. In several states, governors have been identified as one of the most important actors in influencing higher education issues such as affirmative action, college affordability, and postsecondary governance reforms (Gittell and Kleiman, 2000; McLendon and Ness, 2003).

Finally, state governments have undergone structural and cultural changes that have fostered privatization in a larger movement known as "reinventing government" (Thompson and Riccucci, 1998, 231). In the 1980s and 1990s, the longstanding approach to providing public services through top-down bureaucracies began to crumble in the face of critiques alleging inadequate government performance, responsiveness, and accountability. In response to these critiques, government leaders began to turn toward reform ideas inspired by the private sector, such as corporate restructuring, in an effort to improve efficiency, effectiveness, and cost savings. Although different variants of public-sector reform were at work during this period, in general, critics called for decentralized government, flattened hierarchies, enhanced public entrepreneurship, and a greater emphasis on internal markets, organizational competitiveness, and the measurement of performance (McLendon, Deaton, and Hearn, 2007). As state governments pursued reform, four common themes evolved: (1) reducing administrative red tape, (2) paying greater attention to the bottom line, (3) decentralizing management structures, and (4) improving customer service. At the state level, common responses often involved organizational changes, such as providing local agencies with greater autonomy in personnel decisions. Yet this movement has also been accompanied by an ideological shift that has fostered new policy proposals (e.g., school choice initiatives) that may influence how states think about the role of public colleges and universities in providing higher education.

Five Privatizing Trends in State Policy for Higher Education

The context of state policymaking over the past three decades has been subject to new ideological and political dynamics due to the previously identified changes involving state tax limitations, partisan composition of the legislature, term limits, educational governors, and the movement toward reinventing government. State legislatures across the country responded to this changing environment by altering the ways in which they allocated resources and proposing new policy initiatives that indicate a general trend toward the privatization of public higher education. The particular policy trends on which we will focus include: (1) declining state funding effort for public higher education, (2) deregulation of tuition setting authority, (3) growth of prepaid tuition and college savings programs, (4) advent of merit aid scholarship programs, and (5) governance decentralization.

Declining State Funding Effort for Higher Education

Traditionally, public colleges and universities have received the majority of their funding in the form of direct appropriations allocated by the state government (Mumper, 1996). These appropriations support the institutions' operating budgets and are used to provide tuition subsidies that allow state residents to attend college at a substantially reduced price relative to the institutions' actual expenditures per pupil. Total appropriations of state tax funds for higher education operating expenses has increased 21% from $54.2 billion in 1985 to $66.5 billion in 2005 (Southern Regional Education Board, 2006). Yet, despite these gains in real growth, state investment in higher education has substantially declined relative to changes in enrollment, in state wealth, and in the growth of institutional budgets. During the past three decades, trends in state funding for higher education indicate greater privatization as institutions grow less dependent on state appropriations to meet increasing demand and rising operating costs (Okunade, 2004; Rizzo, 2004).

Because of changes in student enrollments, state appropriations for higher education have fluctuated over time relative to institutional needs for funding per full-time equivalent (FTE) student. Over the past 20 years, state appropriations per FTE were highest in the late 1980s and late 1990s, with a particularly dramatic decline in funding per FTE over the past five years. Between 2001 and 2005, state funding per student decreased nearly 20% from $7,124 to $5,825. This figure for 2005 represents the lowest level of state funding per FTE in real dollars over the past 20 years. State governments have not been able to keep pace with the escalating growth in college enrollments spurred by the rapidly increasing number of high school graduates, as well as the growing number of nontraditional students (Mumper, 2001). To provide the same level of service, institutions must find new sources of revenue from nongovernmental sources to slow the rate of passing the costs along to students in the form of increased tuition.

State funding for higher education has also declined in terms of funding per $1,000 personal income (Mortenson, 2005). Since 1985, this measure has declined over 150% in real dollars, from $17.77 to only $6.91 per $1,000 of personal income. This indicates that, even though states have become wealthier over time, higher education has become less of a priority in the states' budgets.

Lastly, public colleges and universities are increasingly turning to nongovernmental sources as a proportion of institutional revenues. At public degree-granting institutions, the average percentage of current fund revenues from state appropriations has declined from 43.2% in 1985 to 31.9% in 2000. Among larger, research-oriented institutions, revenues from their home states have declined to as little as one-third or even one-tenth of total institutional revenues (Hearn, 2003). The decline in state support for higher education has increased the importance of institutional autonomy among public institutions and raised the importance of securing more nontraditional forms of revenue. As state appropriations become a smaller proportion of institutional revenues, public institutions are trying to increase operational autonomy and reduce the level of government control in fiscal policies, such as tuition setting. In South Carolina in 2003, Governor Mark Sanford even proposed an option for public universities that would eliminate state appropriations in exchange for freedom from all state regulations (Couturier, 2005). Even though no public universities in South Carolina selected the option of distancing itself fully from the state, this proposal represented a notable change in thinking about resource allocation for public higher education. Although greater institutional autonomy may improve the competitive position of state flagship institutions, it poses a particular challenge for public comprehensive universities and two-year colleges that may lack the ability to substantially increase revenues through sources such as the endowment, alumni giving, research grants, or patents from research findings (Ehrenberg, 2005).

Decentralization of Tuition Setting Authority

One policy response made by states to compensate for the declining role of state appropriations in financing higher education has been to decentralize tuition setting authority. State appropriations and tuition/fees are the two primary sources of revenue for public colleges and universities; because universities lack control over appropriations, tuition setting authority provides these institutions with an important policy lever for ensuring that adequate revenue is available for financing operating costs. Traditionally, tuition in most states has been set by a combination of actors, including the state legislature, statewide or multi-institution higher education governing boards, and individual institutions (Christal, 1997; Lenth, 1993). These decisions pertaining to student costs occur in a highly politicized process due to the often conflicting interests of the multiple actors involved, and no entity can be held fully accountable for the outcomes. The recent movement toward decentralizing tuition setting authority provides public colleges and universities with greater control over their own budgets. In addition, an implicit assumption among actors in the higher education policy arena is that decentralization of tuition setting is accompanied by greater institutional autonomy and declining government support (see chapter 6).

The introduction of state policies to provide institutions with greater authority in the collection of revenues from student tuition and fees began in the 1980s (Deaton, 2006; Morphew, 2007). New Jersey became an early leader in the movement toward decentralization of tuition setting authority by adopting a policy in 1986 that allowed all four-year colleges and universities to set their own tuition levels as long as they received approval from the state board of higher education. Sixteen states had adopted their own policies to decentralize tuition setting authority by 2003. Among the states that adopted these types of policies, there was considerable variation in the amount of authority given to institutions. For example, the policy in Texas allowed all four-year institutions to determine their own differential tuition levels, while the policy in Georgia only allowed the state's two research universities to adjust tuition for nonresident students. Yet despite these differences in the degree of autonomy granted to colleges and universities in each state, together these policies represent a general movement away from the more highly centralized tuition setting processes of the past and toward greater institutional control.

Prepaid Tuition and College Savings Plans

The increasing cost of tuition has raised concerns among state policymakers because of the implications for access to higher education for low-income students, economic development, and the public benefits from the externalities of higher education (see chapters 3 and 4). In response to these concerns about tuition inflation and the affordability of higher education, states have responded by providing an incentive for families to save for college through the use of college savings or prepaid tuition plans (Baird, 2006a). These plans have helped to institutionalize the shift of paying for college as a public responsibility to a private one. College savings plans are state-sponsored investment accounts that are designed to generate a tax-sheltered return on investment, which can be used to pay for college expenses. Prepaid tuition plans allow families (or other individuals) to pay for a child's future college tuition expenses at today's prices by making a lump sum payment or a series of systematic payments into a state-sponsored investment account. These programs are usually designed to guarantee that an individual's investment will cover the full cost of tuition at in-state public institutions, by a specified date. If a child decides to attend an out-of-state or private institution, the equivalent value of the funds can typically be transferred to the receiving institution.

Prepaid tuition and college savings programs are inherently market-based mechanisms because they rely on individual investments in financial securities, such as mutual funds or bonds, to generate a return on investment. Incentives from the private market are used to encourage consumers to save for higher education by offering professionally managed accounts with potential rates of return that meet or exceed the returns that the average American could expect from the stock market (Olivas, 2003). However, in the case of college savings plans, there is no guarantee on the rate of return, so most of the risk is undertaken by the individual investor (Roth, 1999). By shifting more of the risk and responsibility of financing higher education from the state to individuals, these plans represent a fundamental change in state policy from a "welfare state" toward an "ownership society" (Doyle, McLendon, and Hearn, 2005).

Most states strongly rely on the private sector to provide management or oversight of prepaid tuition and college savings programs, which represents a movement toward the privatization scheme of "contracting out," which is discussed in chapter 7. Some states use private consulting firms to assist in the operation of state plans, while other states have turned over the management of their programs to private investment firms or financial institutions (Olivas, 2003). Furthermore, many states allow both residents and nonresidents to participate in their prepaid tuition and college savings program, which has generated competition across states. To gain a competitive advantage, states may offer features such as reduced fees or fewer transferability restrictions, in an effort to attract new clients (Dynarski, 2004; Olivas, 2003).

Perhaps the most important market implication for institutions of higher education is that prepaid tuition and college savings plans represent diminishing state control over the management of fiscal resources and an increasing reliance on market mechanisms (Baird, 2006b). Typically, state appropriations for higher education are allocated for specific purposes and subject to budgetary review. Since payments from prepaid tuition plans are not distributed through the state budgetary process, they are not subject to the same constraints and can be used at the institution's discretion. One potential concern amid the growth of these programs is that state governments may feel less pressure to maintain the same level of appropriations or keep tuition costs down as the number of fully funded college applicants increases (Olivas, 1996). In addition, these programs may change the ways in which policymakers think about how to help students to finance their education as reliance on government financial aid declines (Mumper, 1996). Overall, the role of prepaid tuition and college savings plans in encouraging private investment, promoting market-based competition, increasing institutional autonomy, and reducing the dependence on state support indicates a trend in the privatization of financing higher education.

Growth of Prepaid Tuition Plans

The origins of prepaid tuition plans can be traced back to private institutions rather than state policies. In 1985, Duquesne University started an Alumni Tuition Plan that allowed alumni to prepay four years of their children's tuition at a highly discounted rate (Mumper, 1996). Similar programs were quickly adopted by several other private universities in the region but did not have much success because there were few participants and the returns from the bond market were lower than the universities expected (Roth, 1999). However, the innovative nature of the programs received national attention and policymakers began to consider the feasibility of adopting similar programs at the state level.

Policymakers in Michigan proposed the first statewide prepaid tuition program, which was introduced by Governor James Blanchard in 1986 (Lehman, 1990). The Michigan Educational Trust was adopted by the state legislature during the same year, but before any contracts could be sold the legislation required verification from the Internal Revenue Service that participants would not be subject to any additional income tax. While Michigan was waiting on the ruling from the IRS,

Wyoming in 1986 became the first state to implement a prepaid tuition program (Mumper, 1996). By 1995, only five states had implemented prepaid tuition programs. Many states were confused about the tax status of prepaid tuition plans and were also concerned that investment returns would not be large enough to cover the rising cost of tuition (Mumper, 1996). In 1996, the U.S. Congress enacted legislation that would provide tax deferment for returns that accumulated from prepaid tuition and college savings plans. Many states followed suit by providing state-level tax exemptions for annual earnings from prepaid tuition and colleges savings programs or by allowing tax deductions for contributions to qualified plans (Baird, 2006b; Ma, 2003). The extension of these tax benefits to prepaid tuition and college savings plans greatly increased the demand for these programs, bringing the total number of prepaid tuition policies to 19 by 2005.

Growth of College Savings Plans

Shortly after the first prepaid tuition program was adopted in the late 1980s, Kentucky developed a prototype for a college savings plan by proposing an investment portfolio managed by the state that families could invest in to earn money for qualified college expenses (Olivas, 2003). The plans were designed as a more flexible alternative to prepaid tuition plans by allowing beneficiaries to use funds at any public in-state institution (Ifill and McPherson, 2004). Furthermore, the plans were particularly attractive to state governments because they had low administrative costs and involved little to no risk for the state (Roth, 1999). The first college savings plan was implemented in Ohio in 1989 but had a slow initial rate of adoption with only four states implementing policies by 1995. The rise of the stock market in the mid- to late 1990s made college savings plans a more attractive alternative to the states and also provided investors with more disposable income to contribute to the plans (Ifill and McPherson, 2004). Moreover, the tax benefits from the 1996 addition of section 529 of the Internal Revenue Code and the Economic Growth and Tax Reconciliation Act of 2001 contributed to the growing popularity of college savings programs (Ma, 2003). As of 2005, all 50 states and the District of Columbia had implemented college savings plans, with several states providing more than one type of plan to provide consumers with greater choice in policy terms (Olivas, 2003).

Trends in Prepaid Tuition and College Savings Plans Investment

During the 1990s, the majority of money invested in prepaid tuition or college savings plans was in the form of prepaid tuition. However, by 2001, the rapid growth of college savings plans led these programs to outpace investments in prepaid tuition programs. This shift in the relative popularity of these programs is attributed to concerns about the long-term sustainability of prepaid tuition plans due to enrollment fluctuations, rising tuition costs, and low returns on investment (Ifill and McPherson, 2004). During the 10-year period from 1996 to 2005, the amount of money invested in both prepaid tuition and college savings programs increased by nearly 3,000% from $2.4 billion in 1996 to $72.3 billion in 2005 (College Savings Plan Network, 2005). By this time, consumers had invested in 7.6 million Section 529 plans with an average investment amount of $9,481 (College Board, 2005). The demonstrated growth and success of these programs indicates that these market-based plans are expected to continue to serve as an important source of funding for higher education in the future.

State-Based Merit Scholarship Programs

The advent and subsequent growth of broad-based, state merit scholarship programs represents one of the most notable and controversial developments in postsecondary financing over the past two decades. State-based merit scholarship programs provide high school graduates meeting certain academic criteria with financial awards to cover all or part of the tuition and fees required to attend in-state institutions. The rationales used by policymakers to justify these policies include increasing access to higher education, reducing the "brain drain" by keeping the most talented students in-state, and providing students with an incentive to improve academic performance (Cornwell and Mustard, 2006b; Cornwell, Mustard, and Sridhar, 2006; Heller, 2004).

State merit scholarship programs may be viewed as a form of policy privatization as they represent a fundamental shift in the conceptualization of higher education from a public good to a private benefit. Traditionally, state subsidies for higher education have been provided directly in the form of need-based grants or indirectly through reduced costs of in-state public tuition (Dynarski, 2004; Ganderton and Binder, 2000). Yet, state merit scholarship programs send a message to students that they must work hard on their academic performance to reap the financial rewards of a college education. Free and reduced tuition are used as the incentive to alter student behavior, which also enhances competition among students for academic performance and admissions in the top in-state universities. In fact, Dynarski (2002b) hypothesizes that the reason these types of programs have gained political support is that "voters are fiercely supportive of transfers that they perceive as earned rewards rather than unconditional requirements" (Dynarski, 2002b, 21).

Furthermore, state merit scholarship programs follow similar trends of privatization in that they increase competition among the public and private institutions within the state. Policies in Florida, Georgia, Kentucky, Louisiana, Michigan, Missouri, Nevada, South Carolina, Tennessee, and West Virginia allow students to apply merit scholarships toward private tuition charges (Heller, 2004). Although states have traditionally only provided subsidies to offset the costs of in-state public tuition, the advent of state merit scholarship programs essentially requires public institutions to compete with private colleges and universities for state dollars.

Growth of State-Based Merit Scholarship Programs

Using a state-funded lottery to support a college scholarship program was first proposed by Georgia Governor Zell Miller in 1991 (Cornwell and Mustard 2006a; Cornwell and Mustard, forthcoming; Dynarski, 2004). In 1992, the Georgia General Assembly passed legislation for the state lottery, and the citizens voted for an amendment to the state constitution that would require lottery proceedings to be used as a supplement, rather than a substitute, for traditional funding for education. The first scholarships for Helping Outstanding Pupils Educationally (HOPE) were awarded in the fall of 1993 to students achieving a "B" grade-point average or higher. These scholarships covered the full cost of tuition and fees at all public, in-state institutions and provided a stipend for books. Students could also elect to use the scholarships to cover part of the cost of private institutions in-state (Cornwell and Mustard, forthcoming).

State-based merit scholarship programs quickly gained popularity among policymakers and voters. By 2005, policies had been implemented in Georgia, Mississippi, New Mexico, Florida, South Carolina, Louisiana, Alaska, Washington, Kentucky, Maryland, Nevada, West Virginia, Tennessee, and Massachusetts (Heller, 2004). Although these programs are similar in nature, they vary notably along several important dimensions, including funding sources, award amount, and eligibility criteria. Merit scholarship programs are funded by different sources across states, including state lotteries, general revenues, tobacco settlements, land lease sales, and even taxes on amusement devices (Heller, 2004). Although most state scholarship programs cover the full cost of tuition and fees, some programs provided smaller award amounts, such as a one-time award up to $2,500 in Michigan or an annual award up to $1,000 in Kentucky. The eligibility criteria for merit scholarship programs also differ by state in terms of rigor and requirements but usually include some combination of minimum grade-point average, ACT or SAT scores, or high school standardized test scores (Dynarski, 2002a).

Trends in State-Based Merit Scholarship Programs

The trends in the state adoption of merit scholarship programs accelerated from 1995 to 2005. Georgia was the only state with a merit scholarship program in 1995, but 10 additional states, primarily in the South, had adopted programs by 2000. The recent addition of merit scholarship programs in West Virginia, Tennessee, and Massachusetts brought the number of state merit aid programs to 14 by 2005.

The growth of merit aid programs has also changed the way that states allocate funds for financing higher education. In 1985, less than 10% of all undergraduate grant aid was non-need based, but this amount increased to 27% by 2004 due primarily to the growth of state merit scholarship programs. The total amount of non-need-based grant aid grew more than six times faster than need-based grants, with a 730% change over the 20-year period for non-need-based grants compared with a 119% change for need-based grants. Most of the growth in non-need-based grant aid has occurred in the past five years, indicating that this trend may continue to become more pronounced in the near future.

Governance Decentralization

The fifth trend in state-policy privatization in postsecondary education involves decentralization of higher education governance. The modern era in public higher education governance dates to the late 1950s and early 1960s, when almost every state in the Union redesigned its governance system. Before this period, most public higher education institutions had been governed in a manner similar to their private-college counterparts: lay boards of trustees at the campus level exercised policy and fiduciary responsibility for their respective campuses (Graham, 1989; Hearn and Griswold, 1994). The postwar boom in college enrollments and a corresponding surge in public expenditures on higher education, however, led many states to adopt new governance models capable of bringing to bear greater order, efficiency, and coordinated planning of the sector's rapid expansion. Most states thus created consolidated governing boards or statewide coordinating boards, approaches to governance that emphasized rationalism and hierarchy. The governance patterns established during this time of widespread reform endured well into the 1980s; yet, the past two decades have witnessed great volatility in the governance of U.S. public higher education (McLendon, Deaton, and Hearn, 2007). From 1985 to 2002, for example, state governments considered well in excess of 120 measures to modify their higher education governance systems with a dominant theme of decentralization (Leslie and Novak, 2003; MacTaggart, 1998; McLendon, 2003a). Collectively, these new governance approaches seem to focus on efficiency rather than equity, choice rather than standardization, decentralized rather than centralized decision making, performance rather than process, and outcome rather than input measures.

In many of the governance changes of the 1980s and the 1990s, states appear to have pursued four possible approaches to decentralized governance. One approach, especially popular during the early 1980s, involved the enactment of management-flexibility legislation, which transferred decision authority over areas of institutional management (e.g., budgeting, personnel, purchasing, and revenues) from the state level to the system or campus level, leaving existing coordinating and governing structures intact (e.g., Hyatt and Santiago, 1984; Meisinger, and Mingle, 1983). A second approach states have taken involves the disaggregating of university governance systems. For example, in 1995 Illinois abolished two multicampus systems and created local boards of trustees for seven of the eight institutions comprising the systems (Marcus, 1997). A third approach has involved reconstituting institutions as public corporations vested with greater autonomy from state government. In Oregon (1995), Maryland (1992), Hawaii (1998), Colorado (2004), and Virginia (2005), legislatures designated certain public universities as "quasi-public corporations" or as "charter colleges," thereby loosening state regulation of campus financial management (MacTaggart, 1998; McLendon, 2003a). These types of changes in institutional designations have increased competition in the higher education sector and motivated universities to find new sources of funding. Finally, decentralization has taken the form of weakening statewide coordinating boards. New Jersey's governance redesign of 1994, for example, abolished one of the nation's most powerful (regulatory) coordinating boards and established a new council of state university presidents to coordinate higher education policy voluntarily. Although decentralization of campus governance certainly has not been the goal pursued in every state over this period, nevertheless, the movement toward increased campus autonomy in more than a dozen states represents a significant milestone in state governance policy for higher education.[1]

Collectively, the five policy trends identified indicate a broader movement toward state policies' privatizing public higher education. The declining state funding effort for higher education has resulted in a growing dependence on private sources of revenue, while prepaid tuition and college savings plans indicate a greater reliance on individual choice and on equity markets for financing public higher education. The advent of merit scholarship programs reflects an increasing reliance on market mechanisms to promote competition and to offer incentives for both providers and consumers of higher education. Governance decentralization and deregulation of tuition setting authority represent diminishing direct state control over the governance and management of public institutions. Overall, these policies have resulted in many states in reduced dependence on state support and increased institutional autonomy, embodying a distinctively new approach to the financing and governance of higher education at the turn of the twenty-first century.

Research on the Origins and Spread of Postsecondary Policy Privatization in the United States

Thus far, we have asserted that the political, financial, and structural contexts of the 50 state governments have undergone substantial change over the past three decades. We have also argued that, when viewed collectively, various trends in state postsecondary finance and governance over this same period may represent a wave of policy privatization in postsecondary education. What factors have accounted for the rise of these trends? Why do states vary in the number and types of privatizing initiatives pursued? Rigorous, systematic efforts to understand the determinants of state policy for postsecondary education are a relatively new undertaking. Most of these recent empirical efforts integrate indicators of state demography, economic conditions, political climates, and structural features of the states and of their postsecondary education systems. Increasingly, analysts have turned also to notions of interstate policy *diffusion*[2] as a potential explanation for patterns of policy adoption in the postsecondary arena. Although the overall body of empirical work on state policy privatization is relatively small, the studies that exist provide intriguing evidence about the forces that may be driving recent changes.

Determinants of State Funding Effort

Empirical analysis of factors influencing state spending on higher education enjoys a longstanding tradition in the field of higher education studies (e.g., Clotfelter, 1976; Coughlin and Erekson, 1986; Hossler et al., 1997; Koshal and Koshal, 2000; Leslie and Ramey, 1986; Lindeen and Willis, 1975; Morgan, Kickham, and LaPlant, 2001; Peterson, 1976; Toutkoushian, and Hollis, 1998). More recently, analysts have increasingly focused on examining the determinants of the declining state funding *effort* for higher education, measured either in terms of higher education's share of state budgets or its funding relative to state wealth (Archibald and Feldman, 2006; Delaney, and Doyle, 2007; Humphreys, 2000; Kane, Orszag, and Apostolov, 2005; Koshal and Koshal, 2000; McLendon, Hearn, and Mokher, 2006; Rizzo, 2004). Collectively, they provide useful insights into some of the forces that contribute to the relative decline in the priority given to higher education within the state budget.

In one of the most recent analyses, Archibald and Feldman (2006) examine state appropriations efforts, between 1961 and 2000, measured as appropriations per $1,000 of state personal income. These authors used a fixed-effects model to estimate the influences of various state contextual conditions, including principally, a state's previous adoption of a constitutionally imposed tax and expenditure limitation (TEL) measure. The presence of a TEL was found to explain over half of the observed decline in state funding effort for higher education over the period studied. Notably, the authors also found that state spending on corrections and on health are complements to higher education spending, meaning that where and when states spend more on these two areas, states also tend to spend more on higher education.[3] Among the political conditions of the state, Archibald and Feldman also found the effects of ideology (more liberal states have higher state appropriations effort for higher education) and Democratic control of state houses (Democrats associated with higher funding levels over the past two decades) statistically significant.

In addition to the Archibald and Feldman study, a number of other studies have also found connections between state funding effort for higher education and partisan control of state political institutions (e.g., Koshal and Koshal, 2000; Rizzo, 2004). Yet partisanship is not the only political characteristic of a state that may influence appropriations for higher education. A recent longitudinal study of factors associated with state funding efforts for higher education between 1984 and 2002 points to distinctively new sources of political influence in shaping public choice, in addition to traditional factors such as state demography, enrollment patterns, and state tuition and aid policies[4] (McLendon, Hearn, and Mokher, 2006). Notably, the authors found strong empirical evidence that in addition to partisanship legislative professionalism and term limits have also influenced state funding efforts for higher education over the past 20 years.

Deregulation of Tuition Setting Authority

Deaton's (2006) unpublished dissertation provides the first systematic, empirical investigation of the forces that led states to shift tuition setting authority closer to the campus level. His 50-state event history analysis,[5] covering the period from 1984 to 2004, examined several categories of prospective policy influences, including state funding levels, tuition levels, postsecondary governance, diffusion pressures, the presence in a state of merit scholarship program, enrollment share by control, state wealth, and measures of partisan control of statehouses. Deaton's analysis reveals that higher levels of per capita income, the presence within a state of a weak coordinating board (i.e., ones lacking budget authority), and the presence of a merit scholarship program increased the likelihood that a state would adopt a tuition decentralization policy. Notably, he found no evidence of institutional political forces at work.[6]

Prepaid Tuition and College Savings Programs

At least three studies have empirically assayed the determinants of prepaid tuition and college savings programs, with each study bringing to bear a distinctive conceptual thrust and research methodology. The earliest work, by Hearn and Griswold (1994), examined state adoption of eight different policy "innovations" in postsecondary education, including prepaid and college savings programs. Hearn and Griswold's central hypothesis was that states with more highly centralized postsecondary governance systems would exhibit higher levels of postsecondary education policy innovation. Their results pointed to the role of governance structures, geographic region, educational attainment, and wealth in the state adoption of certain privatizing postsecondary financing and academic policies.

Building on the Hearn and Griswold study, McLendon, Heller, and Young (2005) assessed the factors associated with state adoption of a variety of innovative[7] governance and financing policies, including prepaid and college savings programs, between 1981 and 1998. Although McLendon and colleagues found evidence corroborating Hearn and Griswold's findings on the policy impacts of state wealth and postsecondary governance arrangements, their study also revealed several distinctively new sources of influence on financing innovations, namely, Republican control of the legislature and regional diffusion. The nature of the study design McLendon et al. used, however, prevented them from ascertaining precisely which financing policies were most sensitive to these political and diffusion influences.

To address the methodological limitations of the two previous investigations, Doyle, McLendon, and Hearn (2005) used event history analysis to examine the factors that drove 33 states to adopt college savings programs and 21 states to adopt prepaid tuition programs between 1986 and 1999. These authors found no evidence of a link between adoption of the programs and the educational characteristics of states, partisan control of government, political ideology, or electoral timing. However, they found (counter to their hypothesis) that policymakers in a less competitive electoral environment will be more likely to adopt either a prepaid tuition or a college savings plan. They also found a governance effect: states with weaker coordinating boards were more likely to adopt both plans. Curiously, while savings plans do not appear to diffuse across states, prepaid tuition plans have a negative diffusion effect. Although such an effect is difficult to interpret, it may suggest that the lessons learned from other states about policy innovations may reduce the rate of adoption.

Merit-Aid Programs

Doyle's (2006) recent event history analysis remains the sole published account of factors associated with state adoption of broad-based, merit scholarship programs, although case studies and field-based research on the phenomenon have gathered pace (e.g., Cohen-Vogel and Ingle, 2007; Ness, 2006). Doyle's analysis points primarily to state demography and to the educational characteristics of states as the principal drivers of adoption of the HOPE-style programs between 1990 and 2002. Lower levels of college continuation and educational attainment were found to increase the probability of adoption, whereas higher levels of student migration decreased the probability. This latter finding—that states in which many students leave to attend college out of state are much less likely to adopt merit-aid programs—stands at odds with Doyle's hypothesized relationship, and with most of the anecdotal accounts surrounding the rise and spread of the policies. Why would this be so? "It could be," the author writes, "that in states with small numbers of students leaving to go to college elsewhere, only the very best students leave" (2006, 282). Doyle also found a negative relationship between the contiguous diffusion measure and policy adoption. Notably, he found no evidence of the influence of political factors at work in the adoption of state merit-aid programs.

Governance Decentralization

The extant research on governance change consists largely of case studies of state activity. Indeed, a substantial body of work has accumulated over the past decade, including studies by Mills (forthcoming) on Florida's recent governance changes; by Protopsaltis (2004) on the nation's first voucher and charter college measure in Colorado; by Leslie and Berdahl (2006) on charter legislation in Virginia; by McLendon (2003a, 2003b) on governance decentralization in Illinois, Arkansas, and Hawaii; and, by Leslie and Novak (2003) on governance changes in almost a dozen different states. Although economic climates and problems internal to higher education helped to ripen the conditions leading to governance change, the case studies indicate that factors such as turnover in the political leadership of states also played a crucial role.

Building on this case study literature, McLendon, Deaton, and Hearn (2007) conducted the sole quantitative empirical investigation on the determinants of governance change in the states. Although their work does not focus on decentralization, exclusively, it does provide perhaps useful perspective on the forces that may be at work nationally. McLendon, Deaton, and Hearn used event history analysis to test a proposition for governance change they termed the "political-instability hypothesis,"[8] analyzing the effect of changes in state economic, demographic, structural, and political conditions on enactment of governance reforms. Their analysis yielded an intriguing set of results: while all three of the indicators of change in state political institutions produced statistically significant coefficients in the hypothesized directions, none of the indicators of state demography, of conditions within higher education systems, or of interstate diffusion yielded similar empirical support. "In essence," the authors write, "our analysis points to fluctuations on the political landscape of states as the primary drivers of legislation to reform governance arrangements for higher education." The authors caution, however, that the connection to partisanship may have less to do with the parties' views on higher education, than it does with shifting principal-agent relationships over time.

The Cumulative and Compounded Factors of State Privatization Policy

Collectively, these empirical studies of the antecedents to state policy privatization indicate the importance of several economic and demographic factors in the origin and spread of postsecondary policy privatization in the states. Fiscal indicators, such as unemployment rates and changes in the composition of the state population, may lead policymakers to rethink how to effectively meet the changing needs of its citizenry, given limited fiscal resources. Yet, for many of these policies, we find a greater number of influences from the political context and governance structure within the state than from the panoply of state economic and demographic characteristics that scholars traditionally have examined. Indeed, policy initiatives such as governance decentralization appear to be influenced almost exclusively by changes in politics such as shifts in legislative control. These findings indicate that privatization trends in state policy for higher education cannot be understood in the absence of examining the political contexts of the states and the political processes by which public policy for higher education is formulated.

Conclusion

Throughout this chapter, we have sought to offer a new way of thinking about privatization in public higher education, by expanding the scope of the topic beyond institutional changes and by examining recent developments in the state policy arena. We have identified contextual changes over time that have fostered a supportive environment for policy change, identified and described the proliferation of five state policy privatization trends in postsecondary education, and surveyed the growing empirical literature on the antecedents to state adoption of these policies. Our discussion provides perspectives on the origins and growth of important recent changes in the policy context for higher education in the American states. The topic is highly relevant, as we see many states continuing their march toward privatization, evidenced most recently by the advent of voucher programs in Colorado and of charter colleges in Virginia and elsewhere (McLendon and Hearn, forthcoming). As public universities face a growing dependence on private sources of revenue, increasing competitive pressure from market mechanisms, and diminishing direct state control over governance and management, policymakers and educational leaders should continue to consider the implications of these reforms for the institutional missions of public institutions and for the collective good of the states those institutions serve.

NOTES

1. Certainly, the policy direction in some states has not been that of unadulterated freedom for public higher education. Indeed, the proliferation of new performance-based accountability regimes and creeping procedural regulation in some states have lessened campus autonomy (McLendon, Hearn, and Deaton, 2006). Yet, collectively, the policy developments that we examined in this chapter represent a notable change in the overall policy climate in many American states over the past several decades.

2. Diffusion refers to the influence of a state's policy behavior on its neighbors. Policies are believed to diffuse across state lines because states emulate their neighbors in an effort to "keep up" or to avoid being disadvantaged, relative to their peers (McLendon, Hearn, and Deaton, 2006; McLendon, Heller, and Young, 2005).

3. Archibald and Feldman (2006, 634) argue that this result "likely reflects differences in tastes for public goods that overpower any effect from budget trade-offs."

4. Overall, the literature on factors related to state appropriations for higher education present a mixed set of findings on the importance of these conditions. Although some studies provide evidence of the statistically significant impact of factors such as state income, rate of unemployment, and tuition levels, other studies have found no such evidence (see Toutkoushian and Hollis, 1998).

5. Event history analysis (EHA) is a methodological technique commonly used to examine the factors that influence the timing of a state's adoption of specific policies. A dichotomous dependent variable for whether a state adopted a policy in a given year is used to calculate the hazard function, which estimates how the risk of adopting a certain policy changes over time for states that have not yet adopted. EHA provides several advantages over traditional logistic

regression models by allowing for the analysis of time-dependent variables, taking explicitly into account the length of time until the event occurs, and estimating the risk of an event occurring at any given time period (Box-Steffensmeier and Jones, 2004).

6. Deaton also conducted separate analyses for tuition-*centralization* measures. Here he found that an increase in the proportion of Republicans in the state legislature increased the propensity of a state to adopt a policy centralizing tuition.

7. These works follow in the tradition of state politics and policy scholars who long ago defined an "innovation" as a policy that is new to the unit (state) adopting it.

8. This hypothesis asserts that states that have experienced greater political turbulence will be ones most likely to have enacted reforms in state governance of higher education.

REFERENCES

Alt, James E., and Robert C. Lowry. 2000. A Dynamic Model of State Budget Outcomes under Divided Partisan Government. *Journal of Politics* 62 (4): 1035–69.

Archibald, Robert B., and David H. Feldman. 2006. State Higher Education Spending and the Tax Revolt. *Journal of Higher Education* 77 (4): 618–44.

Baird, Katherine. 2006a. Do Prepaid Tuition Plans Affect State Support for Higher Education? *Journal of Education Finance* 31 (3): 255–75.

———. 2006b. The Political Economy of College Prepaid Tuition Plans. *Review of Higher Education* 29 (2): 141–66.

Barrilleaux, Charles, Thomas Holbrook, and Laura Langer. 2002. Electoral Competition, Legislative Balance, and State Welfare Policy. *American Journal of Political Science* 46 (2): 415–27.

Box-Steffensmeier, Janet M., and Bradford S. Jones. 2004. *Event History Modeling: A Guide for Social Scientists*. New York: Cambridge University Press.

Boyd, Don. 2002. *State Spending for Higher Education in the Coming Decade*. Technical Report. Boulder, CO: National Center for Higher Education Management Systems.

Breneman, David W., and Joni E. Finney. 1997. The Changing Landscape: Higher Education Finance in the 1990s. In *Public and Private Financing of Higher Education*, ed. Patrick Callan and Joni E. Finney, 30–59. Phoenix, AZ: ACE /Oryx Press.

Carey, John M., Richard G. Niemi, and Lynda W. Powell. 2001. *Term Limits in the State Legislatures*. Ann Arbor: University of Michigan Press.

Christal, Melodie E. 1997. *State Tuition and Fee Policies: 1996–1997*. Denver, CO: State Higher Education Executive Officers, 1997.

Clotfelter, Charles T. 1976. Public Spending for Higher Education: An Empirical Test of Two Hypotheses. *Public Finance* 31:177–95.

Cohen-Vogel, Lora, and William K. Ingle. 2007. When Neighbors Matter Most: Innovation, Diffusion, and State Policy Adoption In Tertiary Education. *Journal of Education Policy*, 22 (3): 241–62.

College Board. 2005. *Trends in Student Aid*. Washington, DC: College Board.

College Savings Plans Network. 2005. Available online at www.collegesavings.org/529PlanData .aspx.

Cornwell, Christopher, and David B. Mustard. 2006a. Assessing Public Higher Education in

Georgia at the Start of the Twenty-First Century. In *What's Happening to Public Education*, ed. Ronald G. Ehrenberg, 107–34. Westport, CT: Praeger / American Council Series on Higher Education.

———. 2006b. Evaluating HOPE-Style Merit Scholarships. Federal Reserve Bank of Cleveland Conference Proceedings, Cleveland, OH.

———. Forthcoming. Merit-Based College Scholarships and Car Sales. *Education Finance and Policy*.

Cornwell, Christopher, David B. Mustard, and Deppa J. Sridhar. 2006. The Enrollment of Merit-Based Financial Aid: Evidence from Georgia's HOPE Program. *Journal of Labor Economics* 24 (4): 761–86.

Coughlin, Cletus C., and O. Homer Erekson. 1986. Determinants of State Aid and Voluntary Support of Higher Education. *Economics of Education Review* 5:179–90.

Couturier, Lara K. 2005. The Unspoken Is Being Done: The Market's Impact on Higher Education's Public Purposes. *New Directions for Higher Education* 129:85–100.

Deaton, Steven B. 2006. Policy Shifts in Tuition Setting Authority in the American States: An Events History Analysis of State Policy Adoption. Ph.D. diss., Vanderbilt University.

Delaney, Jennifer, and Will R. Doyle. 2006. The Role of Higher Education in State Budgets. Unpublished Manuscript, Stanford University and Vanderbilt University.

———. 2007. The Role of Higher Education in State Budgets. In *The Challenges of Comparative State-Level Higher Education Policy Research*, ed. Kate Shaw and Donald Heller, 55–76. Stirling, VA: Stylus.

Doyle, William R. 2005. Public Opinion, Partisan Identification, and Higher Education Policy. Ph.D. diss., Stanford University.

———. 2006. Adoption of Merit-Based Student Grant Programs: An Event History Analysis. *Educational Evaluation and Policy Analysis*, 28 (3): 259–85.

Doyle, William R., Michael K. McLendon, and James C. Hearn. 2005. Why States Adopted Prepaid Tuition and College Savings Programs: An Event History Analysis. Annual Meeting of the Association for the Study of Higher Education, November, Philadelphia, PA.

Dynarski, S. 2000. Hope for Whom? Financial Aid for the Middle Class and Its Impact on College Attendance. Working Paper 7756. National Bureau of Economic Research, Cambridge, MA.

———. 2002a. The Behavioral and Distributional Implications of Aid for College. *American Economic Review* 92 (2): 279–85.

———. 2002b. The Consequences of Merit Aid. Joint Center for Poverty Research Working Paper. University of Chicago, Joint Center for Poverty Research, Chicago.

———. 2004. *Tax Policy and Education Policy: Collision or Coordination? A Case Study of the 529 and Coverdell Saving Incentives*. Cambridge, MA: National Bureau of Economic Research.

Ehrenberg, Ronald G. 2005. The Perfect Storm and the Privatization of Public Higher Education. Cornell Higher Education Research Institute, Ithaca, NY.

Ganderton, Philip T., and Melissa Binder. 2000. Who Benefits from a Lottery-Funded College Subsidy? Evidence from the New Mexico Success Scholarship. Working Paper Series. Social Science Research Network. http://ssrn.com/abstract=262024.

Geiger, Roger L. 2002. The American University at the Beginning of the Twenty-First

Century: Signposts on the Path to Privatization. In *Trends in American and German Higher Education*, ed. Robert M. Adams, 38–84. Cambridge, MA: American Academy of Arts and Sciences.

Gittell, Marilyn, and Neil S. Kleiman. 2000. The Political Context of Higher Education. *American Behavioral Scientist* 43 (7): 1058–91.

Gittell, Marilyn, and Laura McKenna. 1999. Redefining Education Regimes and Reforms: The Political Role of Governors. *Urban Education* 34 (3): 268–91.

Graham, Hugh D. 1989. Structure and Governance in American Higher Education: Historical and Comparative Analysis in State Policy. *Journal of Policy History* 1 (1): 80–107.

Hearn, James C. 2003. *Diversifying Campus Revenue Streams*. Report for the American Council on Education Series. Washington, DC: American Council on Education.

Hearn, James C., and Carolyn P. Griswold. 1994. State-Level Centralization and Policy Innovation in U.S. Postsecondary Education. *Educational Evaluation and Policy Analysis* 16 (2): 161–90.

Hearn, James C., Carolyn P. Griswold, and Ginger M. Marine. 1996. Region, Resources, and Reason: A Contextual Analysis of State Tuition and Student Aid Policies. *Research in Higher Education* 37 (3): 241–79.

Heller, Donald E. 2004. State Merit Scholarships: An Overview. In *State Merit Scholarship Programs and Racial Inequality*, ed. David E. Heller and Patricia Martin, 15–22. Cambridge, MA: Civil Rights Project at Harvard University, 2004.

Hossler, Don, Jon P. Lund, Jackie Ramin, Sarah Westfall, and Steve Irish. 1997. State Funding for Higher Education: The Sisyphean Task. *Journal of Higher Education* 68 (2): 160–90.

Hovey, Harold A. 1999. State Spending for Higher Education in the Next Decade. Opinion Paper. National Center for Public Policy and Higher Education, Washington, DC.

Humphreys, Brad R. 2000. Do Business Cycles Affect State Appropriations to Higher Education? *Southern Economic Journal* 67 (2): 123–38.

Hyatt, James A., and Aurora A. Santiago. 1984. *Incentives and Disincentives for Effective Management*. Guide. Washington, DC: National Association of Colleges and University Business Officers.

Ifill, Roberto M., and Michael S. McPherson. 2004. *When Saving Means Losing*. Indianapolis, IN: Lumina Foundation for Education.

Kane, Thomas J., Peter R. Orszag, and Emil Apostolov. 2005. Higher Education Appropriations and Public Universities: Role of Medicaid and the Business Cycle. In *Brookings-Wharton Papers on Urban Affairs*, ed. Gary T. Burtless and Janet R. Pack, 99–145. Washington, DC: Brookings Institution Press.

Koshal, Rajindar K., and Manjulika M. Koshal. 2000. State Appropriations and Higher Education Tuition: What Is the Relationship? *Education Economics* 8 (1): 81–89.

Lehman, Jeffery S. 1990. Social Irresponsibility, Actuarial Assumptions, and Wealth Redistribution: Lessons about Public Policy from a Prepaid Tuition Program. *Michigan Law Review* 88 (5): 1035–41.

Lenth, Charles S. 1993. *The Tuition Dilemma: State Policies and Practices in Pricing Public Higher Education*. Denver, CO: State Higher Education Executive Officers.

Leslie, David W., and Robert Berdahl. 2006. More Freedoms, More Controls Simultaneously in U.S. State Accountability Patterns: The Virginia Experience. Paper presented at the European Association of Institutional Research, Rome, Italy, August.

Leslie, David W., and Richard Novak. 2003. Substance vs. politics: Through the Dark Mirror of Governance Reform. *Educational Policy* 17 (1): 98–120.

Leslie, Larry L., and Garey Ramey. 1986. State Appropriations and Enrollments: Does Enrollment Growth Still Pay? *Journal of Higher Education* 57 (1): 1–19.

Leubsdorf, Ben. 2006. The Problem with Term Limits: In the Dozen States Where Laws Push Legislators Out of Office after a Few Terms, Colleges Must Repeatedly Deal with Newcomers Looking for Quick Fixes. *Chronicle of Higher Education* 52 (47): A13.

Lindeen, James W., and George L. Willis. 1975. Political, Socioeconomic, and Demographic Patterns of support for Public Higher Education. *Western Political Quarterly*, 28 (3): 528–41.

Lyall, Katharine R., and Kathleen R. Sell. 2005. *The True Genius of America at Risk: Are We Losing Our Public Universities to de Facto Privatization?* Westport, CT: Praeger.

Ma, Jennifer. 2003. *Education Saving Incentives and Household Saving: Evidence from the 2000 TIAA-CREF Survey of Participant Finances*. Cambridge, MA: National Bureau of Economic Research, 2003.

MacTaggart, Terrance J., ed. 1998. *Seeking Excellence through Independence: Liberating Colleges and Universities from Excessive Regulation*. San Francisco: Jossey-Bass.

Marcus, Laurence R. 1997. Restructuring State Higher Education Governance Patterns. *Review of Higher Education* 20 (4): 399–418.

McLendon, Michael K. 2003a. Setting the Governmental Agenda for State Decentralization of Higher Education. *Journal of Higher Education* 74 (5): 479–516.

———. 2003b. State Governance Reform of Higher Education: Patterns, Trends, and Theories of the Public Policy Process. In *Higher Education: Handbook of Theory and Research*, ed. John Smart, 57–143. London: Kluwer.

McLendon, Michael K., Russ Deaton, and James C. Hearn. (2007). The Enactment of State-Level Governance Reforms for Higher Education: A Test of the Political-Instability Hypothesis. *Journal of Higher Education* 78 (6): 645–75.

McLendon, Michael K., and James C. Hearn. Forthcoming. Viewing Recent U.S. Governance Reform Whole: "Decentralization" in a Distinctive Context. In *System Governance: Steering, Policy Processes, and Outcomes*, ed. Jeroen Huisman.

McLendon, Michael K., James C. Hearn, and Russ Deaton. 2006. Called to Account: Analyzing the Origins and Spread of State Performance-Accountability Policies for Higher Education. *Educational Evaluation and Policy Analysis* 28 (1): 1–24.

McLendon, Michael K., Donald E. Heller, and Steven P. Young. 2005. State Postsecondary Education Policy Innovation: Politics, Competition, and the Interstate Migration of Policy Ideas. *Journal of Higher Education* 76 (4): 363–400.

McLendon, Michael K., and Eric C. Ness. 2003. The Politics of State Higher Education Governance Reform. *Peabody Journal of Education* 78 (4): 66–88.

Meisinger, Richard J., Jr., and James R. Mingle. 1983. The Extent of State Controls in Maryland Public Higher Education. In *Managing Flexibility and State Regulation in Higher Education*, ed. James R. Mingle, 17–35. Atlanta, GA: Southern Regional Education Board.

Mills, Michael R. 2007. Stories of Politics and Policy: Florida's Higher Education Governance Reorganization. *Journal of Higher Education* 78 (2): 162–187.

Moe, Terry M. 2003. The Politics of the Status Quo. In *Our Schools and Our Future: Are We Still at Risk?* ed. Paul E. Peterson and John E. Chubb, 177–210. Stanford, CA: Hoover Institution Press.

Morgan, David R., Kenneth Kickham, and James T. LaPlant. 2001. State Support for Higher Education: A Political Economy Approach. *Policy Studies Journal* 29 (1): 359–71.

Morphew, Christopher C. 2007. Fixed Tuition Pricing: A Solution That May Be Worse Than The Problem. *Change* 39 (1): 34–39.

Mortenson, Thomas G. 2005. *State Tax Fund Appropriations for Higher Education FY1961 to FY2005.* Oskaloosa, IA: Postsecondary Education Opportunity, 2005.

Mumper, Michael. 1996. *Removing College Price Barriers: What Government Has Done and Why It Hasn't Worked.* Albany: State University of New York Press.

——. 2001. State Efforts to Keep Public Colleges Affordable in the Face of Fiscal Stress. In *The Finance of Higher Education: Theory, Research, Policy, and Practice*, ed. Michael B. Paulsen and John C. Smart, 321–95. New York: Agathon Press.

National Conference of State Legislatures. 2007. Institutional Change in American Politics: The Case of Term Limits. Denver, Colorado: National Conference of State Legislatures.

Ness, Erik C. 2006. Deciding Who Earns HOPE, PROMISE, and SUCCESS: Toward a Comprehensive Model of the Merit-Aid Eligibility Policy Process. Ph.D. diss., Vanderbilt University.

Okunade, Albert A. 2004. What Factors Influence State Appropriations for Public Higher Education in the United States? *Journal of Education Finance* 30 (2): 123–38.

Olivas, Michael A. 1996. Prepaid Tuition Plans Come of Age: Problems and Prospects. *College Board Review* 178:2–5.

——. 2003. State College Savings and Prepaid Tuition Plans: A Reappraisal and Review. *Journal of Law and Education* 32 (4): 475–515.

Peterson, Marvin W., and Michael K. McLendon. 1998. Achieving Independence through Conflict and Compromise: Michigan. In *Seeking Excellence through Independence*, ed. Terrance J. MacTaggart, 147–73. San Francisco: Jossey Bass.

Peterson, Robert G. 1976. Environmental and Political Determinants of State Higher Education Appropriations Policies. *Journal of Higher Education* 47:523–42.

Protopsaltis, Spiros. 2004. The Policy Process of Higher Education Governance and Finance Reform: A Case Study of Colorado's Postsecondary Voucher System. Paper presented at the Annual Conference for the Association for the Study of Higher Education, Kansas City, MO, November.

Richardson, Richard C., Kathy R. Bracco, Patrick M. Callan, and Joni E. Finney. 1999. *Designing State Higher Education Systems for a New Century.* Phoenix, AZ: Oryx Press.

Rizzo, Michael J. 2004. State Preferences for Higher Education Spending: A Panel Data Analysis, 1977–2001: Cornell Higher Education Research Institute. Paper presented at the Federal Reserve Bank of Cleveland's Conference on Education and Economic Development, Cleveland, November.

Roth, Andrew P. 1999. State-Sponsored, Tax-Advantaged College Savings Plans: A Study of

Their Impact on Contemporary Understanding of the Public-versus-Private Responsibility to Pay for Higher Education Issue. Paper presented at the Annual Meeting of the Association for the Study of Higher Education, San Antonio, TX, November.

Southern Regional Education Board. 2006. SREB Educational Data Library. www.sreb.org/main/EdData/DataLibrary/datalibindex.asp.

Thompson, Frank J., and Norma M. Riccucci. 1998. Reinventing Government. *Annual Review of Political Science* 1:231–57.

Toutkoushian, Robert K., and Paula Hollis. 1998. Using Panel Data to Examine Legislative Demand for Higher Education. *Education Economics* 6 (2): 141–58.

CHAPTER THREE

Incomplete Contracts and the Political Economy of Privatization

• ℰℐ •

ROBERT C. LOWRY

Privatization has been a popular strategy for reforming public services in recent decades (Savas, 2000) and has now become an important topic in public higher education (Brown, 2005; Dillon, 2005; Lyall and Sell, 2005; Petkovsky, 2005). To understand the merits and politics of proposals for privatization, it is useful to think about why a given activity is supplied by the public sector, particularly if, as in the case of higher education, private-sector alternatives already exist.

In this chapter, I ask why we have public universities in the first place. More specifically, why do all 50 states and the District of Columbia have universities that are publicly owned and subsidized through appropriations rather than some alternative arrangement for supporting higher education? I explain this prevailing combination of institutions and subsidies in terms of the costs and benefits to state government officials, identify the important empirical assumptions that underlie this explanation, and briefly consider several scenarios for change. By state government officials, I am primarily referring to the governor and members of the state legislature. Unelected administrators concerned with education policy are assumed to reflect the preferences of their political superiors.

The analysis throughout is positive, not normative. That is, I do not ask whether the prevailing paradigm is optimal according to aggregate social welfare or any other metric. Rather, I start from the observation that any change to existing institutional and financial arrangements will require the consent of state government officials.[1] I therefore focus on these actors: What are the advantages of the prevailing arrangement from their point of view, and what concerns would they have when considering proposed changes to the status quo? Although the starting point for my questions differ from those in the chapter 2, the resulting look at the drivers behind state policy is similar in the attempt to identify underlying causes.

First, I will identify four distinguishing characteristics of public and private universities. Altering any one of these characteristics for public universities or any combination could be considered a move toward privatization, although, in practice, some combinations may not be feasible. The next section presents the case for public ownership as compared with a system in which state governments purchase the services they want through grants, contracts, and directed support for individual students. I argue that the most persuasive case for public ownership today comes from the economic literature on incomplete contracts. This argument assumes that state government officials and academics tend to have different preferences for what universities should produce. The following section includes evidence relevant to this assumption from the historical record, empirical studies of public universities in more and less centralized systems, and the allocation of faculty resources and graduate program rankings in different fields of study. The following section addresses the advantages for state government officials of subsidizing universities through appropriations rather than some combination of grants, contracts, scholarships, and vouchers. Finally, I briefly consider several scenarios for change in the direction of privatization and summarize the argument.

Differences between Public and Private Universities

Table 3.1 contrasts important characteristics of public and private universities along four dimensions: (1) ownership of land and capital assets, (2) sources of general operating funds, (3) formal limits to discretion, and (4) legal authority to exercise discretion within those limits. Table entries describe an "ideal type" for each sector. For a private university, land and assets are owned by a private, usually nonprofit corporation. General operating funds come from a combination of student tuition and fees, donations, and endowment income, although income from donations and endowments may be restricted to certain uses.[2] Formal restrictions on management decisions are few, as private corporation laws are permissive rather than proscriptive. A private university can pursue any activity that serves broadly defined educational purposes and does not conflict with laws of general application (Hopkins, 2001). These include such things as occupational safety and health regulations and tax laws applicable to all nonprofit corporations.[3] Legal authority to exercise discretion rests with a board of directors that is either self-perpetuating, meaning that vacancies are filled by a vote of the remaining directors, or elected by alumni from a slate chosen

TABLE 3.1.
Characteristics of Private and Public Universities (Ideal Types)

	Private University	Public University
Ownership of land and capital assets	Private corporation, usually nonprofit	Publicly chartered corporation
Sources of operating funds	Student tuition and fees, private donations, endowment income	Student tuition and fees, state appropriations
Formal limits to discretion	Laws of general applicability	Constitutional or statutory mission statement; procedural laws and regulations
Authority to exercise discretion	Self-perpetuating board of directors or board elected by alumni	Board appointed by state government officials or elected, subject to political oversight

by a nominating committee. In practice, this may mean ratification of a slate that has exactly as many nominees as vacancies.

For a public university, the land and buildings are owned by a state agency or publicly chartered corporation. General operating funds come almost entirely from student tuition and fees and appropriations. The university's substantive mission may be defined by the state constitution but more likely by statute, and managerial discretion may be further limited by procedural laws and regulations that apply specifically to public universities or even individual institutions. Finally, discretionary authority rests with a governor- or legislature-appointed board or, in a few cases, chosen through popular election.

Of course, these are both ideal types, with many variations. Historically, the legal distinction between public and private colleges was not at all clear. The autonomy of private governing boards from state intervention was not established until *Dartmouth College v. Woodword,* 4 Wheaton (U.S.) 518 (1819), a decision that clarified the status of private, nonprofit corporations generally (Brubacher and Rudy, 1976). Rudolph (1990) claims that the short-run effect of this decision was to discourage the development of public institutions because the state legislature could not simply "reshape" an existing private college. In the long run, however, the decision led to a much cleaner distinction between public and private sectors in higher education than had existed before.

Today, many public universities have affiliated foundations that raise money from private sources to finance capital assets and endowments and athletics (e.g., Iowa State University Foundation, 2006). The relative reliance on different sources of general operating funds varies within both sectors. Most private universities receive few donations and have only small endowments (Winston, 1999), while all public universities receive at least some operating revenues from students. Although some states still have laws stating that tuition must be free or tightly limited (Lowry, 2001b), these can be circumvented with mandatory fees for anything except course instruction. Many states provided government subsidies for operating expenses at private colleges before the Civil War, some as late as the 1920s (Rudolph, 1990), and many states provided minimal or no support to public universities until the 1890s (Brubacher and Rudy, 1976; Rudolph, 1990). Some states continue to subsidize instruction at private institutions for specific purposes on a per student basis (Zumeta, 1992).

Formal limits to discretion also vary within the public sector. Some public universities have constitutional autonomy, although courts have interpreted the relevant constitutional provisions differently in different states (Eykamp, 1995). A few extreme cases such as the University of Michigan and the University of California are nearly free of oversight by the legislative and executive branches, though public funding can be withheld. Other public universities are subject to a wide range of statutory and administrative regulations, such that some do not even control their own tuition revenues (Eykamp, 1995; Lyall and Sell, 2005; Volkwein and Malik, 1997). Eykamp (1995) distinguishes between public universities that have full constitutional status, those that have limited constitutional status, those that are public corporations, and those that are state agencies. *Public corporations* are subject only to statutes directed at the university and regulations adopted pursuant to those statutes. *State agencies* are subject to all statutes and regulations directed at the state government bureaucracy generally. Chapter 8 examines the effect of tuition fees on the privatization of European universities, illustrating this phenomenon as global, not merely American.

Governing boards that exercise discretionary authority differ in size and in operation as well as in selection procedures. Private university boards tend to be larger and meet less often than public boards (Madsen, 1998a, 1998b). Another important difference is that each private university has its own governing board, whereas many public boards govern multicampus systems.[4] In addition, many states that have multiple governing boards also have a statewide coordinating board that gathers information, performs planning functions, and may have authority over individual governing board budgets and degree programs. All of the members of these coordinating boards are appointed by the governor or the governor in conjunction with the legislature (Education Commission of the States, 1997; Knott and Payne, 2004; Lowry, 2001b).

The Case for Public Ownership

In this section, I consider the theoretical case for public ownership of universities. The question is not just whether this arrangement has advantages over a system of purely private higher education but whether it has advantages over a system in which the state purchases research and other public services from private universities and supports students through vouchers or scholarships.

Market Failure

The classic case from microeconomic theory for government intervention in the economy is based on inefficiencies due to market failure (Weimer and Vining, 1999). Private (for-profit) markets cannot be expected to operate efficiently in the presence of market power, information asymmetries between buyers and sellers, or public goods. However, none of these arguments fully justify public ownership of universities.

The market for higher education is clearly not a monopoly, although economies of scale and scope exist up to a point (Goldin and Katz, 1999), and individual universities strive to create market power through reputation. In addition, some colleges in the nineteenth century were shielded from competition by the difficulty and expense of travel. However, nearly all private universities are nonprofit organizations, so market power does not necessarily lead to inefficiently high prices. Rudolph (1990) reports that many struggling colleges in the nineteenth century offered ruinous tuition discounts to increase their student enrollments and generate short-term cash flow.

In some cases, it may be competition that leads to higher tuition, as when elite, nonprofit colleges and universities compete on the basis of prestige and amenities rather than price (Clotfelter, 1996; Winston, 1999). One argument for public ownership is that it can be used to create less prestigious but more accessible options for students. Still, state governments could subsidize instruction with vouchers or student scholarships that may only be spent at institutions satisfying certain conditions, such as a maximum sticker price.

With regard to information, consumers of university instruction and research are generally in a poor position to judge quality, and this problem is exacerbated when payment is made by third parties such as parents (Hart, Shleifer, and Vishny, 1997; Winston, 1999). However, again the alternative to publicly owned universities is a market of nonprofit organizations. The absence of a profit motive provides some reassurance to consumers who are not able to evaluate the quality of the goods or services they receive (Hansmann, 1980, 1996; Winston, 1999). In addition, comparative data on reputation and various measures of inputs and performance are increasingly available from sources such as *U.S. News and World Report* (1994) and the National Research Council (1995).

Finally, many of the outputs of universities have at least some of the characteristics of public goods. Knowledge generated by research is a public good, and private industry benefits from the positive spillover effects from university research (Jaffe, 1989). However, governments can and do subsidize research at private universities, directly and indirectly, with policies that incentivize university-based research (e.g., Bayh-Dole in 1980 that paved the way for university ownership of inventions resulting from federally funded research). Similarly, the argument that training engineers, doctors, teachers, and so forth generates positive spillovers for the surrounding region at most justifies targeted help for individual students through financial aid. Today's increased labor mobility diminishes the effect of this argument further. Bound et al. (2004) find only a modest relationship between the numbers of bachelor's degrees awarded per capita in a state and the stock of college-educated workers in later years, and almost no relationship between medical degrees awarded and the stock of physicians.

Capital Constraints

Several of the previous arguments assume the existence of a market of private, nonprofit universities. However, universities require large investments in land, buildings, and equipment, and one weakness of private nonprofit organizations is their relative inability to raise start-up capital (Hansmann, 1980, 1996). Therefore, the private sector simply could not be counted on to raise the necessary capital in all states.

This argument may help to explain the development of public research universities in the late nineteenth and early twentieth centuries (Goldin and Katz, 1999). Many public universities outside the Northeast were founded with capital derived from federal land grants, a practice that predated the first Morrill Act (Brubacher and Rudy, 1976; Rudolph, 1990). Goldin and Katz (1999) argue that changes in technology associated with the development of research universities led to further advantages for public institutions due to economies of scale and scope. They note that only one highly ranked private research university was founded in the twentieth century, and it is a special case: Brandeis was founded in 1948 with contributions from the Jewish community to serve many Jewish academics and students who took refuge in the United States during World War II (Goldin and Katz, 1999).[5]

The capital constraint argument still does not provide a complete explanation for public ownership. The question is not how to build more research universities but whether ownership of existing universities should lie with the public or private sectors. Even given the difficulty of raising private funds for land, buildings, and equipment, many forms of partial privatization might be considered. Some of these are discussed later.

Incomplete Contracts

The most persuasive argument for public ownership of universities today comes from the economic literature on incomplete contracts (Goldin and Katz, 1999; Grossman and Hart, 1986; Hart, Shleifer, and Vishny, 1997; Shleifer, 1998). Grossman and Hart (1986) ask when a business firm should contract with another firm for inputs, and when it should make them in-house (or buy the second firm). They argue that rights to make decisions about production can be divided into "specific" rights and "residual" rights. The former are set forth in a contract (or statute or regulation) and deal with particular foreseeable decisions or events, while the latter stipulate who gets to exercise discretion in situations where there are no specific rights to apply. Grossman and Hart equate ownership with possession of all of the residual rights. For more information, see figure 8.1 in Chapter 8, which maps public funding regimes in Europe.

Hart, Shleifer, and Vishny (1997) apply this analysis to the "make or buy" decision faced by public agencies. They assume demand exists for a good or service that is not being supplied by the private sector and ask whether the government should provide it directly or contract with one or more private firms. They note that it is typically difficult to write an enforceable contract that covers all exigencies for the performance of complicated tasks, and whoever owns assets controls their use when there is discretion. They argue further that managers in private firms have greater incentives than their public-sector counterparts to cut costs in ways that might decrease quality but also greater incentives to make innovations that increase quality. The make or buy decision turns on how these differences balance out. Two other factors that might tilt the decision include the potential for ex post competition among private firms in the case of contracting and the possibility that politically powerful interests such as employee unions will engage in rent seeking in the case of public ownership. Shleifer (1998) argues that a substitute for competition exists if private suppliers are concerned about building a reputation for quality. He concludes that the case for public ownership is strongest when (1) opportunities for cost reductions that lead to lower quality are significant, (2) innovation is relatively unimportant, (3) competition is weak or consumer choice is ineffective, and (4) reputational mechanisms are weak.

Horn (1995) offers a similar analysis using different terminology. He discusses the choice faced by government officials between establishing a "public enterprise" and subsidizing or regulating a private for-profit enterprise in industries such as utilities and telecommunications where the government has noncommercial objectives. He argues that the public enterprise is likely to be preferred when the noncommercial objectives are important but difficult to define and agree on before the fact and when it is important that the government commit to subsidies or special privileges to secure these objectives (Horn, 1995). Chapter 5 in this volume summarizes yet another body of research, which finds that transaction costs associated with contracting out are highest when the tasks to be performed are complex, outputs are difficult to monitor, and potential suppliers face barriers to entry and exit.

None of these scholars, except Mark Stater (chapter 7), discuss universities per se, and the contrast they present is generally between direct government provision and contracting with for-profit firms, whereas nearly all private universities are nonprofit organizations. However, Hart, Shleifer, and Vishny (1997) and Shleifer (1998) give brief attention to vouchers for elementary and secondary education. As long as the managers in a nonprofit organization can consume the difference between revenues and efficient operating costs in some form, the difference in incentives between public and private sectors remains. Private, nonprofit university administrators and faculty can consume this difference through more generous research and travel accounts, faculty clubs, better infrastructure, and discounted or free tuition for family members.

A more important criticism is that the concern private managers may cut costs in ways that decrease quality does not square with common perceptions of private universities. Opportunities for cost reduction exist in theory, as private universities could hire lower-quality faculty or substitute graduate teaching assistants for professors in the classroom. However, some scholars argue that nonprice competition and reputation effects lead to an oversupply of certain kinds of quality and costs that are inefficiently high (Clotfelter, 1996; Winston, 1999). This is consistent with the model of Glaeser and Shleifer (2001), who show that self-interested entrepreneurs who want to take their "profits" in the form of increased quality rather than income might prefer the nonprofit form of organization to a for-profit firm. Winston shows this as well in his article about the relative subsidies provided by colleges. This argument does not negate the basic assumption of the incomplete contracts literature, which is that private sector suppliers face different incentives than public-sector suppliers. It actually simplifies the comparison somewhat by focusing on a straight trade-off between quality attributes associated with private organization and lower cost associated with the public sector.

We can also think about the issue of quality more broadly by considering the question of *what* is to be produced. Absent oversight and control, faculty may tend to pursue a different curriculum or focus on different kinds of research than state government officials would prefer. Academics are often assumed to be motivated by a quest for prestige, professional rewards, and knowledge for its own sake (James, 1990; Winston, 1999). In contrast, state government officials should prefer to support activities that generate tangible benefits for the median voter, ideally before the next election. These include an "all-purpose" curriculum that satisfies the demands of a wide range of students and applied research that can be linked to economic development (Lowry, 2001a; Veysey, 1965). If these sorts of differences exist, then control of residual decision-making authority becomes important and public ownership has advantages for state government officials.

A Simple Spatial Model

The formal models used by Hart, Shleifer, and Vishny (1997) and Glaeser and Shleifer (2001) are not readily applicable to this last argument because they examine differences in the cost or quality of a fixed service or good. I present an alternative spatial model that focuses on differences over what goods and services should be supplied.

Figure 3.1 illustrates the hypothesized situation. Assume that different people have different preferences about the kinds of instruction and research that universities should supply. These are represented as points on a unidimensional scale, which may be thought of as an ideology of higher education.[6] Outputs can be ordered on the scale so that very low values correspond to a combination of low-cost education supplied to a wide range of students to train them for careers and relatively applied research, whereas very high values correspond to a combination of more selective admission, a liberal arts and sciences curriculum, and basic research. Each person has single-peaked preferences, meaning that he or she has a most-preferred point located somewhere on the scale and assigns progressively lower values to outputs as they move farther away from that point in either direction (Hinich and Munger, 1997).

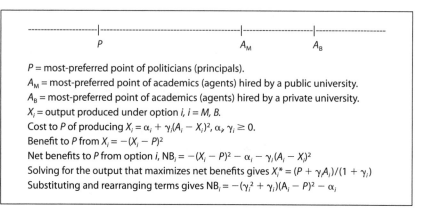

Figure 3.1. A spatial representation of incomplete contracting issues

Point P in figure 3.1 represents the output most preferred by state government officials (the principals). Points A_M and A_B represent the outputs most preferred by academics at universities (the agents) in cases where the public sector "makes" or "buys" higher education, respectively. The distance between A_M and P is less than the distance between A_B and P if academics have heterogeneous preferences and state government officials (or their appointees) can exert influence over the hiring and tenure process such that academics at public universities tend to share their preferences to a greater degree than do those at private universities.

Of course, universities have other principals, including students, private donors, and grant-making agencies. Including them explicitly would complicate the model considerably, but we can interpret A_M and A_B as the agents' induced preferences after taking into account the influence of other principals.

Now assume that P directs or contracts with agents to produce a fixed quantity of output characterized by point X_i, where $i =$ M or B and X_i lies in-between the most preferred points of the principal and the agents ($P \leq X_i \leq A_i$). P cannot easily measure the location of actual outputs on this scale, but he can observe the inputs that are used and the overall production process.[7] P must pay a cost of $\alpha i + \gamma i (A_i - X_i)^2$ with αi and γi greater than or equal to zero and receives benefits of $-(X_i - P)^2$. These cost and benefit functions are assumed to be quadratic to make the math easy, but the logic of the argument applies as long as benefits and costs both decrease as X_i increases (moves away from P and closer to A_i), while marginal benefits decrease and marginal costs increase.

The total costs of producing X_i decrease (increase) as X_i gets farther away from (closer to) P for two reasons. First, the principal may need to pay a premium to induce agents to acquiesce to being directed or agree to supply instruction and research that deviate from their most-preferred point. Second, the principal has to spend resources specifying X_i, overseeing the production process, and enforcing the directive or agreement, given the agents' temptation to shirk and follow their true preferences. The required premium and the temptation to shirk both decrease as X_i gets closer to A_i.

Given these assumptions, we can solve for the output target that maximizes net benefits to the principal under each option: $X_i^* = (P + \gamma_i A_i)/(1 + \gamma_i)$. The principal gets exactly what he wants ($X_i^* = P$) if there is no need to pay a premium and there are no transactions costs of producing outputs that deviate from agents' most-preferred point ($\gamma_i = 0$) but settles for something very close to A_i if these costs are sufficiently high.[8]

The choice whether to make or to buy depends not only on the locations of X_M^* and X_B^* but also on the costs of achieving these outputs. Thus, the principal compares the net benefits for each option, which can be rewritten as $NB_i = -(\gamma_i^2 + \gamma_i)(A_i - P)^2 - \alpha_i$.[9] The crucial variables are the distance between the most-preferred point of state government officials and that of academics at public or private universities ($A_i - P$), the cost of achieving outputs that deviate from academics' most-preferred points ($\gamma_i^2 + \gamma_i$), and other costs related to producing a fixed quantity of output in the public or private sectors (α_i).[10] The first two terms interact. If principals can hire or contract with agents who want exactly what they want ($A_i = P$), contracting, oversight, and enforcement costs are irrelevant. If there are no contracting, oversight, or enforcement costs ($\gamma_i = 0$), then it does not matter whether principals and agents have the same preferences.

This very simple model directs our attention to some key empirical questions. Is it true that the typical public university academic's most-preferred point is closer to the desires of state government officials than the most-preferred point of the typical private university academic; that is, is $A_M < A_B$? If so, then contracting with private universities will be preferred to public ownership only if the total costs per unit of private production are low enough to compensate. However, the cost of achieving outputs that deviate from academics' most-preferred point seems likely to be lower under public ownership ($\gamma_M < \gamma_B$) because the costs of contracting, oversight, and enforcement are likely to be less when the principal adopts a statutory mission statement and procedural regulations and institutionalizes discretionary decision making with a hierarchical governance structure, than under a system of contracts (Horn, 1995; McCubbins, Noll, and Weingast, 1989; Nicholson-Crotty and Meier,

2003; Teske, 1991). In this case, contracting would make sense only if private universities have a large advantage in production costs not related to the exact type of output produced ($\alpha_B < \alpha_M$). If, for example, private universities pay lower salaries to faculty with the same credentials or are able to build and to maintain their physical plant at lower cost or are simply able to operate more efficiently because of increased competition and an absence of oversight, then such a cost advantage would exist. This is the type of argument typically made for privatizing services such as prisons, weapons production, and garbage collection (Hart, Shleifer, and Vishny, 1997; Shleifer, 1998), but it is not at all clear that it holds for higher education, even if we ignore the possibility that elite private institutions may compete on the basis of prestige rather than price.[11] Regardless, the privatization of these once public services has produced mixed results, as Stater documents in chapter 7.

I am not aware of any systematic data that would allow us to answer these empirical questions about preferences and costs associated with contracting, oversight, and enforcement directly. In addition to the technical measurement issues,[12] at least two other factors need to be considered. First, the scenarios we would like to compare do not actually exist anywhere in the United States, because all 50 states and the District of Columbia have publicly owned universities supported by appropriations. Although we could gather data on academics' preferences at private universities, these are not necessarily representative of the data that would exist in a state where there were no public universities and private universities were free to compete for state government grants, contracts, and student subsidies.

The second complication concerns the notion of "typical" costs or preferences. It seems likely that a privatized market for higher education would include a whole range of suppliers. In fact, private universities from elite research institutions to urban commuter schools serving distinct market niches already exist (Lyall and Sell, 2005; Winston, 1999). Under a privatized system, some universities that have sufficient resources from other principals might decline to compete for state government funds (or at least would only compete for those funds that did not require them to alter their existing objectives in any important way), while other universities might specialize in serving state governments. Faculty and administrators would presumably self-select by working for those institutions that best matched their own preferences. The relevant question is not how the "typical" private university under such a system would compare to current public universities but whether there would be sufficient numbers of private universities willing and able to supply the services that state governments want to buy. The law of supply and demand implies that the answer is "yes" provided the price is right, but we cannot be sure how this price (including the cost of making, overseeing, and enforcing contracts) would compare with the cost of supporting and governing public universities under the status quo. Similarly, chapter 4 outlines the factors that might explain the reduction in state funding.

Evidence on Differences in Preferences

One way to shed light on possible differences in preferences between state government officials and academics is to look at the historical record of debates surrounding the early development of public universities. A second way is to look at the variation across different states and assume that outputs of public universities in more centralized systems are closer to the preferences of state government officials than those in less centralized systems. A third method is to compare the allocation of faculty resources and the quality of programs across academic fields at public and private universities. These comparisons are not necessarily predictive of changes that would occur if states were to substitute a system of grants, contracts, and student subsidies for public ownership and appropriations. However, if the evidence suggests that there are real differences, then we have some support for one of the key empirical predicates underlying the incomplete contracts argument.

Historical Evidence

The history of public universities in the United States suggests that the characterization of politicians' and academics' relative preferences is not unreasonable. Disputes between advocates of the classical curriculum taught by most nineteenth-century colleges and a more practical curriculum geared toward economic development were central to the development of public land-grant universities (Brubacher and Rudy, 1976; Rudolph, 1990; Veysey, 1965). Rudolph (1990) concludes, "On the whole, the tendency of the land-grant institutions was to enthrone the practical and ignore the traditional." Lyall and Sell (2005, 52) concur that "America is impatient with musing for its own sake, and many of the reforms that expanded public education in this nation were done to increase the university's involvement in the world." Historian Richard Hofstadter offered a traditionalist's view of these reforms when he argued: "If one had to single out the one feature of the American climate that has been most unfortunate for higher education, it would probably be the implicit assumption that education is something that ought to pay its way, that it is an instrumentality rather than one of the goals of life, that it must justify itself by providing a *quid pro quo*" (Hofstadter, 1952).

Comparisons between state universities and the traditional model may not fully indicate the difference between public and private universities because, for most of the nineteenth century, the traditional model consisted of colleges that were centers of "learning, not research" (Goldin and Katz 1999). The development of the modern research university occurred in both the public and private sectors at roughly the same time. Nonetheless, there were significant differences between the sectors in the emphasis placed on applied research, as well as the importance of making higher education accessible to large numbers of students (Rudolph, 1990).

Indeed, there was little public support initially for many state universities because higher education "did not seem immediately to touch their [taxpayers'] vital interests" (Brubacher and Rudy, 1976, 155). Many states provided minimal or no subsidies for operating expenses until after the Civil War and, in some cases, not until after the second Morrill Act in 1890 provided for federal appropriations to land-grant colleges and universities (Brubacher and Rudy, 1976; Rudolph, 1990). To secure state support and increase enrollments, it was necessary for the new public universities to deviate from the traditional model. Once states started to make appropriations for operating expenses, the amounts appropriated were correlated with the contributions of public universities to the state economy. Goldin and Katz (1999) find that spending by state and local governments on higher education in 1929 was greater in states with larger fractions of the labor force employed in mining, in manufacturing, or in agriculture, three industries that received much more emphasis in the curriculums of public universities than private universities.

Another important conflict in the early days of public universities concerned the role of religion. Most nineteenth-century private colleges were affiliated with religious denominations that dominated their governing boards (Brubacher and Rudy, 1976). This is not surprising, as the founders of nonprofit institutions almost by definition have some nonpecuniary motive (Glaeser and Shleifer, 2001) and perhaps the most common such motive worldwide is the desire to proselytize (James, 1990). It is also not surprising that there was significant opposition to religious influence over public institutions. In some Midwestern states, there was open conflict between members of religious denominations who sought to gain control of public university governing boards and groups that opposed any sort of sectarian influence (Brubacher and Rudy, 1976). Eventually, the latter prevailed and public universities provided an alternative to religiously affiliated private higher education.

Comparing Public Universities in Different States

A number of studies in recent years imply that public universities with more autonomy from state government pursue a different mission than those subject to tighter control, which in turn implies that the preferences of academics are different from those of state government officials. Bowen et al. (1997) compare aggregate measures for seven states having different degrees of centralization and conclude that universities in more centralized systems give greater weight to the interests of the nonacademic public relative to the professional interests of academics. Several econometric studies have found that, controlling for state and local government funding, public universities in less centralized systems generate more revenue per student and charge higher tuition than those in more centralized systems (Knott and Payne, 2004; Lowry, 2001b; Nicholson-Crotty and Meier, 2003; Toma, 1990). Public universities in less centralized systems also tend to spend more on instruction and student services (Lowry, 2001b), have lower total enrollments (Berger and Kostal, 2002), and lower student-to-faculty ratios (Toma, 1990). All of these results are consistent with the notion that state government officials place greater emphasis on cost control and student access to higher education than do academics. See Lowry (2007) for a more extensive summary of this literature.[13]

Differences in Academic Emphasis

Finally, we can compare the fields of instruction and research emphasized by public and private universities. Table 3.2 compares the distributions of faculty members in public and private, nonprofit universities across principal fields of instruction, as estimated by the 2004 *National Study of Postsecondary Faculty* (National Center for Education Statistics, 2004). Panel A shows the estimates for faculty at doctoral universities, while panel B shows the estimates for faculty at master's universities. The last column in each table shows the odds ratio, or the percentage of public university faculty in that field divided by the percentage of private university faculty. This tells us how much more or less likely a randomly chosen faculty member at a public university is to be in each field compared with a randomly chosen faculty member at a private, nonprofit university.

The first line of panel A shows that faculty in public doctoral universities are 7.5 times as likely as faculty in private doctoral universities to have agriculture or home economics as their principal field, 1.8 times as likely to teach education, and 1.3 times as likely to teach engineering. In contrast, faculty at public doctoral universities are only 90% as likely as their private-sector counterparts to teach humanities, about 80% as likely to teach fine arts or health sciences, and 70% as likely to teach business.

Panel B shows the differences in emphasis at master's universities as well. Once again, agriculture and home economics lead the list of fields that receive greater

TABLE 3.2.
Principal Teaching Fields of Faculty, by Type of University and Control

Field	Public (%)	Nonprofit (%)	Odds Ratio
		Doctoral Universities	
Agriculture and home economics	4.5	0.6	7.50
Education	7.1	3.9	1.82
Engineering	6.7	5.1	1.31
Natural sciences	22.2	21.1	1.05
All other	10.1	10.1	1.00
Social sciences	9.9	10.3	0.96
Humanities	10.3	11.5	0.90
Fine arts	5.5	6.8	0.81
Health sciences	18.4	23.5	0.78
Business	5.1	7.1	0.72
		Master's Universities	
Agriculture and home economics	1.3	0.8	1.63
Social sciences	11.5	9.1	1.26
Natural sciences	18.1	14.7	1.23
All other	13.5	13.0	1.04
Humanities	14.5	14.9	0.97
Education	15.5	16.1	0.96
Engineering	2.4	2.5	0.96
Fine arts	9.0	9.8	0.92
Health sciences	5.9	7.3	0.81
Business	8.3	12.0	0.69

Source: National Center for Education Statistics (2004).
Note: Principal fields match the categories used in the 1988 *National Study of Postsecondary Faculty.*

emphasis at public universities, but now they are followed by the social and natural sciences, while the percentages of faculty teaching education or engineering are similar for both sectors. Fine arts, health sciences, and business again are fields that receive relatively more emphasis at private universities.

Graduate program rankings published by *U.S. News and World Report* (2004) imply that there are also differences of quality and emphasis within fields. When medical schools are ranked by research, 28 of the top 50 programs (56%) are at private institutions. When medical schools are ranked by primary care training, 34 of the top 50 programs (68%) are at public institutions. Public institutions also account for 63% of ranked graduate programs in nursing, 74 percent in speech-language pathology, 85% in audiology, and 100% in veterinary medicine. Other fields where private institutions account for relatively large shares of ranked programs include law (52%), business (50%), economics (64%), history (50%), English (48%), and fine arts (55%).[14]

Of course, it does not follow that if all universities were to convert to private ownership, the distribution of faculty would look like the private university column in table 3.2 or that there would be no quality programs in veterinary medicine. The greater emphasis on agriculture and home economics at public universities no doubt reflects the fact that all but two land-grant universities are public institutions (National Association of State Universities and Land-Grant Colleges, 2006).[15] If these universities were to become private but retain their land-grant status, they would likely continue to emphasize these fields. More generally, many current public universities and perhaps some private ones would likely define their market niches by focusing on fields demanded by students like those who currently attend public universities. Nonetheless, the data show that public universities subject to control and oversight by state government officials tend to emphasize different fields of instruction than private universities that have more freedom to define their missions as they choose.

The Advantages of Appropriations

Grossman and Hart (1986) equate ownership with residual rights to exercise discretion regardless of how revenues are obtained, and for much of the nineteenth-century state universities received little or no funding for operating expenses from state governments (Brubacher and Rudy, 1976; Rudolph, 1990). Given this, what is the role of state appropriations in solving the incomplete contracts problem?

First, public ownership without some sort of subsidy or other special privilege may not be a workable model. Public universities struggled mightily in most states until they began to receive subsidies for operating expenses (Brubacher and Rudy, 1976; Rudolph, 1990), and much of the impetus for current calls for privatization comes from the failure of appropriations to keep up with costs (Brown, 2005; Lyall and Sell, 2005). In general, the stick of oversight is rarely enough by itself to sustain an arrangement in which agents have the option of exiting (i.e., working for a different university or leaving academics) and the organization is charged with goals that place it at a competitive disadvantage; some sort of carrot is needed as well (Horn, 1995).

For some kinds of enterprises, there are other kinds of carrots that might be offered. The U.S. Postal Service is a public enterprise that receives no subsidies for operating expenses but is charged with the noncommercial objective of universal mail delivery six days a week. To accomplish this, it is granted a monopoly over the delivery of first-class mail (Geddes, 2005). There are many other examples of public enterprises that receive special privileges that enable them to pursue noncommercial objectives (Horn, 1995). If a single university or university system were granted a monopoly over higher education in a state, it might be feasible to require that university to perform a variety of public services while generating all of its operating revenues from private sources. Given that such a monopoly is politically infeasible, some other subsidy or privilege must be extended.

There may be no one argument that definitively explains why appropriations are used instead of other forms of financial subsidies, but appropriations do have advantages over each of the obvious alternatives. With respect to student subsidies, appropriations should enjoy greater political support than need-based or merit scholarships because only a relatively small subset of the population would benefit from scholarships, whereas all high school graduates and their parents potentially benefit from appropriations. Garratt and Marshall (1994) show it is rational for taxpayers to support subsidized instruction for all public university students even if only some high school graduates actually benefit and admission is based on test scores and other widely used criteria. Of course, the cost per taxpayer of student subsidies increases with the number of beneficiaries. Determining the exact design of a subsidy that maximizes political support is beyond the scope of this chapter, but it seems likely that support for student subsidies will be greater if all public university students benefit rather than a targeted few.

State government officials may also prefer appropriations over vouchers and scholarships because under the latter systems the allocation of revenues across universities is determined by the decisions of individual students. Subsidizing higher education through vouchers or scholarships therefore increases the influence of one set of principals (students) at the expense of another (state government officials). This may alter university outputs, as students are likely to be almost entirely interested in the private benefits of instruction rather than services that supply public goods. Lowry (2004) finds that graduation rates are higher and there are more small classes at universities that rely more heavily on student tuition and fees relative to appropriations, after controlling for public or private ownership.[16]

Finally, funding higher education through contracts, grants and vouchers, or scholarships opens the door to lobbying and other forms of transaction costs for state government officials that may exceed the comparable costs of making appropriations (Horn, 1995; Shleifer, 1998). Appropriations are less likely to be the subject of lobbying in part because they are unrestricted and can be used for any general educational expense. In addition, appropriations are—or at least were until recently—a relatively stable source of funds. The expectation in many states was that higher education appropriations would essentially grow at the same rate as enrollments year after year (Lyall and Sell, 2005). In contrast, grants and contracts have restricted uses and specific end dates, which create incentives for lobbying to secure more favorable terms and future grants or contracts. It is possible that this factor could work in favor of privatization: Although funding universities through grants and contracts would impose additional transactions costs, it would also create opportunities for government officials to direct benefits toward favored political constituencies (Shleifer, 1998).

Scenarios for Change

Assuming that politicians and academics have different preferences, attempts by the former to exert control over the latter will always cause tension. For many years, an institutional equilibrium has prevailed in all 50 states and the District of Columbia that includes publicly owned universities subject to monitoring and oversight and subsidized by appropriations. The net benefits to state government officials under such a system should be higher than under a system of private ownership plus grants, contracts, and student subsidies for several reasons: (1) greater ability to influence the hiring and promotion of faculty and administrators; (2) lower contracting, oversight, and enforcement costs of achieving given outputs; (3) broader political support for appropriations that potentially benefit all high school graduates; (4) less influence by other principals (students); and (5) lower transactions costs when making funding decisions.

The exact arrangements differed by state, and I do not mean to suggest that all parties were fully satisfied with this equilibrium. However, the size of the necessary political coalition and the cost of changing institutional arrangements embedded in statutes and constitutions can be quite large, and no coalition of actors having the ability to change the basic arrangements was sufficiently dissatisfied to incur the costs of making major changes (Horn, 1995; North, 1990).

Recently, the decline in appropriations relative to costs and attempts to impose greater accountability combined with the pursuit of alternative revenue sources by public universities appear to have disrupted this equilibrium in several states, leading to calls for partial or even complete privatization (Brown, 2005; Lyall and Sell, 2005). Although "privatization" is sometimes used to refer to a trend toward decreased reliance on revenues from appropriations relative to private revenue sources, I will focus here on proposals that include a significant shift toward the characteristics associated with private universities along one or more of the dimensions in table 3.1. In considering each proposal, first determine whether it offers advantages to the state government officials who would have to consent to any change and second whether the proposed changes are likely to constitute a new equilibrium or simply the first steps down a slippery slope to something else.

One scenario that does not come under the heading of privatization would be for state government officials to promise increased (or at least sustained) appropriations in the future in exchange for additional oversight powers or accountability regulations. A basic problem with this scenario is that any commitment to future appropriations may not be credible, given the overall political and economic climate and competing demands for state government funding (Lyall and Sell, 2005). Both chapters 6 and 7 examine the potential benefits of privatization on other public resources to question the positive and negative effects it might have on higher education.

The opposite scenario would involve increased autonomy coupled with continued appropriations but at a lower level. The Virginia Charter Status plan allows the University of Virginia, Virginia Tech, and William and Mary to trade fewer procedural regulations for substantive goals and lowered expectations of state funding. To secure a sufficiently large coalition for change, the opportunity to apply for charter status was extended to all public university campuses in the state, but only these three took the bargain (Couturier, 2006; Petkovsky, 2005). For these three universities, the change essentially amounts to a shift from a state agency to what Eykamp (1995) calls a "public enterprise," although the terminology of state agency continues to be used (Couturier, 2006). The University of Colorado also has recently been granted "enterprise" status (Lyall and Sell, 2005), although this may be more an attempt to get around the fiscal constraints of Colorado's Taxpayer Bill of Rights than a change in governance structure or formal constraints on discretion. Three questions arise from this situation: (1) Are these new arrangements stable? (2) Will appropriations shrink relative to costs? (3) Will the universities seek more flexibility in a few years?

A third scenario involves retaining public ownership but ceding some discretionary authority to private-sector actors. Lyall and Sell (2005) argue that because private sources account for a large share of public university revenues, they should have a comparable share of seats on the governing board. Other scholars have argued similarly that the only legitimate stakeholders in nonprofit organizations are the donors and clients who provide revenue, and all revenue sources should be represented on the board of directors (Ben-Ner and Hoomissen, 1994). However, why state government officials would agree to proportional representation is difficult to see. Just as the carrot of financial subsidy may be necessary to secure academics' acquiescence to oversight by state government officials, retention of residual rights to exercise discretion may be a necessary condition for the continuation of significant subsidies by state government. State government officials might agree to give private revenue sources a minority of the voting seats on the board—and this might be sufficient to cause some changes in outputs—but it is not likely that they would surrender control over a majority of seats, given the importance of discretionary authority in governing higher education.

A fourth scenario is to transfer ownership of all or part of a public university's assets to the private sector. Although complete privatization of the University of Colorado has been semi-seriously proposed, the sheer cost of the land and buildings it owns presents a major obstacle (Brown, 2005). This has been proposed in Oregon as well. One could imagine a scenario in which units of the public university not integrally involved in pursuing its public service objectives and whose graduates have high expected incomes[17] might "go private," while those units involved in pursuing public service objectives or training students for lower-paying careers would remain under public control. The University of Virginia law and business schools, for example, do not receive any subsidies for operating expenses (Lyall and Sell, 2005). The result eventually might look something like Cornell University, with its distinction between endowed and statutory colleges charging separate tuitions. Comparably, chapter 8 discusses the United Kingdom's use of "top-up" fees in its privatization scheme.

Literal transfer of the assets for much or all of any large university would raise two substantial problems: (1) How would the transfer be handled, and (2) who would be able to raise the necessary money? The first question is beyond the scope of this chapter but would require careful attention. The second question reintroduces the issues of religion and, more broadly, ideology into the debate. Recall that one of the sources of conflict in the nineteenth century was over religious influence in colleges and universities (Brubacher and Rudy, 1976). Assuming that the privatized university would be a nonprofit organization, entrepreneurs capable of raising the required funds would likely have a religious or other ideological motive (James, 1990). A recent example is the proposed Ronald Reagan University in Colorado, which was intended to emphasize values associated with its namesake but which foundered when Nancy Reagan declined to allow the use of the name (McPhee, 2004). Attempts to prohibit potential bidders who have strong ideological or religious motives would likely raise thorny constitutional issues and (if successful) result in a very "thin" market of buyers. Of course, if the new organization were for-profit, this would raise a host of new issues.

A final scenario would be to retain public ownership of land and buildings but lease them to a private entity for a long period of time. Discretionary authority could also be transferred to the private entity and appropriations could be reduced or eliminated. The private entity might be required as a condition of the lease to perform certain functions and meet certain performance goals, for which it would receive a contractual sum. Municipal sports stadiums, some primary and secondary schools, and some prisons have operated this way. The problem here is that the private entity's incentive to adhere to the public service requirements of the contract might be inadequate in the absence of significant ex post competition from other potential lessees (Shleifer, 1998). In other words, this approach would be subject to objections based on incomplete contracts.

Summary

Equilibrium institutional arrangements do not necessarily arise because they are inevitable or optimal in any normative sense. Rather, they offer feasible solutions to the immediate problems faced by key actors, and once in place, they tend to persist in part because of the transactions costs of overturning them and the uncertainty associated with alternatives (Horn, 1995; North, 1990).

Public universities developed as equilibrium institutions in this sense, with many variations around a common theme. Federal land-grant policies created a comparative advantage for public institutions in overcoming start-up costs in the nineteenth century, and this advantage was magnified by economies of scale and scope given the new technology of the research university (Goldin and Katz, 1999). Public ownership offered a feasible solution to the problem of incomplete contracts given divergent preferences between state government officials who emphasized access to higher education for all taxpayers and economic development, and academics who favored more selective admissions and greater emphasis on the pursuit of knowledge for its own sake. Although tax-funded financial support for public universities was initially scarce, appropriations offer incentives for academics to supply outputs valued by politicians and have a variety of advantages over alternative ways of subsidizing instruction, research, and public service activities. The model eventually was adopted nationwide and has persisted for over 100 years.

It appears that the conditions for a shift to a new equilibrium may be present in some states. This may mean shifting within the existing paradigm, for example, by reducing both formal constraints and appropriations. More fundamental shifts involving transfers of assets or discretionary authority open many possibilities in theory, but in practice, only those that leave state government officials at least as well off as they are now will receive consideration. In addition, some of the proposed changes may only represent the first steps in a long process rather than a new equilibrium arrangement.

NOTES

This chapter was originally prepared for presentation at the State of the Art Conference on "The Privatization of the Public Research University," University of Georgia, September 7–9, 2006. I thank the conference participants for their questions and comments on the earlier version.

1. A few public universities have constitutional status such that changes in their control and governance would require ratification by popular vote. This applies to only a relatively small number of universities, however, and it is unlikely to occur if actively opposed by state government officials.

2. Both private and public universities also seek funds for research from a variety of public and private sources. However, research funds, as well as revenues from auxiliary operations such as hospitals, cannot be used to pay for student instruction (Lyall and Sell 2006).

3. In addition to statutes of general application, all private universities that accept federal research grants—that is, all private research universities—must comply with various regulations regarding equal opportunity, veteran's preferences, and so on.

4. In both sectors, day-to-day discretionary authority is typically exercised by the chief executive officer. The relationship between board structure and operations and the CEO's de facto authority is not simple. On the one hand, larger boards and less frequent meetings imply more authority for private CEOs. On the other hand, each private board governs only one campus, whereas many public governing boards must divide their attention among several campuses.

5. Goldin and Katz do not argue that the private sector is incapable of raising the necessary capital, only that the public sector has a comparative advantage. However, it may be that the private sector was literally incapable of raising sufficient capital in certain parts of the country in the late nineteenth and early twentieth centuries.

6. Alternatively, we could allow for multiple dimensions where the line in Figure 3.1 represents the (possibly weighted) Euclidean distance between two points in a multidimensional space (Hinich and Munger, 1997).

7. McLendon, Hearn, and Deaton (2006) show that states are increasingly incorporating performance measures into their funding decisions for public universities. Although the ability to measure outputs may be increasing, it remains imperfect, and there are costs associated with collecting this information. Moreover, that these measures are being used in funding decisions demonstrates that legislators are willing to pay more for outputs closer to their own preferences.

8. More generally, X_i^* increases with both A_i and γ_i: $\delta X_i^*/\delta A_i = \gamma_i/(1 + \gamma_i) < 0$; $\delta X_i^*/\delta \gamma_i = (A_i - P)/(1 + \gamma_i)^2 < 0$, since $A_i < P$.

9. Technically, the principal would not take either option unless net benefits exceed those of the next best use of resources. We could assume that benefits are actually $\beta - (X_i - P)^2$, where β is large enough to satisfy this condition, then safely ignore β for the rest of the exercise.

10. In the terminology of principal-agent models, $(A_i - P)$ represents costs that are related to issues of adverse selection, while $(\gamma_i^2 + \gamma_i)$ represents costs associated with moral hazard. In standard principal-agent models, adverse selection arises because the agent's innate attributes such as preferences or competence are not easily observed. In higher education, academics' attributes may be well known based on their training and professional socialization, but they still do not match the preferences of state government officials. Moral hazard issues involve the design and implementation of incentives for agents to conform to the principal's expectations, given an underlying difference in preferences (Weimer and Vining, 1999).

11. Although there are systematic differences in labor inputs between the sectors, it is not clear how they affect overall costs and quality. In 2003–4, 51.1% of full-time instructional staff at public four-year universities were tenured, compared with just 40.5% at private four-year universities, but the average salary was 22% higher at private universities (National Center for Education Statistics, 2005, tables 236, 242).

12. Technical measurement issues regarding preferences are not necessarily insurmountable. Political scientists have devoted a great deal of effort to measuring the "ideal points" of members of Congress on a spatial scale and determining whether the relevant scale has one, two, or more dimensions. See, e.g., Poole (2006).

13. None of the studies cited here explain why different states adopted systems with different degrees of centralized control.

14. Author's calculations from *U.S. News and World Report* (2004) based on the top 50 programs plus ties, except for fields where fewer than 50 programs are ranked.

15. The exceptions are the Massachusetts Institute of Technology and Tuskegee Institute in Alabama.

16. I do not mean to suggest that state government officials are opposed to high graduation rates or small classes. It is a question of trade-offs: What are they willing to surrender to achieve these results?

17. Higher expected incomes should translate into greater willingness by students to pay higher tuition and more donations from alumni.

REFERENCES

Ben-Ner, Avner, and Theresa Van Hoomissen. 1994. The Governance of Nonprofit Organizations: Law and Public Policy. *Nonprofit Management and Leadership* 4 (Summer): 393–414.

Berger, Mark C., and Thomas Kostal. 2002. Financial Resources, Regulation, and Enrollment in U.S. Public Higher Education. *Economics of Education Review* 21 (April): 101–10.

Bound, John, Jeffrey Groen, Gabor Kezdi, and Sarah Turner. 2004. Trade in University Training: Cross-State Variation in the Production and Stock of College-Educated Labor. *Journal of Econometrics* 121 (July–August): 143–73.

Bowen, Frank M., Kathy Reeves Bracco, Patrick M. Callan, Joni E. Finney, Richard C. Richardson Jr., and William Trombley. 1997. *State Structures for the Governance of Higher Education.* San Jose: California Higher Education Policy Center.

Brown, Jennifer. Strapped Colleges Weigh Autonomy. *Denver Post*, September 26, 2005, A-1.

Brubacher, John S., and Willis Rudy. 1976. *Higher Education in Transition: A History of American Colleges and Universities, 1636–1976.* 3rd ed. New York: Harper & Row.

Clotfelter, Charles T. 1996. *Buying the Best: Cost Escalation in Elite Higher Education.* Princeton, NJ: Princeton University Press.

Couturier, Lara K. 2006. *Checks and Balances at Work: The Restructuring of Virginia's Public Higher Education System.* San Jose. National Center for Public Policy and Higher Education.

Dillon, Sam. 2005. At Public Universities, Warnings of Privatization. *New York Times,* October 16, sec. 1, 12.

Education Commission of the States. 1997. *State Postsecondary Education Structures Sourcebook.* Denver, CO: Education Commission of the States.

Eykamp, Paul W. 1995. Political Control of State Research Universities: The Effect of the Structure of Political Control on University Quality and Budget. Ph.D. diss., University of California, San Diego.

Garratt, Rod, and John M. Marshall. 1994. Public Finance of Private Goods: The Case of College Education. *Journal of Political Economy* 102 (June): 566–82.

Geddes, Richard. 2005. Reform of the U.S. Postal Service. *Journal of Economic Perspectives* 19 (Summer): 217–32.

Glaeser, Edward, and Andrei Shleifer. 2001. Not-for-Profit Entrepreneurs. *Journal of Public Economics* 81 (July): 99–115.

Goldin, Claudia, and Lawrence F. Katz. 1999. The Shaping of Higher Education: The Formative Years in the United States, 1890 to 1940. *Journal of Economic Perspectives* 13 (Winter): 37–62.

Grossman, Sanford, and Oliver Hart. 1986. The Cost and Benefits of Ownership: A Theory of Vertical and Lateral Integration. *Journal of Political Economy* 94 (August): 691–719.

Hansmann, Henry B. 1980. The Role of Nonprofit Enterprise. *Yale Law Journal* 89 (April): 835–901.

——. 1996. *The Ownership of Enterprise.* Cambridge, MA: Belknap Press of Harvard University Press.

Hart, Oliver, Andrei Shleifer, and Robert W. Vishny. 1997. The Proper Scope of Government: Theory and Application to Prisons. *Quarterly Journal of Economics* 112 (November): 1127–61.

Hinich, Melvin J., and Michael C. Munger. 1997. *Analytical Politics.* New York: Cambridge University Press.

Hofstadter, Richard. 1952. *The Development and Scope of Higher Education in the United States.* New York: Columbia University Press.

Hopkins, Bruce R. 2001. *Starting and Managing a Nonprofit Organization: A Legal Guide.* 3rd ed. New York: John Wiley & Sons.

Horn, Murray J. 1995. *The Political Economy of Public Administration: Institutional Choice in the Public Sector.* New York: Cambridge University Press.

Iowa State University Foundation. 2006. About ISU Foundation. 2006. www.foundation .iastate.edu/site/PageServer.

Jaffe, Adam B. 1989. Real Effects of Academic Research. *American Economic Review* 79 (December): 957–70.

James, Estelle. 1990. The Public/Private Division of Responsibility for Education: An International Comparison. *Economics of Education Review* 6 (1): 1–14.

Knott, Jack H., and A. Abigail Payne. 2004. The Impact of State Governance Structures on Management Performance of Public Organizations: A Study of Higher Education Institutions. *Journal of Policy Analysis and Management* 23 (Winter): 13–30.

Lowry, Robert C. 2001a. The Effects of State Political Interests and Campus Outputs on Public University Revenues. *Economics of Education Review* 20 (April): 105–19.

——. 2001b. Governmental Structure, Trustee Selection, and Public University Prices, and Spending: Multiple Means to Similar Ends. *American Journal of Political Science* 45 (October): 845–61.

——. 2004. Markets, Governance, and University Priorities: Evidence on Undergraduate Education and Research. *Economics of Governance* 5 (April): 29–51.

——. 2007. The Political Economy of Public Universities in the United States: A Review Essay. *State Politics and Policy Quarterly* 7 (Fall): 303–324.

Lyall, Katharine R., and Kathleen R. Sell. 2005. *The True Genius of America at Risk: Are We Losing Our Public Universities to de Facto Privatization?* Westport, CT: Praeger.

Madsen, Holly. 1998a. Composition of Governing Boards at Independent Colleges and Universities, 1997. Occasional Paper No. 36, Association of Governing Boards of Colleges and Universities, Washington DC.

——. 1998b. Composition of Governing Boards at Public Colleges and Universities, 1997. Occasional Paper No. 37, Association of Governing Boards of Colleges and Universities, Washington DC.

McCubbins, Matthew D., Roger G. Noll, and Barry R. Weingast. 1989. Structure and Process, Politics and Policy: Administrative Arrangements and the Political Control of Agencies. *Virginia Law Review* 75:431–82.

McLendon, Michael K., James C. Hearn, and Russ Deaton. 2006. Called to Account: Analyzing the Origins and Spread of State Performance-Accountability Policies for Higher Education. *Educational Evaluation and Policy Analysis* 28 (Spring): 1–24.

McPhee, Mike. 2004. Nancy Reagan Derails University Plan. *Denver Post*, April 30, B3.

National Association of State Universities and Land-Grant Colleges. 2006. About NASULG, www.nasulgc.org/About—Nasulgc/members—land—grant.htm.

National Center for Education Statistics. 2004. National Study of Postsecondary Faculty. http://nces.ed.gov/surveys/nsopf/.

——. 2005. Digest of Education Statistics. http://nces.ed.gov/programs/digest/.

National Research Council. 1995. *Research-Doctorate Programs in the United States: Continuity and Change.* Washington, DC: National Research Council.

Nicholson-Crotty, Jill, and Kenneth J. Meier. 2003. Politics, Structure and Public Policy: The Case of Higher Education. *Educational Policy* 17 (January): 80–97.

North, Douglass C. 1990. *Institutions, Institutional Change, and Economic Performance.* New York: Cambridge University Press.

Petkovsky, Andrew. 2005. University Autonomy Measure Approved. *Richmond Times Dispatch*, March 31, B-1.

Poole, Keith. 2006. NOMINATE data. http://voteview.com/dwnl.htm.

Rudolph, Frederick. 1990. *The American College and University: A History.* Athens: University of Georgia Press. (Original publication 1962.)

Savas, Emanuel S. 2000. *Privatization and Public-Private Partnerships.* New York: Chatham House, 2000.

Shleifer, Andrei. 1998. State versus Private Ownership. *Journal of Economic Perspectives* 12 (Fall): 133–50.

Teske, Paul. 1991. Interests and Institutions in State Regulation. *American Journal of Political Science* 35 (February): 139–54.

Toma, Eugenia Froedge. 1990. Boards of Trustees, Agency Problems, and University Output. *Public Choice* 67:1–9.

U.S. News and World Report. 2004. America's Best Graduate Schools. Washington, DC.

——. Various Years. America's Best Colleges. Washington DC.

Veysey, Laurence R. 1965. *The Emergence of the American University.* Chicago: University of Chicago Press.

Volkwein, James Fredericks, and Shaukat M. Malik. 1997. State Regulation and Administrative Flexibility at Public Universities. *Research in Higher Education* 38:17–42.

Weimer, David L., and Aidan R. Vining. 1999. *Policy Analysis: Concepts and Practice.* 3rd ed. Upper Saddle River, NJ: Prentice Hall.

Winston, Gordon C. 1999. Subsidies, Hierarchy, and Peers: The Awkward Economics of Higher Education. *Journal of Economic Perspectives* 13 (Winter): 13–36.

Zumeta, William. 1992. State Policies and Private Higher Education. *Journal of Higher Education* 63 (July): 363–417.

CHAPTER FOUR

An Economist's Perspective on the Privatization of Public Higher Education

• ℰℳ •

ROBERT TOUTKOUSHIAN

Researchers and academics have a long history of grouping institutions of higher education (IHE) in various ways, on the basis of their size, selectivity, mission, highest degree offerings, and geographic location. Perhaps the most common distinction, however, has been between public and private institutions.[1] Public IHE are typically defined as those that receive direct financial support in the form of appropriations from state governments. At the other extreme are private institutions that do not receive state appropriations. There are also institutions that fall somewhere between these extremes. For example, some private institutions receive appropriations from their states to help support academic programs that require particular state needs in areas such as medicine.

The evidence from the past 20 years, however, shows that while state funding for public higher education has generally increased over time, the growth has failed to keep pace with the rising cost of educating students in public institutions (chapter 4; Toutkoushian, 2001) or the ability of states to fund higher education (chapter 2; Grapevine, 2006). In more recent years, the level of state funding for public education has increased in all but three fiscal years between 1992 and 2005 (Grapevine, 2006; Heller, 2006). The shares of public educational revenues obtained from state funding, however, have fallen considerably over time, from 45% in 1980–81 to 35% by 2000–2001 (National Center for Education Statistics, 2006). Accordingly, as several contributors to this volume have noted, it is more correct to say that it is the *relative* state funding for higher education, and not the level of state funding, that has decreased over time. Policymakers have expressed concerns over this trend because it has shifted the burden of paying for higher education toward students and their families at a time when policymakers are devising strategies to enable more high school graduates to pursue a postsecondary education.

The reduction in relative state support for higher education has led some education observers to conclude that public higher education is becoming more "privatized." As Priest, St. John, and Boon (2006, 2) noted, "For public colleges and universities, privatization involves becoming more like for-profit corporations and nonprofit colleges, which have functioned for centuries without state subsidies to reduce tuition." Although state support for higher education is the focus of this chapter, other signs of privatization also affect public IHE. In recent years, a number of public institutions, including the University of Minnesota and the University of New Hampshire, have adopted incentive-based budgeting systems to entice academic units to become more competitive and cost-efficient (Priest, Becker, Hossler, and St. John, 2002; Priest and Boon, 2006). Likewise, some institutions have turned to outsourcing certain functions and services to private enterprises (Priest, Jacobs, and Boon, 2006).

The decline in relative state support for higher education has been well documented (Hearn, 2006); yet, policymakers have struggled to understand why this has occurred and how it will affect the academy. Academics from different disciplines would approach this problem in a variety of ways. For example, Michael K. McLendon and Christine G. Mokher (chapter 2) rely primarily on a political science framework to examine state funding for higher education, and Gabriel Kaplan (chapter 6) centers his analysis of state funding on the effects of governance and ownership. In this chapter, I focus on economists' perspectives. Economists typically use theoretical models and optimization techniques to explain the behavior of states with regard to funding for higher education and to determine how sensitive the results are to changes in key variables and parameters in the model. These models are based on three fundamental questions: (1) Who are the decision makers? (2) What are their goals and objectives? (3) What constraints do they face? Given answers to these questions and a set of behavioral and simplifying assumptions, the economist would then construct a model to determine how the decision makers could best attain their goals, given the constraints on their actions.

This approach differs from how a sociologist or a political scientist would attempt to explain state funding for higher education. Nonetheless, even several of the "noneconomic" contributions in this volume draw on methodologies similar to economists' methodologies to examine state funding. The chapters by Robert C. Lowry (chapter 3), Kaplan (chapter 6), and McLendon and Mokher (chapter 2), for example, focus on the roles of particular decision makers in state funding. Furthermore, both Lowry and Kaplan specify objectives that the decision makers seek to optimize and use this to frame their arguments regarding state support for higher education.

In this chapter, I explore the issues surrounding state support for public higher education from an economist's perspective. First, I describe how economists think about subsidies for higher education, and then I document key changes that have occurred in funding both public and private institutions over the past 30 years. In the next section, I explore economic models that have been used to justify public subsidies of higher education and what factors might account for the decline in relative state funding over time. The third section considers in more detail the various options that states can use to support higher education and how economists would examine the costs and benefits of these alternatives. This is followed by a brief discussion of the economic literature on the costs and benefits of state support for higher education from the perspective of taxpayers.

Economic Framework for Higher Education Financing

Perhaps the best place to start is to review the framework advanced by economists for understanding the similarities and differences in how public and private institutions of higher education are funded. Gordon Winston (1999) presents the economist's view of the pricing and financing of higher education institutions (also see Hansen and Weisbrod, 1969, 1971; G. Johnson, 1984; W. Johnson, 2006). He observed that most education institutions charge prices (tuition rates) below their costs of providing education services because they use subsidies from various sources, including governments and private sources, to cover a portion of education costs. He expresses the pricing equation for educational institutions as

$$\text{Price} = \text{Cost} - \text{Subsidy}, \tag{1}$$

where Price = net price charged to students and their families, Cost = per pupil cost to institutions of providing education services, and Subsidy = total per pupil subsidies from all (nonstudent) sources.

This simple equation illustrates that institutions with more subsidies at their disposal are able to use the subsidies to reduce the price charged to students and that rising prices could be due to rising costs, falling subsidies, or some combination of the two. The equation shows that prices can rise even when subsidies increase if education costs rise at an even faster rate than subsidies. The effect of subsidies on the numbers of students enrolling, and hence the social benefits derived from them, depends on the elasticity of the supply curve. Figure 4.1 shows that the number of

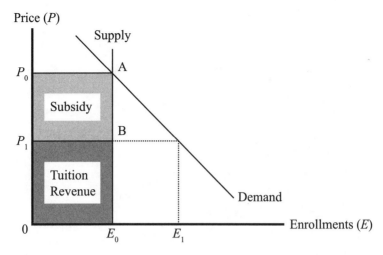

Figure 4.1. Subsidies in higher education pricing—perfectly inelastic supply

available spaces in higher education is fixed (perfectly inelastic supply curve) in the short run. This might be the case for a selective institution, many of whom set enrollment targets for the academic year and then through the admissions process decide how to fill these seats.

The downward-sloping demand curve shows that the institution could enroll more students if it reduced the price charged to students; however, this does not occur because the number of seats is held constant. The market-clearing price without subsidies is denoted by P_0; at this price, the quantity of spaces demanded is equal to the quantity supplied. The institution uses subsidies from federal, state, and local governments, as well as private donations, investment gains, and auxiliary services to cover some portion of its costs and thus charge students a reduced price P_1. In this example, the institution has total subsidies equal to the area (P_0, P_1, A, B) and distributes this subsidy equally to all students.[2] At the price P_1, however, the institution would have E_1 students willing and able to enroll and thus only a fraction E_0/E_1 of students would be admitted.

Figure 4.2 is similar to figure 4.1, except that in this graph the supply curve is assumed to be perfectly elastic. This means that all students who are willing and able to pay the price of admission would be enrolled. A number of institutions of higher education use "open admissions"; they will enroll every qualified applicant regardless of the implications for their size. This depiction also characterizes the aggregate higher education market because students who are willing and able to pay the price of admission can find an institution that will enroll them, even if it is not their first

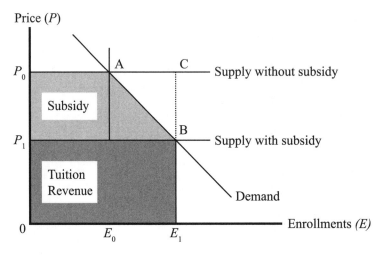

Figure 4.2. Subsidies in higher education pricing—perfectly elastic supply

choice. Thus, one can think of figure 4.2 as applying to either an open admissions institution or the higher education system as a whole.

In the open admissions model, the education supply curve shifts downward because of the subsidy, and the subsidy covers the lost revenue that the institution would have received if the supply curve did not change and E_1 students enrolled. The subsidy is given by the area (P_{0}, P_1, A, B), and tuition revenue becomes (P_1, B, E_1, o). In this instance, the subsidy leads to an increase in enrollments from E_0 to E_1. This is important because I argue that one reason states provide financial assistance to IHE is to entice more students to attend college so that society can reap the social benefits. In the example of a selective institution, the subsidy leads to greater numbers of applicants to the institution but not additional students.

Perhaps the first question of interest to an economist is why institutions—public and private—might be concerned with their mix of revenues, holding constant the level of total revenues. The economist would begin by identifying the decision maker (in this case, the college or university), the decision maker's constraints (total revenue is fixed but can be obtained from different sources), and its goals and objectives. Economists have struggled, however, to provide a generally accepted model of the goals that institutions of higher education are trying to achieve. Bowen (1980), for example, suggests that institutions seek to maximize revenues, while Paulsen (2001a) counters that institutions attempt to maximize their discretionary income. I have argued elsewhere (Porter and Toutkoushian, 2006) that postsecondary institutions seek to maximize their knowledge production through teaching, research, and service and that institutions with more selective admissions pursue reputation maximization as a way of securing more resources to achieve this goal.

This framework rationalizes why both selective and open admissions institutions would have an interest in securing state appropriations. Beginning with selective institutions as the decision makers, and assuming that they seek to maximize their reputations, then an economic argument can be made that state appropriations help selective institutions achieve their goal. An increase in the share of education costs covered by subsidies allows selective institutions to build excess demand for their services ($E_0 - E_1$) and admit a smaller proportion of applicants (figure 4.1). This in turn enables the institution to raise the profile of students who are admitted and enroll, which has a subsequent positive effect on the perceived quality and reputation of the institution. This does not hold true for open admissions institutions (figure 4.2) because all applicants are admitted. However, by replacing tuition revenue with subsidies, open admissions institutions are able to enroll more students and thus produce more knowledge through their various activities.

These descriptions of institutional behavior are based in part on the notion that IHE must operate in a competitive market. Even though most IHE do not compete with one another for profits, as would be true in many nonacademic markets, institutions compete with one another for students, faculty, staff, and research funding. Likewise, colleges and universities that do not attempt to maximize profits still need to be concerned about generating enough revenues to fund their operations adequately because these revenues are used to enhance their goals such as contributing to knowledge production in society. In this view, selective institutions are not presumed to use subsidies so that they can support broader societal goals relating to increasing access to higher education for underrepresented segments of the population or increase the social benefits from higher education. Rather, increasing the number of applicants is in the selective institution's self-interest because it enables them to increase the pool of students from which to choose, and hence raise their reputation and the resources that they can acquire to carry out their mission. Similarly, open admission institutions seek financial resources not because it leads to benefits for society, but because through enrolling more students, they can produce more knowledge, which is consistent with their own goals and objectives.

Another reason that both selective and open admissions institutions might prefer state funding over other income options is that it provides institutions with a relatively stable source of revenue. This stability fits well with enterprises such as institutions of higher education where expenditures are fairly predictable. Most institutional expenditures are for compensation, and the tenure system requires institutions to make long-term employment commitments to its faculty and thus

TABLE 4.1.
*Comparison of Net Expenditure and General (E&G) Revenues by
Source for Public and Private Institutions, 1994–95*

Revenue Source	Revenue per Pupil, Public Institutions ($)	Revenue per Pupil, Private Institutions ($)	Share of Net E&G Revenues, Public Institutions (%)	Share of Net E&G Revenues, Private Institutions (%)
Net tuition and fees	1,532	6,850	20.7	54.8
Government appropriations	4,029	188	54.5	1.5
Private gifts, grants, and contracts	418	1,897	5.7	15.2
Endowment income	61	1,016	0.8	8.1
Government grants and contracts	1,345	2,557	18.2	20.4
Net E&G revenues per student	7,386	12,507	100	100

Source: The figures in the first two columns originally appeared in table 6 of Toutkoushian, R. 2001. Trends in Revenues and Expenditures for Public and Private Higher Education. In *The Finance of Higher Education: Theory, Research, Policy, and Practice*, ed. M. Paulsen and J. Smart, 11–38. New York: Agathon Press, 2001. Data were obtained from IPEDS Finance Survey FY95, as reported by WebCASPAR. Net tuition and fees represent gross tuition and fees minus scholarship and fellowship expenditures from state, local, private, and institutional sources.

reduces an institution's flexibility to lower costs in the event that demand for its services falls. Other sources of subsidies such as endowment income do not offer the same level of stability as state funding.

The heavy reliance on subsidies to help fund their operations cuts across both public and private institutions. However, public and private institutions differ significantly in how they obtain these subsidies. Examining trends in revenue sources in the public and private sectors was made more difficult in the past 10 years because of changes in the accounting standards used by institutions. In 1995, private institutions were no longer required by the Financial Accounting Standards Board to report revenue and expenditure data using the generally accepted fund accounting categories of public institutions. In 2002, public institutions changed to the same categorization scheme as private institutions. As a result, the trends in revenues within each sector through 2006 are difficult to examine and the distributions of revenues for public and private institutions cannot be strictly compared with one another between these years.

In an earlier study (Toutkoushian, 2001), I examined the trends in revenue sources for public and private institutions between 1975 and 1995, when both sectors were using the same revenue and expenditure categories for federal reporting purposes. In table 4.1, I used data from this study to compare the net expenditure

TABLE 4.2.
Percentage Distribution of Current Funds Revenues by
Source for Public Institutions, Selected Years

	Percentage Share of Current Fund Revenues		
Revenue Source	1980–81	1990–91	2000–2001
Tuition and fees	12.9	16.1	18.1
Federal government	12.8	10.3	11.2
State government	45.6	40.3	35.6
Local government	3.8	3.7	4.0
Private gifts, grants, contracts	2.5	3.8	5.1
Endowment income	0.5	0.5	0.8
Sales and services	19.6	22.7	21.7
Other income	2.4	2.6	3.7

and general (E&G) revenues by source for public and private institutions in fiscal year 1994–95.[3]

All of the nontuition revenues shown in table 4.1 can be viewed as subsidies that effectively reduce the net price charged to students. In total, almost four-fifths of the net E&G revenues per pupil in public institutions were subsidies, as compared with less than half for private institutions. Private institutions relied more heavily than public institutions on funding from their endowment income and from private gifts, grants, and contracts to help cover educational costs. Public institutions, however, received a significant portion of their net E&G revenues from state, federal, and local governments.

State governments have traditionally played a major role in financing public higher education. In fiscal year 2005, states appropriated more than $63 billion for higher education (Grapevine, 2006). The falling relative level of higher education subsidies from state governments is not a recent phenomenon. From 1975 to 1995, the share of total E&G revenues in public institutions that were subsidized fell from 87% to 79% (Toutkoushian, 2001). Table 4.2 provides an updated calculation of the shares of current fund revenues for education services in public institutions coming from sources such as tuition and fees, state appropriations, and other categories.

The data show that the share of current fund revenues in public institutions covered by state funding has fallen from 45% in 1980–81 to 35% by 2000–2001. This does not mean, however, that the level of financial support from states for higher education has fallen (see also chapters 2 and 6). In fact, the National Center for Education Statistics (2006, table 333) shows that between 1990–91 and 2000–2001 total state appropriations for higher education increased from $35.9 billion to $56.3 billion and that every state experienced a notable rise in total state appropriations over this period. The annual Grapevine survey of the states also collects data on state tax appropriations for higher education and examines how they are changing over time. They found that the increase in total state appropriations for higher education between fiscal year 1995 and fiscal year 2005 was nearly twice the rate of inflation for the same period (47% to 28%). The Grapevine data also show that while total appropriations for public higher education have grown, the growth has been uneven. Total state appropriations for higher education fell in the early 1990s, increased by an average of 4% to 7% annually through the rest of the decade and then increased by smaller amounts in most subsequent years.

Despite the growth in total state dollars appropriated for higher education, the reduced share of education costs subsidized by state governments shows that states are playing an increasingly smaller role in financing public higher education. The increase in total state funding has not kept pace with changes in states' ability to pay for higher education. Grapevine (2006) reported that the median level of state appropriations per $1,000 personal income in the United States fell from $9.49 in 1991–92 to $6.89 by 2004–5. Using the pricing equation shown by Winston (1999), that higher education prices have risen faster than subsidies suggests that higher education costs have grown at an even faster rate than subsidies. Increasingly, public institutions have turned to tuition and fees; private gifts, grants, and contracts; and sales and services to help compensate for the relative reduction in state support.

Private institutions also rely heavily on subsidies and have experienced a substantial decline in the share of their educational costs subsidized by various entities. In previous calculations, I found that the share of net E&G revenues in private institutions that were subsidized (i.e., not covered by net tuition and fees) fell from 53% in 1975 to 45% in 1995 (Toutkoushian, 2001). Therefore, over this period, both the public and private sectors experienced similar declines in the shares of education revenues that were subsidized by nontuition sources, and both have had to turn increasingly to students and their families to pay for a larger portion of their education costs. Table 4.3 contains a breakdown of current fund revenues by source for private institutions in selected recent years. Private institutions are highly dependent on students and private giving to finance their costs of education. On the basis of the more recent data and different accounting standards, private institutions have continued to experience a decline in the share of subsidized education revenues (72% in 1997–98 to 66% in 2002–3).

In contrast to state funding, the revenues from sources such as endowment income and private gifts, grants, and contracts can fluctuate considerably, depending on the health of the economy. This variability can be clearly seen in table 4.3. In

TABLE 4.3.
Distribution of Current Fund Revenues by Source for Private Institutions, Selected Years

Revenue Source	Percentage Share of Current Fund Revenues		
	1997–98	2000–2001	2002–3
Tuition and fees	27.8	38.1	34.1
Federal appropriations, grants, and contracts	11.7	16.3	15.7
State appropriations, grants, and contracts	1.0	1.4	1.4
Local appropriations, grants, and contracts	0.6	0.6	0.5
Private gifts, grants, and contracts	13.9	19.3	13.6
Investment return	23.4	−4.4	8.8
Educational activities	2.8	4.2	2.9
Auxiliary enterprises	8.0	10.6	9.3
Hospitals	6.6	8.7	8.5
Other revenues	4.2	5.1	5.2

1997–98, for example, more than 23% of education current fund revenues at private institutions were obtained from investment returns. When the national recession began in 2000, however, private institutions realized an aggregate loss in investment return (−4.4%) and had to dramatically raise tuition and fees and rely more heavily on private giving to make up for the loss. State funding for higher education therefore is an appealing source for financing institutions of higher education because it offers more stability in funding. At the same time, revenue sources such as endowment income and private gifts, grants, and contracts have the potential to provide larger revenue increases and thus enable institutions to make substantial programmatic additions.

Economic Models of State Support of Higher Education

Given the clear trend toward decreased relative state support of public higher education institutions, from an economic perspective, is this good or bad? Economists are accustomed to arguing in favor of privatizing markets for goods and services because privatization would increase the level of competition between providers and lead to gains in efficiency and ultimately lower prices for consumers. In K–12 education, Milton Friedman and other economists have been leaders in support of vouchers for students to attend private schools. In many smaller communities, public K–12 schools essentially operate as monopolies in that students and their families would have to either move or provide homeschooling if they were dissatisfied with the public schools. Microeconomic theory suggests that, in most instances, a monopolized market would provide fewer goods/services and charge higher prices than would be true in a more competitive market because there is less incentive for producers to find ways to become more efficient.

At first glance, it might seem as though the same arguments could be made for privatizing the higher education market. Public higher education institutions enjoy a significant price advantage over their private counterparts, due to the large portion of costs that are covered by state funding. Likewise, the fact that state appropriations have risen faster than inflation and yet have not been able to keep pace with rising education costs (Toutkoushian, 2001) could be taken as evidence that IHE are not being very cost efficient in the delivery of education services (see also chapter 6). However, the geographical scope of K–12 markets for students is generally much smaller than the postsecondary market because students at the K–12 level typically live at home while attending school. As a result, there are very few substitutes for public K–12 schools within the market. In the postsecondary market, many traditional-aged students normally live away from home and thus consider a larger geographic area for their postsecondary education, although working adults who are continuing their education will be more place-bound than their younger counterparts. Despite the significant price advantage for public IHE, the postsecondary education market already contains a fair amount of competition. Students typically have a number of providers of postsecondary services to consider and thus the market should be more competitive than is true at the K–12 education level. The substantial growth in the use of technology to deliver higher education services through distance education has furthered the competition for both traditional and nontraditional students. In chapter 6, Kaplan also provides an excellent discussion of the effects of competition and privatization on the higher education market.

Public-sector economists have long been interested in explaining the behavior of governments and their interaction in specific markets. According to Browning and Browning (1994), as cited by Paulsen (2001b), "The economics of the public sector can be defined as 'the study of how government policy, especially tax and expenditure policy, affects the economy and thereby the welfare of its citizens.' " Much of this work focuses on the efficiency and equity of governmental funding (Browning and Browning, 1994; McMahon, 1991; Stiglitz, 2000). Public-sector economists in general attribute government support for higher education as a means of rectifying inefficiencies, inequities, or failures in the higher education market. By giving financial support for higher education, it is believed that governments can help make the market more equitable with regard to educational opportunities for all citizens and lead to a more efficient provision of higher education services.

To explain the change in state support for higher education, an economist would ask, Who makes the decisions about state support? What goals are these decision makers trying to achieve? What constraints do they face? The constraint faced by decision makers in this context is that limited funding is available to distribute among competing demands for state dollars, such as Medicaid, transportation, corrections, K–12 education, and higher education. States are often required by law to spend specific amounts on particular items in the budget. Higher education is usually not one of these items and thus must compete with other "discretionary" items for the remaining state support. Economists have used two specific approaches to examine state support for higher education: (1) the positive externalities approach and (2) the median voter model.

Positive Externalities of Higher Education

In the first approach, economists identify the state as the decision maker, and states view financial support to education, to corrections, and to other areas as investments that will generate benefits to citizens of the state (Creedy and Francois, 1990). From the economist's perspective, government intervention in a competitive market may be desirable when the market fails to lead to the optimal allocation of resources from society's point of view. Market failure could arise when either the good/service is a "public good" or the good/service leads to positive or negative externalities. As noted by Kaplan (see chapter 6), higher education does not appear to meet the criteria for a public good because students can be excluded from receiving the service, and one student's use of the service may preclude another from receiving the service. Kaplan observed, "There are few of the typical market failures that would justify public ownership and provision which seem to apply to higher education"; however, he overlooks the positive externalities thought to be created by education. Lowry (chapter 3) focuses on how the knowledge created by research might be viewed as a public good and describes the "positive spillover effects" from education, which economists would label as positive externalities.

Higher education can be thought of as a service that provides both direct benefits to those who receive the services (primarily students) and indirect benefits to others who do not receive the services (Acemoglu and Angrist, 2001; Bowen, 1977; W. Johnson, 2006; Moretti, 2004; Paulsen, 2001b; Paulsen and Peseau, 1989; Schultz, 1963; Weisbrod, 1968; Wolfe, 1995). These indirect benefits are referred to as *positive externalities*. A positive externality is a benefit accrued by one group of individuals when another group consumes a good or service. In the case of higher education, as state residents acquire more education, not only are direct (private) benefits provided to them but also indirect (social) benefits are provided to other state residents.

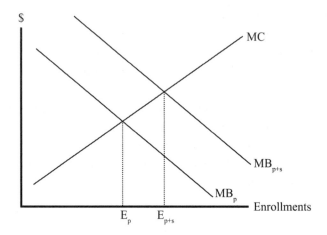

Figure 4.3. Annual percentage changes in state funding for higher education, fiscal years 1992–2005

These social benefits may be economic gains from attracting better-paying jobs to the state that result in higher tax revenues or less-tangible benefits such as crime reduction, reduced demand for social services, improved health, and increased civic engagement.

Economists argue that if the production of a good or service leads to positive externalities, and the funding of the good or service was left to the competitive market, then from society's point of view not enough of the good or service would be produced (see figure 4.3, adapted from McEachern, 1994).

The line MC represents the marginal cost of higher education. The line MB_p shows the private marginal benefits received by students from pursuing higher education, and MB_{p+s} is the combined private and social marginal benefits received when students pursue higher education. The negative slope of the marginal benefit curves reflects the assumption of diminishing marginal returns to education. That is, the private and social gains from enrolling additional students increase at a decreasing rate. This would arise if the students with the largest private or social benefits from higher education are the first to pursue it. Subsequent students may still have marginal benefits that exceed the marginal cost, but the differences would become progressively smaller. Eventually, a point would be reached in which the benefits from enrolling additional students would be exceeded by the cost of enrolling them.

Comparing only MB_p and MC, the optimal number of students who should pursue higher education would be E_p because at enrollment levels above this quantity, the cost of providing additional higher education exceeds the private benefits received by additional students from higher education. However, this ignores the social benefits that others obtain when students pursue higher education. As a result, states would have an incentive to provide funding to help entice more students to pursue postsecondary education, not because of the private benefits received by those students but because it would lead to positive externalities for the state.

From the economist's perspective, state governments are simply acting in their self-interest in that they support higher education because it enables the state to reach its goal of maximizing the social benefits for its citizens. The optimal amount of financial support for higher education is found at the point where the ratios of marginal (social) benefits to marginal costs are the same for all discretionary items (Bowen, 1980; Hoenack, 1982; Paulsen, 2001b). If the ratio of marginal benefits to cost for higher education exceed the ratio for corrections, for example, then the state could increase the total social benefits received by reallocating some dollars away from corrections and toward higher education.

Median Voter Model

The median voter model of public choice theory offers an alternative—and perhaps more pessimistic—view of the legislative decision-making process. A number of researchers have used the median voter model to identify factors that cause legislative demand for higher education to change (Borcherding and Deacon, 1972; Bös, 1980; Clotfelter, 1976; Coughlin and Erekson, 1986; Hoenack and Pierro, 1990; Strathman, 1994; Toutkoushian and Hollis, 1998). In the median voter model, individual legislators are the decision makers because they vote on the levels of state funding to appropriate to competing interests. The goal of legislators is to act in ways that will maximize ability to be reelected (Coughlin and Erekson, 1996). According to this model, the preferences of the median voter would dominate the preferences of other voters when majority rule is used to decide issues. As a result, legislators would vote in accordance with the demands of the median voter in their region. Others such as Becker (1983) have modified the median voter model to show how special interest groups (such as teachers' unions) can exert influence on legislators. Furthermore, McLendon and Mokher (chapter 2) review many different ways in which the political composition of a state may affect its relative support for higher education. Although the authors approach the problem through a political science lens, much of their work could be equally interpreted through an economic lens by focusing on the goals and constraints of legislative decision makers.

Studies that rely on the median voter model specify the legislative demand for higher education to be a function of factors that would affect the median voter's preferences for public higher education support. These factors would include the price of public higher education services, the size of the population that might benefit from public higher education, the ability of citizens to provide financial support for higher education, and the size of competing interest groups such as corrections, K–12 education, and Medicaid. Using this framework, I examined the legislative demand for higher education over the period 1982 to 1996 (Toutkoushian and Hollis, 1998). Many of the results supported the notions of the median voter model. I found that state support for higher education was positively related to the ability of citizens to pay for education and to the size of the population that would use public higher education services. Of the special interest groups considered in the study, only K–12 education was shown to detract funding away from public higher education, suggesting that K–12 and higher education were viewed as substitute services by legislators.

Explanations for Declining Relative State Support of Higher Education

An economist would hold that the decision maker—either the state or the median voter—is able to form a demand function for each competing use of state funds. The demand function represents the various quantities of higher education that the decision maker would be willing and able to purchase at different prices. In this view, the quantity of higher education demanded by the decision maker would fall as the price of higher education rises, holding all else constant. The demand curve for higher education support can also shift (increase or decrease) for all prices as various factors affecting demand change. Table 4.4 lists possible "demand shifters" for the median voter's higher education preference. For example, if the health of the state's economy were to improve, then the state could afford to provide support for higher education as well as other needs. This change would be viewed by an economist as a rightward shift (increase) in the legislative demand for higher education because the state could now more easily afford to support higher education at all prices.

In the positive externality approach, falling relative state support for public higher education would be attributed to perceived reductions in the social benefits from either higher education, increases in the marginal cost of public higher education, gains in the social benefits from competing items in the state budget, or increases in the marginal cost of these items. Obtaining empirical evidence to test these conjectures, however, is a difficult exercise because measuring many of the social benefits derived from alternative uses of state dollars is difficult (Behrman,

TABLE 4.4.
Examples of Possible Demand Shifters for the Median Voter's Preference for Higher Education

General Demand Shifter	Predicted Impact on Demand	Examples for Higher Education
Change in the price of substitute goods/services	As the price of substitute goods/services increases, the demand curve is predicted to increase (shift to the right)	Change in the price of delivering K–12 education services, corrections, etc.
Change in the ability to pay for goods/services	As the ability to pay for goods/services increases, the demand curve is predicted to increase (shift to the right)	Change in median family incomes or poverty levels in the state
Change in the size of the population	As the number of demanders in the market increases, the demand curve is predicted to increase (shift to the right)	Change in the size of the population; change in the age distribution of the population

1997; Paulsen, 2001b). Education stakeholders at both the K–12 and postsecondary levels have had particular trouble quantifying the extent to which educational services lead to positive externalities for society. Economists often focus on measuring the positive externalities through economic impact studies and gains in output or earnings that are due to higher education (Acemoglu and Angrist, 2001; Caffrey and Isaacs, 1971; Leslie and Brinkman 1988; Leslie and Slaughter, 1992; Moretti, 2004; Wolfe, 1995). Using the state's demand function for higher education, factors could be identified that might shift the state's demand to the left and thus give rise to a decline in state funding. Possible factors might include a decrease in state income/wealth, a decrease in the price of alternative public services, or decreased preferences for higher education.

The median voter's demand function for higher education could likewise be used to select factors that might have led to a leftward shift in demand for supporting higher education. Falling levels of state support for higher education could therefore be due to changes in variables that would negatively affect the preferences of the median voter for financially supporting higher education. For example, a decline in median family incomes or in the size of the population may lead to reductions in relative state support for higher education.

Taken together, changes in the health of the economy have clearly contributed to variations in state funding for higher education. The latter half of the 1990s was characterized as a time of robust economic growth, which contributed to rising

TABLE 4.5.
K–12 Public School Enrollments in the United States,
Selected Years

Year	Enrollments (millions)
1959	36.1
1969	45.6
1979	41.7
1989	40.5
1990	41.2
1991	42.0
1992	42.8
1993	43.5
1994	44.1
1995	44.8
1996	45.6
1997	46.1
1998	46.5
1999	46.9
2000	47.2
2001	47.7
2002	48.2
2003	48.5

Source: National Center for Education Statistics. 2006.
Digest of Education Statistics 2005 (Tables 032 and 036).
Washington, DC: U.S. Department of Education.

family incomes and hence rising state tax collections. With the 2001 recession, however, the growth in family incomes decreased, as did state tax collections in subsequent years because of the lagged relationship between economic growth, incomes, and tax collections. This does not fully account for the longer-term decline in relative state support for higher education but is certainly a factor that economic theory would point to in helping explain recent variations.

Demographic trends also may explain some of the decline in relative state support for higher education (table 4.5). Enrollments at the K–12 level peaked in the late 1960s because of the baby boomer generation and then declined from the late 1970s through the 1980s, as these cohorts of students were replaced by smaller cohorts. In the 1990s, K–12 enrollments began to rise again as the children of baby boomers entered school. These variations in the size and in the distribution of the nation's population predictably would affect the demand for higher education services.

There are some important similarities and differences in the approach I have outlined and the approaches discussed by Kaplan (in chapter 6) and Lowry (in chapter 3). In all three cases, we focus on state support by asking who are the decision makers and what are their goals and objectives. Kaplan describes a general situation in which an institution is the decision maker that seeks to maximize benefits to be distributed over a range of benefactors, including investors, consumers, and society. Kaplan's primary focus, however, is on the effects of institutional ownership on the achievement of its goals and objectives. Part of the argument used by Kaplan for public ownership of institutions is that it encourages the production of "spillover benefits," which are viewed by economists as positive externalities due to the failure of the competitive market.

Lowry's analysis centers on the notion that different decision makers at the legislative and institutional levels may have different goals and objectives. Economists refer to this as a "principal-agent" problem. In this case, the legislature would be the principal and the institution would be the agent. Lowry uses this framework to argue that states fund higher education so that they can entice institutions to produce outputs the state desires. The analysis could be reconciled with the ideas presented here by noting that the outputs desired by state governments are those that lead to positive externalities for the state. Although there are aspects of higher education that fit the principal-agent model, the concept may have limited value in explaining state funding because most states have not tried to influence the delivery of higher education services to the same extent that they have the K–12 education market. At the same time, the principal-agent problem could help explain the decline in subsidies for higher education if principals believe that they have little influence over institutions (agents).

Options for State Support of Higher Education

The tools of economics can also be used to investigate states' choices regarding how they will provide support for higher education. As McLendon and Mokher (chapter 2) noted, states can distribute funding in several ways to help finance higher education. The most recognized approach is to appropriate funds directly to institutions to support their general educational activities. These are often given to institutions as block grants that at least implicitly are intended to reduce the net prices charged to state residents (also see chapter 3). In response, most public IHE charge resident students lower prices than they charge nonresident students. To illustrate, table 4.6 shows the tuition and fees charged to undergraduate students by Big 10 public universities in 2005–6.

States can likewise provide higher education institutions with appropriations for specific academic programs directly related to state needs. Through the Morrill Act, states established land-grant public universities in which the institutions received

TABLE 4.6.
*Resident and Nonresident Tuition and Fees for Undergraduate Students at
Big 10 Public Institutions, 2005–6*

Institution	Resident Tuition and Fees ($)	Nonresident Tuition and Fees ($)	Nonresident Tuition Premium ($)
Pennsylvania State University	11,024	21,260	10,236
University of Michigan	9,609	28,381	18,772
Ohio State University	7,509	18,732	11,223
Michigan State University	7,161	18,861	11,700
University of Minnesota	7,140	18,770	11,630
University of Illinois	7,042	21,128	14,086
Purdue University	6,320	19,686	13,366
Indiana University	6,291	18,687	12,396
University of Wisconsin	5,618	19,618	14,000
University of Iowa	4,890	16,276	11,386

Source: 2005 University of Missouri Tuition and Fees Study.

Notes: Tuition and fees are generally based on 30 credit hours per year. Undergraduate fees for Indiana University are based on a flat fee of 12–17 credit hours. The averages of upper- and lower-division fees are used for the University of Michigan, Michigan State University, and Pennsylvania State University.

state funding to help operate research and service programs in agriculture. States also distribute funding to institutions with other academic programs such as medicine. In most cases, appropriations to support state programmatic needs are combined with general appropriations into a single block grant. It can be argued, however, that both are related to the positive externalities that states are thought to accrue from on another.

Finally, although most state funding for higher education is in appropriations to institutions, states can also provide support for higher education through state-directed financial aid. In this instance, financial assistance is given directly to students rather than to a subset of predetermined institutions. Some states, such as Vermont, provide a significant portion of state funding directly to students as financial aid, whereas other states, including New Hampshire, provide most funding as appropriations to institutions. According to the two models discussed earlier, the dollars are provided to either help generate the positive externalities associated with higher levels of educational attainment for the citizenry or to increase the probabilities of elected officials.

Whether state support should be direct appropriations or student aid is controversial. Those who advocate that states allocate a higher share of funding directly to students suggest that this would allow the state model to more closely parallel with the federal model of support and provide students with more feasible choices of

TABLE 4.7.
Descriptive Statistics for Selected Variables, 1994

Variable	Mean ($)	Standard Deviation ($)	Minimum ($)	Maximum ($)
Appropriations per student	5,087	1,422	2,752	10,531
State financial aid per student	194	256	10	1,410
Median family income	30,593	5,147	20,271	42,113
Average public tuition rates	2,513	884	1,409	5,536

postsecondary institutions by reducing the net prices students pay at all institutions. They would also argue that it is inefficient for public institutions to use the appropriations to lower the prices for all students because some of those who receive the benefit would have attended college anyway. Therefore, only a portion of state funding actually leads to an increase in the social benefits obtained from higher education. Opponents assert that if state dollars were given to students rather than institutions tuition rates at public institutions would likely rise because the subsidy level has fallen. It is also possible that the increased state aid would lead public and private institutions to simply lower the level of institutional aid offered to students, and thus there would be no change in the net price faced by students.

To examine some of these issues, I obtained data for 1994 from Halstead (1996) on the following four variables for each state: average tuition rates at all public institutions (T), state appropriations per student (A), state financial aid per student (F), and median family income (Y). The calculations for variables T, A, and F are for all (two-year and four-year) public institutions within each state. Table 4.7 contains descriptive statistics for each of these variables.

In 1994, state public IHE charged an average of $2,512 in tuition for in-state students. State support such as direct appropriations is, on average, twenty-five times greater than state support for financial aid. The average level of family income also varies considerably across states.

To examine the possible trade-offs between state support for higher education and public tuition rates, I specified a multiple regression model of the form:

$$T = \alpha_0 + \alpha_1 A + \alpha_2 F + \alpha_3 Y + \varepsilon, \tag{2}$$

where α_0 to α_3 are coefficients to be estimated using the 1994 data for all 50 states. If public IHE use state appropriations to reduce in-state tuition rates, then $\alpha_1 < 0$. Likewise, $\alpha_2 < 0$ implies that public IHE increase their in-state tuition rates when states provide more support such as financial aid to students, holding state appropriations and median family income constant. The main results from the model are shown in equation (3). The estimated coefficients appear in front of each variable, and the standard errors are shown below each coefficient:

$$T = 1182.44 - 0.330*A + 1.485*F + 0.089*Y, \quad R^2 = 0.64 \quad\quad (3)$$
$$(493.6) \quad\ (0.059) \quad\ (0.312) \quad\ \ (0.016)$$

The three variables used here account for 64% of the variations in average public tuition rates across states, and each of the variables was found to have a statistically significant effect on average public tuition rates at the 1% significance level. First, the results for median family income show that states with higher income levels for families have higher average tuition rates at their public institutions. The coefficient -0.330 for appropriations per student suggests that a $1 increase in state appropriations to public institutions leads to a 33-cent decline in average public tuition rates. This is consistent with the notion that public institutions use state appropriations to partially offset the prices charged to state residents. Turning to the next variable, the results show that a $1 increase in state financial aid per student is associated with a surprisingly large $1.49 increase in average public tuition rates. Every dollar of state funding reallocated away from appropriations and given to financial aid would result in sizable price increases at public institutions of about $1.82.

Another concern with state-supported financial aid programs is that some portion of state dollars is likely to go to higher education institutions located in other states. This could lead to reductions in the positive externalities from state funding because fewer state dollars are spent in the same state, and students who attend out-of-state universities may be less likely to return to their home state after graduation; thus they take their positive externalities to other locales. The net effect depends on whether the lost benefits from students staying out of state are more than made up by additional students from other states who could now enroll at in-state institutions as nonresident students and then opt to reside in the state following graduation.

Distributional Effects of State Support of Higher Education

Some economists have focused on the manner in which taxes for higher education are collected and benefits distributed among individuals. In 1969, Hansen and Weisbrod published a study that argued, among other things, that the net benefits from higher education subsidies tend to be higher for wealthy families than for poor families. One implication of this work is that state support for higher education could serve to widen income disparities between families within a state. Other articles that relate to the debate on this subject include Hansen and Weisbrod (1971),

Pechman (1970, 1972), Hartman (1972), Moore (1978), and Kane (1999). In these studies, the general notion is that families pay taxes to their state government for funding initiatives such as subsidizing some of the cost of higher education. This tax burden represents a direct cost to families. As described earlier, families with children in college also receive benefits in the form of price subsidies (where subsidy equals cost minus net price) because the subsidies effectively reduce the net prices paid by families for their children's education.

The main policy questions of interest to an economist then become: (1) do the private returns from state support for public institutions of higher education offset the tax burden, and (2) do the net benefits vary based on a family's income level? Family income is likely to be a factor in the cost-benefit analysis because state tax burdens are calculated as percentages of family income. Even in states with regressive income tax structures, families with higher levels of income normally pay more in taxes than other citizens, make larger dollar contributions toward state funding, and have larger tax burdens. On the benefit side, families only receive the private benefits from their tax contributions when they have children enrolled in institutions of higher education. Subsidies at both public and private institutions are substantial, and the sources of these subsidies vary greatly across sectors.

In their study, Hansen and Weisbrod (1969) examined the levels of subsidies and tax burdens for families in California. They focused on the benefits received by families who sent their children to one of the public institutions within the state (University of California System, State College System, and Junior College System) and found that families who sent their children to University of California institutions received the largest subsidies and also tended to have the highest income levels. In contrast, families who did not send their children to any public in-state institution received no benefits and thus experienced negative net benefits after accounting for their tax burden. They concluded that "families with children enrolled in public higher education receive positive net transfers (subsidy less taxes paid) and that these net transfers are an increasing fraction of average family money income" (Hansen and Weisbrod, 1969, 2).

In limiting their focus to public institutions, however, Hansen and Weisbrod (1969) ignored the subsidies that families receive from sending their children to either private institutions or out-of-state public institutions. If revenues from sources other than state appropriations can be considered subsidies for public in-state institutions, then the same argument could be made for counting them for private institutions and out-of-state public institutions. W. Johnson (2006) argues for the full consideration of private subsidies in this type of analysis because "private subsidies, which are financed by donations past and present to private institutions, are also relevant to policy discussions because of the tax preferences given to charitable contributions, the earnings of endowment funds of private colleges and universities, and the real property of private colleges" (297–98). Expanding the range of institutions under consideration could also alter the conclusions about net benefits. Not only are wealthy families more likely than poor families to send their children to college, they are also more likely to send them to private institutions.

W. Johnson's study (2006) considered the full subsidies received by families sending their children to both public and private institutions. Not surprisingly, his data showed that wealthier families received the largest share of private subsidies. After segmenting the sample on the basis of family income, and not the type of institution attended by their children, W. Johnson (2006) concluded that the net public subsidies were greater for lower-income families than for upper-income families. He argued that this finding largely reflects the fact that the college-going rates for children from lower-income families have historically been lower than for children from higher-income families and that Hansen and Weisbrod's conclusions were due to the manner in which they stratified families in the dataset.

Conclusion

In this chapter, I have attempted to describe some of the ways that an economist would consider questions relating to state support for higher education. Economists draw from public choice theory to explain how governments decide on their support for a wide range of services, including higher education. Their work focuses on identifying the decision maker with regard to state funding, their goals and objectives, and the constraints they face when making allocation decisions. Despite having a similar approach to this issue, economists can derive a wide range of specific models and hence policy recommendations, depending on how they answer questions about the decision maker and its goals and the simplifying and behavioral assumptions that they use when specifying a model. Economists also rely heavily on empirical data to test predictions in these models and quantify relationships of interest to policymakers.

These models suggest several explanations for the decline in relative state support for public higher education. First, the slower growth in incomes beginning in 2000 surely contributed to declines in state tax collections. When states face budget shortfalls, they often are forced to cut or reduce the rate of growth in discretionary items in the budget, such as higher education. Second, the significant enrollment increases at the K–12 level beginning in the mid-1990s increased legislative demand for K–12 funding. I had found earlier (Toutkoushian and Hollis, 1998) that K–12 education is a competing interest group for higher education in terms of state funding. This demographic trend in recent years, however, has led to a rightward shift in the demand for higher education as the children of the baby boomers began to move out of the K–12 system and became eligible for postsecondary education, thus partially offsetting the other demand shifters.

The decline in relative state support for higher education has led to net price increases for many students, which is certainly a negative for some individual students who can no longer afford to go to college and for society in terms of reduced social benefits. This movement upward along the demand curve for education means that there will be reduced student demand for higher education at a time when policymakers are striving to raise the college participation rate. The increased price of higher education has not led to enrollment declines in more recent years, however, because of the rising number of college students. Looking ahead, public higher education may benefit from having less competition with the K–12 sector for state funding as K–12 enrollments decline and larger numbers of students reach the typical age of college enrollment. More important, as these students move out of the postsecondary market beginning around 2010 and are replaced by smaller classes of students, the price increases caused by falling state subsidies and enrollment declines may lead to more severe financial problems for institutions. If enrollments begin to decline by the end of the decade, it could lead to substantial reductions in the social benefits produced by higher education.

Although difficult to document, it is also possible that the decline in relative state support for higher education is at least partially attributed to a growing perception among many policymakers that higher education is a good that produces mainly private and not social benefits. This work points out the importance of higher education researchers to focus their efforts on finding better ways of documenting the presence of positive externalities from higher education. Educators often argue that, as a nation, we do not supply "enough" support for education at all levels. From an economic point of view, however, the level of financial support for education is already based on the collective perceptions of taxpayers, legislators, and states of the costs and benefits of education. If society believed that the benefit/cost ratio for education was higher than in other areas, then more funds would be redirected toward education. That this does not appear to be happening suggests that perceptions of the benefits from education, particularly social benefits, may be understated because of the difficulty in measuring them. To date, economists and others have not done an adequate job of showing decision makers why they should reallocate funds away from other activities and direct them instead to higher education or collect more funds from citizens for this purpose. Simply listing potential externalities, such as reduced demand for public services, is a poor substitute for empirically based estimates of the social benefits when it comes to convincing decision makers to increase financial support for higher education.

Additional research is needed to examine the costs and benefits of alternative options for providing state financial support for higher education. Critics on both sides of the debate have expressed legitimate concerns with either direct state appropriations to public institutions and state financial aid programs that are portable beyond state boundaries. One policy option to consider is to provide state support mainly through financial aid that could only be used at in-state, public institutions. In this way, states could target financial support to those students who are less likely to participate in higher education, namely, students from lower-income families, and states would get a larger return on investment in terms of gains in higher education participation rates. Because fewer students would receive the state subsidy than is true when state appropriations are used to lower the price for all in-state students, this could result in larger net price discounts for students from lower-income families. Furthermore, by stipulating that the dollars could only be used at in-state public institutions, there is a greater chance that the tax dollars would be spent within the state and that the students who receive the benefit would stay in-state following graduation. Such a policy might be difficult to implement, however, because fewer voters in the state would receive benefits under this plan.

Finally, in pulling together the discussions here with the debate regarding the distributional effects of state support for higher education, several potential avenues for further work emerge. First, it would be interesting to consider how the results from the various models might change if only state funding for higher education were considered in the subsidy calculations. The argument given for a broader definition of subsidy is based on the notion that tax contributions from families allow the state and federal governments to offer tax incentives for other revenue forms used by institutions. However, these considerations certainly vary by family income, and their inclusion may have an effect on whether higher-income families are net benefactors or contributors to higher education support. At a minimum, it would be helpful to see an analysis of whether state support contributes differently to income inequality than other sources of subsidies. Second, how could the model be expanded to consider state-funded financial aid? In particular, the model could be used to provide more insight into the costs and benefits to states from reallocating financial support away from appropriations and toward state financial aid. Together, these refinements might yield valuable information to policymakers regarding how alternative state financial policies affect citizens.

NOTES

1. For simplicity, I label institutions as either public or private, where private generally refers to "not-for-profit" institutions.

2. In a more complex treatment of the problem, one could allow a portion of subsidies to be distributed unequally among students as need-based or merit-based financial aid.

3. E&G revenues are a subset of total (current funds) revenues. Current fund revenues are defined as expenditure and general revenues plus revenues from the sales and services of educational activities, auxiliary enterprises, hospitals, other sources, independent operations, and Pell Grant revenues.

REFERENCES

Acemoglu, Daron, and Joshua Angrist. 2001. How Large Are Human Capital Externalities? Evidence from Compulsory Schooling Laws. In *NBER Macroeconomics Annual 2000*, ed. Ben Bernanke and Kenneth Rogoff, 9–59. Cambridge, MA: MIT Press.

Becker, Gary S. 1983. A Theory of Competition among Pressure Groups for Political Influence. *Quarterly Journal of Economics* 98:371–400.

Behrman, Jere. 1997. Conceptual and Measurement Issues. In *The Social Benefits of Higher Education*, ed. Jere Behrman and Nevzer Stacey, 17–68. Ann Arbor: University of Michigan Press.

Borcherding, Thomas E., and Robert T. Deacon. 1972. The Demand for Services of Non-Federal Governments. *American Economic Review* 62:891–901.

Bös, Dieter. 1980. The Democratic Decision on Fees versus Taxes. *Kyklos* 33:76–99.

Bowen, Howard R. 1977. *Investment in Learning: The Individual and Social Value of American Higher Education.* San Francisco: Jossey-Bass.

———. 1980. *The Costs of Higher Education: How Much Colleges and Universities Spend per Student and How Much They Should Spend.* San Francisco: Jossey-Bass, 1980.

Browning, Edgar K., and Jacquelene Browning. 1994. *Public Finance and the Price System.* Englewood Cliffs, CA: Prentice-Hall.

Caffrey, John, and Herbert Isaacs. 1971. *Estimating the Impact of a College or University on the Local Economy.* Washington, DC: American Council on Education.

Clotfelter, Charles T. 1976. Public Spending for Higher Education: An Empirical Test of Two Hypotheses. *Public Finance* 31:177–95.

Coughlin, Cletus C., and O. Homer Erekson. 1986. Determinants of State Aid and Voluntary Support of Higher Education. *Economics of Education Review* 5:179–90.

Creedy, John, and Patrick Francois. 1990. Financing Higher Education and Majority Voting. *Journal of Public Economics* 43:181–200.

Grapevine. 2006. *State Rankings on 1-Year, 2-Year, 5-Year, and 10-Year Percent Changes in State Tax Appropriations for Higher Education,* www.grapevine.ilstu.edu, accessed August 1.

Halstead, Kent. 1996. *State Profiles: Financing Public Higher Education 1978 to 1996 Trend Data.* 19th ed. Washington, DC: Research Associates of Washington.

Hansen, W. Lee, and Burton A. Weisbrod. 1969. The Distribution of Costs and Direct

Benefits of Public Higher Education: The Case of California. *Journal of Human Resources* 4 (2): 76–191.

———. 1971. On the Distribution of Costs and Direct Benefits of Public Higher Education: Reply. *Journal of Human Resources* 6 (3): 363–74.

Hartman, Robert W. 1972. Equity Implications of State Tuition Policy and Student Loans. *Journal of Political Economy* 80 (3): S142–S171.

Hearn, James C. 2006. Alternative Revenue Sources. In *Privatization and Public Universities*, ed. Douglas M. Priest and Edward P. St. John, 87–108. Bloomington: Indiana University Press, 2006.

Heller, Donald E. 2006. State Support of Higher Education: Past, Present, and Future. In *Privatization and Public Universities*, ed. Douglas M. Priest and Edward P. St. John, 11–37. Bloomington: Indiana University Press.

Hoenack, Stephen A. 1982. Pricing and Efficiency in Higher Education. *Journal of Higher Education* 53 (4): 403–18.

Hoenack, Stephen A., and Daniel J. Pierro. 1990. An Econometric Model of a Public University's Income and Enrollments. *Journal of Economic Behavior and Organization* 14:403–23.

Johnson, George E. 1984. Subsidies for Higher Education. *Journal of Labor Economics* 2:303–18.

Johnson, William R. 2006. Are Public Subsidies to Higher Education Regressive? *Education Finance and Policy* 1 (3): 288–315.

Kane, Thomas J. 1999. *The Price of Admission*. Washington, DC: Brookings Institution.

Leslie, Larry L., and Paul T. Brinkman. 1988. *The Economic Value of Higher Education*. New York: ACE/Macmillan.

Leslie, Larry L., and Shelia Slaughter. 1992. Higher Education and Regional Economic Development. In *The Economics of American Higher Education*, ed. William E. Becker and Darrell R. Lewis, 223–52. Boston: Kluwer Academic.

McEachern, William A. 1994. *Microeconomics: A Contemporary Introduction*. 3rd ed. Cincinnati, OH: South-Western.

McMahon, Walter W. 1991. Efficiency and Equity Criteria for Educational Budgeting and Finance. In *Financing Education: Overcoming Inefficiency and Inequity*, ed. Walter W. McMahon and Terry Geske, 1–30. Urbana: University of Illinois Press.

Moore, Gary A. 1978. Equity Effects of Higher Education Finance and Tuition Grants in New York State. *Journal of Human Resources* 13 (4): 482–501.

Moretti, Enrico. 2004. Estimating the Social Return to Education: Evidence from Longitudinal and Repeated Cross-Section Data. *Journal of Econometrics* 121:175–212.

National Center for Education Statistics. 2006. *Digest of Education Statistics, 2005*. Washington, DC: U.S. Department of Education.

Paulsen, Michael B. 2001a. Economic Perspectives on Rising College Tuition: A Theoretical and Empirical Exploration. In *The Finance of Higher Education: Theory, Research, Policy, and Practice*, ed. Michael B. Paulsen and John C. Smart, 193–263. New York: Agathon Press.

———. 2001b. The Economics of the Public Sector: The Nature and Role of Public Policy in the Finance of Higher Education. In *The Finance of Higher Education: Theory, Research,*

Policy, and Practice, ed. Michael B. Paulsen and John C. Smart, 95–132. New York: Agathon Press.

Paulsen, Michael B., and Bruce A. Peseau. 1989. Ten Essential Economic Concepts Every Administrator Should Know. *Journal for Higher Education Management* 5 (1): 9–17.

Pechman, Joseph A. 1970. The Distributional Effects of Public Higher Education in California: A Review Article. *Journal of Human Resources* 5:361–70.

———. 1972. A Note on the Intergenerational Transfer of Public Higher Education Benefits. *Journal of Political Economy* 80:S256–S259.

Porter, Stephen R., and Robert K. Toutkoushian. 2006. Institutional Research Productivity and the Connection to Average Student Quality and Overall Reputation. *Economics of Education Review* 25:605–17.

Priest, Douglas M., William E. Becker, Don Hossler, and Edward P. St. John. 2002. *Incentive-Based Budgeting Systems in Public Universities*. Northampton, MA: Edward Elgar.

Priest, Douglas M., and Rachel D. Boon. 2006. Incentive-Based Budgeting Systems in the Emerging Environment. In *Privatization and Public Universities*, ed. Douglas M. Priest and Edward P. St. John, 175–188. Bloomington: Indiana University Press.

Priest, Douglas M., Bruce A. Jacobs, and Rachel D. Boon. 2006. Privatization of Business and Auxiliary Functions. In *Privatization and Public Universities*, ed. Douglas M. Priest and Edward P. St. John, 189–202. Bloomington: Indiana University Press, 2006.

Priest, Douglas M., Edward P. St. John, and Rachel Boon. 2006. Introduction. In *Privatization and Public Universities*, ed. Douglas M. Priest and Edward P. St. John, 1–10. Bloomington: Indiana University Press.

Schultz, Theodore W. 1963. *The Economic Value of Education*. New York: Columbia University Press.

Stiglitz, Joseph E. 2000. *Economics of the Public Sector*. 3rd ed. New York: W. W. Norton.

Strathman, James G. 1994. Migration, Benefit Spillovers, and State Support of Higher Education. *Urban Studies* 31:913–20.

Toutkoushian, Robert K. 2001. Trends in Revenues and Expenditures for Public and Private Higher Education. In *The Finance of Higher Education: Theory, Research, Policy, and Practice*, ed. Michael B. Paulsen and John E. Smart, 11–38. New York: Agathon Press, 2001.

Toutkoushian, Robert K., and Paula Hollis. 1988. Using Panel Data to Examine Legislative Demand for Higher Education. *Education Economics* 6:141–57.

Weisbrod, Burton A. 1968. External Effects of Investment in Education. In *Economics of Education I*, ed. M. Blaug, 156–82. Baltimore: Penguin Books.

Winston, Gordon C. 1999. Subsidies, Hierarchy, and Peers: The Awkward Economics of Higher Education. *Journal of Economic Perspectives* 13 (1): 13–36.

Wolfe, Barbara L. 1995. External Benefits of Education. In *International Encyclopedia of Economics of Education*, ed. Martin Carnoy, 159–163. 2nd ed. Tarrytown, NY: Elsevier, 1995.

CHAPTER FIVE

The Organizational Dynamics of Privatization in Public Research Universities

• ☙ •

PETER D. ECKEL AND CHRISTOPHER C. MORPHEW

Research universities are unique in their form, behavior and choice processes, having been described famously as organized anarchies (Birnbaum, 1988; Cohen, March, and Olsen 1972; March and Olsen, 1976). They also are evolving into quasi-private organizations—or what the University of Texas president calls the "hybrid public research university, one with roots in both the public and private spheres" (Yudof, 2002, 24)—as they replace considerable portions of their traditionally publicly funded revenues with funding from private sources (Hearn, 2003; Lyall and Sell, 2005). Such drastic changes in funding and governance must surely alter the key functions of universities. What does such a transition mean for how research universities behave as organizations?

This chapter adopts an organizational behavior view to explore the intersection of privatization trends in the American public research university and the unique organizational decision-making behaviors of that type of institution. This approach sets this chapter apart from the others in this volume that discuss key drivers shaping such trends and explore the policy implications of privatization. It suggests that such changes may well be transformational organizationally and wonders what the consequences might be for how public research universities behave. It specifically pursues the following conceptual questions and offers a set of propositions about how university decision making might evolve because of privatization:

- What are the predicted effects of privatization on the decision-making processes of public research universities?
- How might the organized anarchy and "garbage can" decision making, familiar to these types of institutions, be altered by privatization?

To accomplish this task, we adapt Cohen, March, and Olsen's (1972) conceptual framework of the garbage can decision making that exists in the organized anarchy. We describe that theory and provide several examples of how the theory has been applied to relevant studies of organizations. Second, we explore how the privatization of the public research university might affect the dynamics of its framework by suggesting several propositions for future research. Finally, we conclude with a discussion of what these possible changes might mean for university decision making.

University Response to a Dynamic Environment

A deeper and more nuanced understanding of how privatization interacts with the organizational structure of public research universities is needed. Much of the existing literature focuses on privatization as a fiscal or economic phenomenon (see chapters 3, 4, and 7) or as a policy matter (see chapter 1). Authors typically acknowledge that privatization includes "the growing importance of private resources to public colleges and universities" (Eckel, Couturier, and Luu, 2005, 5). To be sure, public monies are playing a smaller and smaller part in institutions' financial portfolios. According to Kane, Orzag, and Gunter (2003), funding for higher education has dropped from 7.2% of overall state expenditures in 1977 to 5.3% of state expenditures in 2000. They argue that if funding had remained constant at 1977 levels higher education would have gained an additional $21 billion. As a percentage of institutional revenue, state funding has also declined, from 46.5% in 1977 to 35.9% in 1996 (Kane, Orzag, and Gunter 2003). Furthermore, the future financial outlook for all 50 states looks bleak. Recent data suggest that no state will have a surplus in baseline revenues, and 29 states will face a gap of 5% or more (Jones, 2006). These predicted shortfalls are due to insufficient tax revenue as economic growth and sales and excise taxes do not keep pace with demand for governmental programs and services; increased spending, mostly due to Medicaid growth; and reduction in federal grants to states. And if more public dollars become available, the backlog of underfunded projects means that higher education still will not immediately benefit (National Association of State Budget Officers, 2007).

However, the strong focus on the fiscal dimensions of privatization shortchanges other key aspects of this phenomenon, including changing state oversight and regulatory agreements between the states and public institutions that include such elements as autonomy regarding lease agreements, human resources policies, procurement and capital projects, changing involvement in selecting governing board members, and different accountability procedures and metrics (Couturier, 2006).

Privatization is more than just the money, as many of the other chapters in this book also suggest.

Little discussion exists about the organizational behavior dynamics privatization might create for public research universities. Most of the discussion focusing on privatization does not address the organizational and administrative dimensions this trend suggests. A few scholars have examined ways research universities have changed organizationally to accommodate and react to privatization, although key studies exist (Clark, 1998, 2004; Marginson and Cosidine, 2000; Slaughter and Rhodes, 2004); however, none has addressed the effect privatization might have on key, core processes that span the organization, such as decision making.

These points suggest that higher education would benefit from a conceptualization of how privatization might affect universities' behavior beyond a description of this changing fiscal environment and often a corresponding call to arms. As it is, higher education leaders are often told that privatization represents a "threat" or signals a "crisis" (Lyall and Sell, 2006), and rarely are they engaged in a substantive discussion about how and why replacing public revenue with private monies might affect how research universities behave. We aim to develop propositions about how privatization may change (and won't change) the way public research universities behave, emphasizing their decision-making processes.

Throughout this book and widely in the literature, the effects of privatization on university funding, organizational structures, personnel, and curriculum are already documented. These four key organizational aspects reflect, in reverse order—(1) what is done (the curriculum), (2) where it is done (organizational structures), (3) who does it (personnel), and (4) how it is paid for (funding). What is missing, of course, is the analysis of *how* this is all accomplished within the public research university, which is the focus of this chapter.

First, the focus is very much about the money. Public dollars have not kept pace with institutional need (Breneman 2005, 3; Hearn, 2006, 87; Kane, Orzag and Gunter, 2003). Institutions are very much concerned with identifying and pursuing diverse streams of revenue (see, for example, Bok, 2003; Kirp, 2003; Slaughter and Leslie, 1998). In a synthesis of the literature on revenue-generating strategies, Hearn (2003) identifies eight traditional and innovative revenue streams (which sometimes are only tributaries) that institutions are pursuing:

- Instruction, including online programming and niche-oriented nondegree programming.
- Research and analysis, including technology-transfer initiatives, business incubators, and e-commerce initiatives.

- Pricing, including differentiated pricing and user fees.
- Financial decision making and management, including venture capital investment, as well as participation in arbitrage and options markets.
- Human resources, including compensation incentives for entrepreneurship and retirement/rehiring incentives for faculty.
- Franchising, licensing, sponsorship, and partnering arrangements with third parties, including logo-bearing clothing, tours and camps, and event sponsorships.
- Auxiliary enterprises, facilities, and real estate, including on-campus debit cards, facility rentals, and alumni services.
- Development, including appeals to donors abroad and other efforts.

Public colleges and universities are becoming entities in the market, a trend gaining speed among many nonprofits, including hospitals and museums (Weisbrod, 1998, 1).

Second, this emphasis on generating revenue can be linked to altered organizational structures (Clark, 2004; Slaughter and Leslie, 1998) that may change internal campus dynamics. For instance, although research institutes and centers have long been a way of life in research universities, their number and importance are growing, creating, in some instances, strong new dynamics on campuses, particularly between institutes and traditional academic departments. Mallon (2006, 55) identifies what he calls "power centers" as a subset of institutes that have the ability to reshape institutional behavior because of their "considerable reach and resources" (2006, 27). As he notes, "Although many centers and institutes remain on the margins of academic life, some have accreted significant influence and power. In turn, this growth on the edge of the university creates a centrifugal force, shifting away from the traditional norms and pathways of academic decision making" (Mallon, 2006, 16).

Furthermore, colleges and universities create new units to tap the marketplace. For instance, the rise of "wholly owned subsidiaries" is not uncommon, even if their success is difficult (Bleak, 2006, 35), and new institutional units such as those concerned with technology transfer, patents and licensing agreements, and intellectual property are proliferating (Clark, 1998; Slaughter and Rhodes, 2004). Colorado State University, University of North Carolina, and the University of Illinois have each created spin-offs to offer online education and generate revenue for their "parent companies."

The internal dynamics may change as those units able to garner and to control resources rise in influence and stature. Such structural change may well influence institutional dynamics shifting power to those units able to generate and to control resources. In some instances, this may be to centralize influence in the administrative core as it coordinates budget allocations and oversees revenue-generating activities, particularly auxiliary services that fund core teaching and research activities. However, in other cases, revenue-garnered influence may move away from the central administration to specific academic departments and institutes because they are able to develop and control significant resources (Kirp, 2003; Slaughter and Leslie, 1998). Their ability to control resources means that these units may demand greater autonomy from central oversight, decide to contribute less to university-wide activities, set their own strategies and priorities, and even relocate themselves physically from the rest of campus. Kirp's (2003) case study of the University of Virginia's Darden School of Business is a prime example of a business school doing all of these things.

Third, research institutions are changing their staffing arrangements. Rhoades (1998) identifies a growing subset of professional employees who, while not fulfilling traditional faculty jobs, nonetheless play important roles in the intellectual life of campus and strongly influence academic work and priorities. These "managerial professionals" include directors of technology transfer, chief information officers, and university attorneys. In addition, research universities are seeing changes in hiring patterns among their faculty. New positions, such as research professor, professor of practice, and other such titles were not widespread 25 years ago. Institutions continue to rely on part-time and non-tenured-track faculty (although not to the same extent as other higher education sectors, such as community colleges). Finally, the roles of traditional faculty continue to evolve with increased emphasis on applied research and heightened pressure for external support. A stark illustration is the recent adoption by the Texas A&M University System Board of Regents of a policy that considers success with patents and the commercialization of research in tenure reviews (Lipka, 2006).

Finally, privatization is having an effect on the curriculum. Institutions now pursue master's and professional programs, continuing education and certificate programs, and corporate and contract education. These new initiatives often focus on fields and disciplines in which students (or their employers) can and are willing to pay higher tuition costs or, alternately, where new graduates readily earn high starting salaries. Examples include professional master's degrees in engineering, executive MBAs, and even the University of Pennsylvania's executive doctorate in higher education. In this manner, curriculum decisions are being entered into—even controlled by—administrators, chairs, and market-savvy faculty members who are keen to create academic programs that fit a fiscal niche. They are "capitalizing on the curriculum" (Eckel, 2003, 865).

Public research institutions are also pursuing partnerships with other research universities domestically and abroad to offer courses that each could not offer or could do so only at a lower level of quality. These are often undertaken to penetrate new educational markets in the United States and increasingly abroad. Domestic examples include the Great Plains Interactive Distance Education Alliance, an alliance of 10 land-grant universities in the Midwest offering a series of online graduate programs in areas related to human ecology, and the Worldwide Universities Network, a group of 16 research universities from the United States, Europe, and China, which offer graduate-level courses in addition to fostering student and faculty exchange and cooperative research (Eckel, Green, and Affolter-Caine, 2002). International efforts include partnerships between U.S. and Chinese universities such as Benedictine College (Kansas) and the Hong Kong Institute of Continuing Education; Fordham University and Peking University; and Missouri State University and Liaoning Normal University (Green, Eckel, Calderon, and Luu, 2007). However, many other similar partnerships exist in the U.S. and elsewhere.

The Organization of the Public Research University

The American public research university is a complex organization made up of many subunits, inhabited by professionalized specialists, and designed (or evolved) to perform a large number of seemingly unrelated tasks that support a highly differentiated mission. Though laypersons might answer "teaching" or "research" when asked about the activities of research universities, this type of organization produces hundreds of products, many intangible, some more easily evaluated and measured.

The modern public research university is charged by its state and policymakers with, among other things, teaching skills to a diverse group of student learners, serving as an economic driver for the region and state, competing with other research universities for research funding and prestige, providing public service to the state's citizens, beating the neighboring state's football team (or even more fiercely, its in-state rival), and doing all of this with a shrinking piece of the state's budget pie. Its organizational actors both artificially inseminate livestock and publish poetry (not, it should be pointed out, at the same time). One outcome of this obtuse mission is an organizational form that is unlike those assumed by organizations with more focused purposes. The organization is obscenely decentralized, and specialized subunits are nested under one another with apparently no means of communicating information above, below, or sideways on the organizational chart (Weick, 1976). As former president of the University of Chicago famously noted, "The university is a collection of departments tied together by a common steam plant" (as cited in Birnbaum, 2004, 185).

Critics of higher education look at the way colleges and universities behave and wonder how such an organization could be so effective (Birnbaum, 1988a). Others strike out to "fix" what on the surface seems like a dysfunctional organization, only to do potentially more damage because they have little appreciation for its complexity (Birnbaum and Eckel, 2005). But, the research university's organizational form is perverse precisely because such a form allows it to pursue its many goals without acknowledging their inconsistency, lack of connection, and even outright discord (Weick, 1976). Form follows function: just as research universities' goals, values, and tools are incongruent, so to are the structures and behaviors they use to reach their goals, and, in the case of these public entities, to contribute to their success (Birnbaum, 1988a).

Researchers who have studied the organizational form of research universities have recognized the seemingly irrational structures and behavior of this institution and, given the success of the research university, invented and applied new scholarly terms to describe it. These characteristics highlight the differences between research universities and other more rational organizations with less complexity and easily identified and measured goals (Mintzberg, 1993).

Chief among the terms adopted by organizational researchers who have studied research universities is "organized anarchy," originally coined by Cohen, March, and Olsen (1972, 1) in their seminal article. The authors focus on the choices organizations make and argue that, because of their unique attributes, specifically, poorly defined goals, unclear technology (i.e., how things work, not the debate between open source and proprietary information technology), and fluid participation of key constituents, these organizations are less likely to make decisions akin to other organizations and more likely to be organized as "a loose collection of ideas" (Cohen, March, and Olsen, 1972, 1). The goals of research universities are both poorly defined and can be in conflict with each other. For instance, they seek both the unfettered pursuit and dissemination of knowledge and the financial gain that comes from scientific breakthroughs through patents and licensing. Second, they are unclear in how they actually realize their goals: How many faculty really understand how students become civic minded or develop as global citizens as so many mission statements purport? Finally, organizational actors must choose among many simultaneous activities competing for their attention; they cannot attend to all organizational priorities concurrently. Instead, decision makers have to choose where to put their attention and efforts. Any new provost quickly learns that she cannot be everywhere at once and that all commitments are top priorities.

Cohen, March, and Olsen (1972) argue that all organizations have some part that is structured in this fashion; however, research universities are their poster child. This conceptualization of organizational behavior contrasts with more traditional theories, which assumed organizations had clear goals and priorities, agreed-upon methods for achieving goals, and determined priorities and preferences before they act, and not that preferences were determined through their action, as with universities (Cohen and March, 1986) given the earlier three characteristics.

These three organizational characteristics shape organizational processes. Instead of clearly defined processes in which those at the top set strategy and make decisions to pursue the strategy, organized anarchies are dominated by a specific and different type of decision making, the aptly labeled "garbage can" choice process. Here streams of problems, solutions, and participants converge in the metaphoric garbage can to shape and to dictate choice opportunities. Decisions are rendered by the coupling of solutions, actors, and problems. Decisions tend to be made by chronological proximity and timing rather than by rationality to maximize outcomes: problems, solutions, and people bump into one another and stick together. Within the plentiful garbage cans that comprise a given research university, decisions are made by one of three ways (Cohen and March, 1982). First, decisions can be made by *resolution*, in which participants make a concerted effort to apply solutions to recognized and agreed-upon problems. This type of decision making most closely resembles the rational organizational perspective in which possible options are considered and then one is selected that will maximize outcomes. Second, decisions can be made by *flight*, when problems become attached to other unintended solutions or participants or when something leaves the choice arena, which removes a bottleneck. For example, a suggested foreign language requirement can cascade into a debate and decision about faculty hiring or the decline of the humanities and the need for more investment. Finally, decisions can be achieved by *oversight* when key decision makers are too busy to participate in all decisions so problems and solutions are coupled when, seemingly, no one is paying attention. Organized anarchies (not to mention other organizations) do not consistently make decisions by first identifying all of the possible choices, then by speculating about the outcomes of each, and finally, by choosing the solution that most likely will maximize decision outcomes. Rather, in garbage can decision making, solutions are in search of problems as much as problems are in search of solutions.

Cohen, March, and Olsen (1972) state that both public (e.g., social service) and educational organizations are particularly prone to garbage can decision making.

They use universities as the application case in their article: "If the implications of the [garbage can] model are applicable anywhere, they are applicable to a university" (Cohen, March, and Olsen 1972, 11). They point out that universities are quite likely to make no decision even after devoting considerable resources to the processes of decision making (flight) or to make big decisions with a small amount of participation on the part of key constituents (oversight).

In *Ambiguity and Choice in Organizations,* March and Olsen (1976) feature a number of case studies that highlight the utility of the organized anarchy / garbage can model of decision making in organizations. Most of these cases take place in colleges and universities. These cases make the point that the choices organizations make may defy common organizational sense: As participants change and prospective solutions and problems interact, the product of a decision-making process may look nothing like a decision at all, or it may bear little relation to the process that produced it. Or, as the authors put it, "Indeed the activities within a choice situation may be explicable only if we recognize the other major things that take place within the same arena at the same time" (March and Olsen, 1976, 11). Decisions are not always understandable without knowledge of the context that produced the decision; this notion is at the core of the garbage can framework.

Olsen's (1976) case study of the selection of a new dean is illustrative. Like other searches on university campuses, the players are fluid, with new members entering and exiting the search committee at various times, often in response to other "problems" or "solutions" in their units. Choices, such as the decision to offer the position to a candidate, are made, but no outcome is produced because the candidate in question does not make a decision about whether to accept the offer. A chance meeting introduces candidates to the search committee and an unrelated decision related to faculty evaluation procedures causes one member to "withdraw from all administrative work" in protest (Olsen, 1976, 99). In the end, the decision to appoint the search chairperson as dean meets with dissension and confusion but is still made. A similar point is made about presidential searches by Birnbaum (1988b), a process that he deftly describes as "the search and postdecision surprise" (Birnbaum 1988b, 505),[1] which describes both the selection and the behaviors of the chosen candidate. His research illustrates garbage can decision making at its best (and most confusing).

Garbage Can Decision Making and Privatization

The focus of this chapter is the intersection of organized anarchy's garbage can decision making and privatization. Put another way, we hypothesize what privatization might do to the choice processes in public research universities. We have documented some of the changes in organizational form and behavior that other scholars have already pointed out, but our goal is to focus specifically on the decision-making process and not on other organizational phenomena or characteristics and to develop a set of ideas that might apply to a range of institutions and limited to a specific site or case study. Interesting conceptual questions exist about how the garbage can model may change as privatization encroaches on the public research university beyond a single site. When broken down into its elements, Cohen, March, and Olsen's (1972) garbage can decision-making concept is illuminating and can be used to construct several interesting propositions.

Enhancing Responsiveness and Competitiveness

University garbage cans may well provide a means for universities to be increasingly responsive and, in turn, competitive. Privatization and corresponding entrepreneurial activities present both untraditional and an expanded array of traditional choice opportunities. While institutions are seeking to expand online or niche instruction; engage in technology-transfer initiatives, business incubators, and e-commerce initiatives; explore venture capital investments; pursue franchising, licensing, sponsorship, and partnering arrangements with third parties; and develop auxiliary enterprises, facilities, real estate, on-campus debit cards, facility rentals, and alumni services, they must also continue (if not expand) their traditional functions of teaching, research, and service. As revenue becomes a new priority, universities still must pursue their core activities vigorously. Thus, because the range and amount of activities increase, the number and variety of garbage cans expand as well.

In their discussion of the how Regional Bell Operating Companies (RBOCs) restructured and behaved following their deregulation in Canada, Smith and Zeithaml (1996) argue that garbage cans served as an effective means for the RBOCs to create new business ventures apart from their core business in the monopolistic local telephone business. Their study documented how, in response to their regulated ability to offer other services outside local phone service, the RBOCs created units that were unlike the larger units involved in the firm's traditional core business of telephone service. What resulted in these new and chaotic units, which were characterized by changing goals, uncertain technology, and the fluid participation of organizational actors, was ultimately assessed as worthwhile and, just as importantly, allowed the organizations' leaders to focus on the core business during a time of transformational change in the telephone industry. They concluded that "organizations that have gone through a discontinuous organizational change should consider the development of dual trajectories . . . [and] may find the creation of a few garbage can activities to be a long-term hedge" (Smith and Zeithaml, 1996, 398). In other words, organizations such as the RBOCS, with organizational slack in their primary enterprise, would be wise to do two things to respond to such a change. First, focus on responding to such change in their core but, second, and more important, create means for dealing with opportunities that fall outside the core but are essential to the organization's long-term survival.

The environment faced by public research universities seems in many ways to mirror that which faces the RBOCs. Both organizations are facing a reduction of what Cohen, March, and Olsen (1972) would refer to as their organizational slack. For public universities, this is a result of diminished state support and an increasing need to find substitute resources elsewhere. Thus, their ability to respond in a coordinated way is reduced, and a high priority of the central administration is securing new resources, which occupies much of administrators' time. A useful response to such a dilemma is to create subunits that act as garbage cans so that problems, solutions, and participants deemed to be outside the technical core of the institution can be relegated there. Such cans would yield opportunities that can be acted on more readily rather than need central coordination and approval. Decisions to act are decentralized, rather than centralized creating more flexibility to take advantage of the environment. This means that organizations become simultaneously more responsive; yet, more uncoordinated in the ways they respond. They create better sensing mechanisms but do not always act consistently or know of other decisions made.

Furthermore, this kind of garbage canning buffers the organization's technical core from further disruption (Meyer, Scott, and Deal, 1981). Each subunit can respond, adapt, or take risks without jeopardizing the whole. In effect, multiple garbage cans help contribute to loose coupling that fosters local adaptation, taps dispersed expertise and interest (rather than rely on central approval), and avoids the cost of central coordination in addition to creating more responsive organizations (Weick, 1976). Thus, our first proposition.

PROPOSITION 1: Universities will create new units to interface with external audiences that will serve as receptacles for more streams of actors, problems, and solutions, allowing more decisions to be rendered more quickly because of increased opportunities for interaction.

Just as Smith and Zeithaml (1996, 388) argued that "companies facing dramatic external changes . . . may find value in creating garbage cans" (Smith and Zeithaml,

1996, 398), we might expect that public research universities dealing with the evolution of privatization would create similar garbage cans for choice opportunities. Clark's (1998, 6) notion of "expanded developmental periphery" for entrepreneurial campuses reflects these characteristics. In the institutions he studied, each created units outside the traditional academic core that interact with external actors to best position the institution in a dynamic environment.

Garbage Cans Are Not Created Equal

Cohen, March, and Olsen (1972) hint that all cans are not the same when they note that decision-making apparatuses will differ according to a number of factors, including "the allocation of energy by potential participants in the decision" (Cohen, March, and Olsen 1972, 4). Research on the effects of privatization or the rise of academic capitalism in higher education argues much the same: The relative proximity of garbage cans to "the market" will be correlated with the same unit's attention and interest by high-level organizational decision makers (Slaughter and Leslie, 1998; Kirp, 2004). Furthermore, not all choice opportunities in an organized anarchy may remain garbage can processes. Senior campus leaders would be remiss to let high-profile and potentially profitable units go unattended. The result is that university units dealing with central aspects of privatization (e.g., research institutes, fundraising, technology transfer, admissions) are likely to receive a disproportionate share of the attention of administrators. For example, Mallon (2006, 55) found that "power centers" have the ear of university administrators to such an extent that "their directors do not feel the need to [participate in traditional campus governance], given their other means to connect to prominent decision makers." Entrepreneurial strategies have associated academic as well as reputational and financial risk (Shattock, 2005). These activities are often high stakes, requiring significant university investment for a sizable return, attracting the attention of key decision makers. Thus, while the number of decision opportunities expands and constraints on their time grows because the number of decisions grows, key decision makers will only be able to attend to an increasingly finite set of decisions. In contrast, units more closely associated with some of the drudgery of privatization (e.g., student advising, general education curriculum) are less likely to receive the same level of attention.

In the parlance of the garbage can model of decision making, we would expect that such disparate levels of attention would likely result in different kinds of decision-making processes. Specifically, we would expect that high-profile units in close proximity to large or new revenue streams would be likely be the focus of administrators in their decision making.

> PROPOSITION 2: Privatization and the establishment of new units closely linked to new revenue streams will result in increased attention by key decision actors, resulting in more decisions made by resolution. Concurrently, decisions elsewhere, particularly those not associated with privatization strategies, will more likely be made by flight or oversight because senior decision makers will be elsewhere.

Such differences in decision-making processes are consistent with Cohen, March, and Olsen's (1972) claim that decision making by flight is quite common in university environments "except under conditions where flight is severely restricted (for instance, specialized access" (Cohen, March, and Olsen 1972, 9). They suggest, as does our proposition, that more rational decision making is unlikely in the privatized university except where organizational attention is focused.

The Number of Actors Will Increase and Influence Outcomes

As the research university becomes more privatized, it opens its borders to a range of external influences, factors beyond the well-documented impact of professional and scholarly groups (Alpert 1985; Clark 1998). Government funding agencies, such as National Institutes of Health, the National Science Foundation, and the Department of Defense set conditions for university behavior as a condition of support. For example, the National Cancer Institute mandates that university-based comprehensive cancer centers have a structural position in the university hierarchy with authority that usurps traditional academic departments (Mallon 2006). Beyond the government, private corporations are exerting increased external influence that create more permeable boundaries between university and funder. The University of California's relationship with Novartis is one high-profile example (Rudy et al., 2007). The Alfred Mann Foundation for Biomedical Engineering has conditions regarding access to intellectual property that have made more than a few universities nervous (Blumenstyk, 2006). On a smaller scale, partnerships and alliances between universities—both in the labs and in the classrooms—means that faculty and administrators from different institutions will have a strong interest in and potential influence over a different university's activities (Eckel, 2003).

As scholars of strategic alliances note, a key decision is the extent to which each partner's governance structure has legitimacy over the shared work of the collective.

In privatized instances, those increasingly involved in the decision-making process may come from different institutional cultures, are unfamiliar with one another, or have a different understanding of the environment (Boyrs and Jemison, 1989). Furthermore, not all partners share the same objectives. In many instances, partnerships are undertaken because of complementary but not consistent goals (Gulati and Singh, 1998).

The issues that create large and attractive garbage cans likely will involve multiple units even within a single university. For example, the broad focus of many entrepreneurial activities makes it possible for various stakeholders, such as faculty, administrators, and even board members, to set their claims on the same piece of the governance pie. Activities that seek to capitalize on university capital, such as leveraging the curriculum or research through contract education or for-profit subsidiaries, cross the domains of all three traditional governance stakeholders: (1) faculty because of their primacy in developing and overseeing the curriculum; (2) administrators because of their responsibility to secure revenue and design and implement new institutional arrangements; and (3) trustees because of their fiduciary and strategic responsibility (the governance roles for each outlined by the American Association of University Professors in the 1966 Statement on Government).

Thus, the internal and external dynamics of privatization mean that both the number and types of potential actors may grow as universities pursue external resources more vigorously. In this instance, many hands may not make light work but instead add more anarchy to the decision process.

PROPOSITION 3: The abilities and common understandings of actors involved will decrease as their numbers increase, resulting in increased flows of solutions seeking problems and less decisions made by resolution.

The Currents of the Three "Streams" Will Vary

Higher education is commonly criticized as slow moving. "Academic time" seems to follow its own pace. Decision-making committees deliberate and debate, explore options, and seek input. (They also relive histories, rehash injustices, and exert status.) However, strategies associated with privatization most likely will not abide by academic time and instead adhere to a market-driven sense of time. Institutions will increasingly try to react quickly to emerging opportunities and respond quickly to competitors encroaching on their turf. The result may be that varying streams of people, problems, and solutions moving through choice opportunities (the stuff in the garbage can at any one time) will pass through at different rates accelerated by external market pressures. In some instances, solutions, problems, and actors may be swift currents driven by the marketplace. In other instances, academic traditions will continue to create meandering streams. Furthermore, the streams present in a garbage can, at any one time, may not be limited to people, to problems, or to solutions. Other streams flowing from privatization may exist, such as regulations that act to limit solutions, problems, or people.

Three potential implications exist for the changing streams, each with its own propositions. First, the mix in the garbage can may change rapidly as some fast-moving streams will flow quickly through decision opportunities. Actors, solutions, and problems may change on a moment's notice. Hesitations may mean that a completely different set of elements are now present in the decision process and a hoped for outcome may have passed. Decisions delayed even slightly may look differently than if they were resolved earlier. Therefore:

PROPOSITION 4: Time and timing, something March and his colleagues (1976) did not address, will play an increasingly central role in determining which decisions are made at what point in time.

Second, various actors will have different, competing expectations of what constitutes legitimate time spent on problems. Those individuals with a market-driven sense of timing will expect decisions to be quick. While those from traditional academic perspectives may believe decisions are rendered too quickly and intentionally slow the process, creating disruption or allowing a higher proportion of unintended solutions to be coupled with problems. Therefore:

PROPOSITION 5: Actors will be less able to render decisions by resolution because it will be more difficult to predict the solutions and problems in the can at any given time.

Third, because of compressed time schedules, particular actors often may try to force together problems and solutions when relatively little natural "sticking" would occur. Thus, decisions thought to be made may come undone and institutions could spend scarce time and attention rehashing decisions. Issues will continue to ride the "issue carousel" in which they come around and around again rather than be implemented (Julius, Baldridge, and Pfeffer, 1999, 113).

PROPOSITION 6: Decisions made by flight and oversight and pushed to conclusion, given time constraints, will re-cycle and continue to need attention and resolution even though key actors will think the decisions have been made.

Less Organization, More Anarchy

Heightened frustration by university decision makers seems to be the likely sum effect of the previously articulated propositions. The effects of privatization on university behavior, as viewed through the organized anarchy decision-making framework, are more choice opportunities (i.e., more cans) that encompass a greater scope of decisions; a wider group of uninformed decision makers who most likely will have increasingly diverse perspectives, understanding, priorities, and objectives, and familiarity with the institution and its culture; increasingly distracted leaders who must choose where to invest their time and energy among an increasing number of decisions, and high-stakes situations that will require resolution within a shrinking time frame. This does not bode well for the university decision maker trying to move a campus strategically. Contemporary advice to university leaders is to articulate a clear agenda, set priorities, and evaluate progress toward that agenda. They are repeatedly chided to not be all things to all people and to have an overly broad set of activities that take the university in dispersed directions. The effects of the trends discussed here, all fostered by privatization, is in the opposite direction: toward a trajectory that will only increasingly frustrate those trying to lead their institution— the faculty, the administration, or the trustees. The likely bottom line for decision making, given the increasingly privatized public research universities, is *more* anarchy and *less* organization at a time when leaders are trying to pursue the opposite. This is occurring at a time when policy makers are trying to hold leaders more accountable and promote efficiency and effectiveness.

What are the solutions for university decision makers? In *How Colleges Work*, Birnbaum (1988) builds on the ideas of Cohen and March and offers the following strategies for effective leadership in the anarchical university:

- *Spend time.* People willing to invest their scare time on any particular decision are likely to have a disproportionate effect on its outcomes.
- *Persist.* Decision makers who don't like the outcome of a particular decision because of the mix in the garbage can have multiple opportunities to reintroduce their issue. With enough persistence, the right people, solutions, and problems can come together. To savvy leaders, it is one thing to make a decision and quite another to see it implemented.
- *Exchange status for substance.* Within anarchical universities, people are often more concerned about recognition and appreciation than effecting outcomes, which is why faculty fight to participate in a decision and then not show up at the meeting. Thus, decision makers can allow others the glory and recogni-

tion as long as the outcomes are desired. Create and charge that high-profile committee and get out of its way. If the mix of actors, problems, and solutions is right, the outcomes will reveal themselves.

- *Overload the system.* When too many decisions exist, at least some of them will be resolved through flight or oversight. By continuing to put numerous decisions into the process, leaders only hedge their bets that eventually a decision on one will be rendered unobtrusively.

- *Provide garbage cans.* By increasing the opportunities for choice, leaders can further hedge their bets that inappropriate solutions will be attached to their pet problems. The extraneous garbage cans serve as magnets to attract undesired solutions, reducing the odds that an unfavorable solution will be attached to the problem.

- *Manage unobtrusively.* By focusing on a series of small scale changes that have a cumulative effect, leaders can avoid the attractiveness of a high stakes garbage can.

Many of these suggestions hold if our propositions reflect the emerging reality as public research universities become increasingly privatized. However, some modifications and additions are called for. First, the system may be naturally overloaded and thus there is no need for leaders to do this. The expanded periphery of universities, the broadened range of decisions, and the increased number of cans may overload the system organically. Second, leaders may instead focus on getting the right actors to pay attention to the right decision opportunities. Those thought to be able to affect key outcomes may need to be steered to the right cans. At the same time, those actors who easily disrupt the system might be guided to less important decisions where those garbage cans can become "deep freezes" (Birnbaum, 2000, 237). Finally, leaders might put their efforts into getting key decisions implemented rather than on getting the right outcomes articulated. Because the time and attention of leaders is limited, many of those decisions rendered will never be acted on. Thus, identifying the right implementable decisions may be a better use of leaders time and social capital. Leaders should use an action rationality—a focus on getting things accomplished even if it is not the most desired outcome—rather than a decision rationality, which is based on maximizing outcomes that might not be too difficult to implement (Brunsson, 1982).

All of these ideas rest on the large assumption that the proposed propositions are on target. However, we cannot ensure that this is so. What is needed is solid, empirical research to test, to modify, to support, and to refute our ideas. We encourage active researchers to tell us whether we've got it right and to help shed more light on this important and understudied phenomenon.

NOTE

1. This phrase was originally used by Harrison and March in the article in *Administrative Science Quarterly* 29 (1984): 26–42.

REFERENCES

Alpert, Daniel. 1986. Performance and Paralysis: The Organizational Context of the American Research University. *Journal of Higher Education* 56 (3): 241–81.

American Association of University Professors. 2001. *Policy Documents and Reports*. 9th ed. Washington, DC: AAUP, 2001.

American Council on Education. 2004. *Rewriting the Rules of the Game: State Funding, Accountability and Autonomy in Public Higher Education*. Paper 2 in The Changing Relationship between States and Their Institutions Series. Washington, DC: American Council on Education.

Birnbaum, Robert. 1988a. *How Colleges Work*. San Francisco: Jossey-Bass.

——. 1988b. Presidential Searches and the Discovery of Organizational Goals. *Journal of Higher Education*, 59 (5): 489–509.

——. 2000. The Latent Organizational Functions of the Academic Senate. In *Organization and Governance in Higher Education*. 5th ed., ed. M. Christopher Brown III, 232–43. Boston, MA: Pearson Custom.

——. 2004. *Speaking of Higher Education: The Academic's Book of Quotations*. Westport, CT: ACE / Praeger Series on Higher Education.

Birnbaum, Robert, and Peter D. Eckel. 2005. The Dilemma of Presidential Leadership. In *American Higher Education in the Twenty-First Century*. 2nd ed., ed. Phil G. Altbach, Robert O. Berdahl, and Patricia J. Gumport, 340–365. Baltimore: Johns Hopkins University Press.

Bleak, Jared. 2006. Charging into the Market: Governance Challenges Created by the Fit and Fitness of Commercial Activities. In *The Shifting Frontiers of Academic Decision Making: Responding to New Priorities, Following New Pathways*, ed. Peter D. Eckel, 35–54. Westport, CT: ACE/Praeger.

Blumenstyk, Goldie. 2006. Universities Forgo Millions over Strings Attached to a Foundation's Grants. *Chronicle of Higher Education* 52, no. 28 (March 17): A1.

Bok, Derek C. 2003. *Universities in the Marketplace: The Commercialization of Higher Education*. Princeton, NJ: Princeton University Press.

Boyrs, Bryan, and David B. Jemison. 1989. Hybrid Arrangements as Strategic Alliances: Theoretical Issues in Organizational Combinations. *Academy of Management Review* 14:234–49.

Breneman, Davis W. 2005. Entrepreneurship in Higher Education. In *Arenas of Entrepreneurship: Where Nonprofit and For-Profit Institutions Compete*, ed. Brian Pusser, 3–10. New Directions for Higher Education Report 129. San Francisco: Jossey-Bass.

Brunsson, Nils. 1982. The Irrationality of Action and Action Rationality: Decisions, Ideologies, and Organizational Actions. *Journal of Management Studies* 19:29–44.

Clark, Burton R. *Creating Entrepreneurial Universities: Organizational Pathways of Transformation.* New York: Pergamon, 1998.

———. 2004. *Sustaining Change in Universities: Continuities in Case Studies and Concepts.* New York: Open University Press / McGraw-Hill Education.

Cohen, Michael D., and James G. March. 1986. *Ambiguity and Leadership.* 2nd ed. Boston: Harvard Business School Press.

Cohen, Michael D., James G. March, and John P. Olsen. 1972. A Garbage Can Model of Organizational Choice. *Administrative Science Quarterly* 17:1–25.

Couturier, Lara K. 2006. *Checks and Balances at Work: The Restructuring of Virginia's Public Higher Education System.* San Jose, CA: National Center for Public Policy and Higher Education.

Eckel, Peter D. 2003. Capitalizing on the Curriculum: The Challenge of Curricular Joint Ventures. *American Behavioral Scientist* 46 (7): 865–82.

Eckel, Peter D., Britany Affolter-Caine, and Madeline Green 2003. New Times, New Strategies: Curricular Joint Ventures. The Changing Enterprise Occasional Paper No. 2. American Council on Education, Washington, DC.

Eckel, Peter D., Lara Couturier, and Dao T. Luu. 2005. Peering around the Bend: The Leadership Challenges of Privatization, Accountability, and Market-Based State Policy. Paper 4 in The Changing Relationship between States and Their Institutions Series. American Council on Education, Washington, DC.

Green, Madeleine. F., Peter D. Eckel, Lourdes Calderon, and Dao T. Luu. 2007. Venturing Abroad: Delivering U.S. Degrees through Overseas Branch Campuses and Programs. U.S. Higher Education in a Global Context. Working Paper 1. American Council on Education, Washington, DC.

Gulati, Ranjay, and Harbir Singh. 1998. The Architecture of Cooperation: Managing Coordination Costs and Appropriation Concerns in Strategic Alliances. *Administrative Science Quarterly* 43:781–814.

Harrison, J. Richard, and James G. March. 1984. Decision Making and Postdecision Surprises. *Administrative Science Quarterly* 29:26–42.

Hearn, James C. 2006. Alternative Revenue Sources. In *Privatization and Public Universities,* ed. Douglas Priest and Edward St. John, 87–108. Bloomington: Indiana University Press.

———. 2003. *Diversifying Campus Revenue Streams: Opportunities and Risks.* Washington, DC: American Council on Education, 2003.

Jones, Dennis. 2006. State Shortfalls Projected to Continue Despite Economic Gains: Policy Alert. Report for the National Center for Public Policy and Higher Education. San Jose, CA, February.

Julius, Daniel J., J. Victor Baldridge, and Jeffery Pfeffer. 1999. A Memo from Machiavelli. *Journal of Higher Education* 70 (2): 113–33.

Kane, Thomas J., Peter R. Orszag, and David L. Gunter. 2003. *State Fiscal Constraints and Higher Education Spending: The Role of Medicaid and the Business Cycle.* Washington, DC: Brookings Institution.

Kirp, David L. 2003. *Shakespeare, Einstein, and the Bottom Line*. Cambridge, MA: Harvard University Press.

Lipka, S. 2006. Texas A&M: Patents to Count for Tenure. *Chronicle of Higher Education* 52, no. 40 (June 9): A12, http://chronicle.com/weekly/v52/i40/40a01201.htm.

Lyall, Katherine C., and Kathleen R. Sell. 2005. *The True Genius of America at Risk: Are We Losing Our Public Universities to De Facto Privatization?* Westport, CT: Praeger.

March, James G., and Johan P. Olsen. 1976. *Ambiguity and Choice in Organizations*. Bergen, Norway: Universitietsforlaget.

Marginson, Simon, and Mark Considine. 2000. *The Enterprise University: Power, Governance, and Reinvention in Australia*. New York: Cambridge University Press.

Mallon, William T. 2006. Centers, Institutes and Academic Decision Making: Addressing "Suburban Sprawl" through Strategies for "Smart Growth." In *The Shifting Frontiers of Academic Decision Making: Responding to New Priorities, Following New Pathways*, ed. Peter D. Eckel, 55–74. Westport, CT: ACE/Praeger.

Meyer, J. W., W. R. Scott, and T. E. Deal. 1981. Institutional and Technical Sources of Organizational Structure: Explaining the Structure of Educational Organizations. In *Organization and the Human Services*, ed. H. D. Stein, 151–78. Philadelphia: Temple University Press.

Mintzberg, Henry. 1993. *Structure in Fives: Designing Effective Organizations*. Englewood Cliffs, NJ: Prentice-Hall.

National Association of State Budget Officers. 2007. *The Fiscal Survey of States*. Washington, DC: National Association of State Budget Officers.

Olsen, Johan P. 1976. Choice in an Organized Anarchy. In *Ambiguity and Choice in Organizations*, ed. James G. March and Johan P. Olsen. Bergen, Norway: Universitietsforlaget.

Rhoades, Gary. 1998. *Managed Professionals: Unionized Faculty and Restructuring Academic Labor*. Albany, NY: SUNY Press.

Rudy, Alan P., Dawn Coppin, Jason Konefal, Bradley T. Shaw, Toby Ten Eyck, Craig Harris, and Lawrence Busch. 2007. *Universities in the Age of Corporate Science: The UC Berkeley-Novartis Controversy*. Philadelphia: Temple University Press.

Shattock, Michael. 2005. European Universities for Entrepreneurship: Their Role in the Europe of Knowledge. The Theoretical Context. *Higher Education Management and Policy* 17 (3): 13–25.

Singh, Mala. 2001. Reinserting the "Public Good" in Higher Education Transformation. *Kagisano, CHE Higher Education Discussion Series*, no. 1 (Summer): 7–22.

Smith, Anne D., and Carl Zeithaml. 1996. Garbage Cans and Advancing Hypercompetition: The Creation and Exploitation of New Capabilities and Strategic Flexibility in Two Regional Bell Operating Companies. *Organization Science* 7 (4): 388–99.

Slaughter, Sheila, and Larry L. Leslie. 1997. *Academic Capitalism: Politics, Policies, and the Entrepreneurial University*. Baltimore: Johns Hopkins University Press.

Slaughter, Sheila, and Gary Rhoades. 2004. *Academic Capitalism and the New Economy*. Baltimore: Johns Hopkins University.

Weick, K. E. 1976. Educational Organizations as Loosely Coupled Systems. *Administrative Science Quarterly* 21 (1): 1–19.

Weisbrod, Burton A. 1998. The Nonprofit Mission and Its Financing: Growing Links between Nonprofits and the Rest of the Economy. In *To Profit or Not to Profit: The Commercial Transformation of the Nonprofit Sector*, ed. Burton A. Weibrod, 1–22. New York: Cambridge University Press.

Yudof, Mark G. 2002. Is the Public Research University Dead? *Chronicle of Higher Education* 48, no. 18 (January 11): 24.

CHAPTER SIX

Governing the Privatized
Public Research University

• ☙ •

GABRIEL KAPLAN

The current crisis over evaporating state funding in public higher education is unique for a sector seemingly ever on the verge of crisis. There are crises over the content of the canon, over freedom of expression, over the politicization of the academy by the Left and the Right, over too much or too little enrollment diversity, over the increase in tuition and the burden of postgraduate debt, to name only a few. But as crises go, states and institutional stakeholders have been remarkably quiescent before a steady withering of the public's share of ongoing operating support to public institutions and the implications for the operation and governance of these once great pinnacles of state intervention. In many cases, institutional leaders have been at the forefront of the effort to change the governing relationships between states and institutions as state dollars go to other needs.

Perhaps the leadership of public universities and state officials should not be faulted. For one, the decline in the state's share of institutional support is somewhat misleading, for much of this decrease can be attributed to the growth in revenues from nonstate sources. Furthermore, the decrease in the degree of public funding has meant little in the way of marked changes in staffing or organization on public campuses (Kaplan, 2006b).[1] This crisis has elicited little relative concern or action across campuses among students, faculty, and other stakeholders. But the difficulty of finding the dollars they feel they need to keep their institutions competitive has led state leaders and institutional officials to pursue a strategy that has come to be called *privatization*, or *deregulation*[2] (see chapter 6; McGuinness, 2005). By achieving greater distance from the state and more flexibility in budgeting and price setting, leaders at the state level and within institutions have argued that they can offset the loss of state dollars while maintaining important public goals such as maintaining research productivity, attracting quality students and faculty, and maintaining institutional competitiveness.

In essence, institutions are seeking greater stability and predictability of their revenues (AGB, 2005). Deregulation or achieving greater distance from and flexibility from the state, it is hoped, will allow institutions to focus on revenue sources such as tuition, endowments, contracts, and grants—the lifeblood of the private research institution. And already, some leading public institutions such as the University of Colorado and Pennsylvania State University have altered their revenues structures such that less than 10% of their overall funding is derived from state subsidies for full-time enrollments. Almost all states allowed or encouraged their public institutions to respond to the recessionary downturn in public funding by sharply increasing tuition, but as the revenue mix of these institutions changes, the degree to which they remain public becomes a subject of interest and discussion. As public support wanes, some states have sought to alter the states role in higher education by dissociating the state from those institutions' operational matters.

This chapter looks at a commonly held but implicit understanding among higher education watchers that as public funding declines, the public role in governance should too. In other words, many observers and leaders in the sector think that privatization should consist of a backing off of the public role in funding and decision making (Lyall and Sell, 2006; Selingo, 2003). But others have raised concerns about tuition increases and governors in Massachusetts, New York, and Colorado have taken steps to keep them down. McGuinness (2005) argues that when tuition increases are constrained and state-provided revenues are flat state institutions are going to seek research and contract dollars, which has severe implications for teaching. The Association of Governing Boards (AGB) has warned that altering the basic relationships between states and institutions has implications for access, participation, affordability, and higher education's role in equipping states to deal with economic and technical change (AGB, 2005). Research suggests that much of this concern is well founded. Studies have shown that public and private institutions have some real difference in outcomes and some real differences in governance structures (Kaplan, 2002a). We know that ownership is significantly associated with lower operating costs and other differences (Kaplan, 2002a, 2002b). And it seems logical that the public role has affected how state institutions have grown and where they have placed their emphases. So concerned policy analysts should keep in mind that significant policy differences may arise from differences in the way the public expresses its ownership interests. If we want to realize particular policy objectives, especially in the areas of operating costs, program overlaps, and efficiencies, we may want to reconsider how the state lets go of its role in higher education policymaking.

The chapter proceeds by reviewing what privatization has meant so far among public higher education institutions in the first section. It goes on to look at the benefits from privatization that are predicted by theory. This discussion also looks at the drawbacks from privatization that are predicted from theory. The next section looks at the empirical evidence related to this question. It then considers the implications of this review for policymaking in this area and the final section concludes with some thoughts about reform options.

Background

In the context of general public policy discussions, privatization consists of the selling off of state-owned assets to the private sector by government (Donohue, 1991). Thus far, no state has auctioned off their state campuses to the highest bidder or sought to take a public institution truly public by issuing shares and trading them on a major stock exchange. Nevertheless, the concept of privatization within public higher education occurs in numerous discussions over science and social science policy, tuition setting, and state budget debates.

What then does privatization mean within this context? It begins with the perceived decline in state funding for higher education. I say perceived because state funding dollars for higher education have increased relentlessly over the past 30 years. What has changed has been the proportion of dollars that fund the institution's day-to-day operations, which are received from the state. Between 1980 and today, the proportion of state dollars that went toward public higher education declined from 44% to 32% (Selingo, 2003). As with many public funding declines, most, when they occur, consist of declines in real funding rather than declines in nominal funding. Real funding levels or baseline funding represents the amount of money needed to keep the university operating at the same level as in the previous fiscal year. Since labor costs are expected to at least keep pace with inflation, and many wage benefits increase faster than inflation, baseline funding increases can be relentless.

Nevertheless, institutions have faced serious shortfalls between what they expected to receive from the state and what they defined as their need, on the one hand and what they received, on the other. The future prospects for states are improving in the short term as they emerge from the recessionary revenue contractions of 2001–4. However, state revenue projections from two leading studies suggest that in the long term, the picture for state higher education is bleak, as state revenue structures are challenged by changes in the structure of state economies and sectors such as prisons, health care, and K–12 education impose continued budget pressures (Boyd, 2002; Hovey, 1999). Higher education is usually the largest component of discretionary state budgets that politicians feel they can cut, and it is often the first place they look. As state sector revenues wither, institutions turn to other sources and pay heed to the dictates that obtaining such funds impose on their funding structures, making them less distinguishable from their private counterparts.

A second feature of privatization, then, consists of the institutional reaction to the perceived decline in state contributions. In many states, there exists an implicit understanding between state officials and institutional leaders that cuts to the expected amount of state funding will be offset at the institutional level by increases in tuition (Kaplan, 2006b). In addition, many institutions, particularly research institutions, have become more aggressive and creative about finding sources of institutional funding from their scientific and social scientific endeavors: Indirect costs associated with such grants provide valuable support for institutional infrastructure; agreements with corporate entities such as pharmaceutical and agribusiness to fund research in exchange for licensing agreements have become a feature of higher education finance; and patents from discoveries are a not inconsequential source of further revenues, for instance.

A further feature of privatization in this context consists of changes in institutional practice such as increased competition for students or greater attention to donated resources. Public research institutions have set up honors colleges and generous merit-based scholarship programs to attract students who typically would have attended a top-flight Ivy League or other selective private institution. These same institutions have sought to grow the endowment base of their affiliated foundations by aggressively pursuing donations from wealthy individuals and foundations following strategies of their independent peers.

A third manifestation of privatization has been the effort to seek changes in the legal relationships between state and institution. The two main forms that this effort has taken at the state level to explicitly alter the relationship between university and the state are the designation of public institutions as enterprises or charter universities (AGB, 2005). In Virginia, the leading research institutions in the state approach political officials to seek charter status after successive years of budget cuts and gubernatorial proscriptions on tuition increases. Echoing a burgeoning movement in K–12 education, the University of Virginia, the College of William and Mary, and Virginia Tech petitioned state officials to dissolve many of their ties to state government to gain flexibility and the chance to operate at a greater distance from the state. They promised that this would actually save the state money in the long run since they could find new ways of funding their services (Couturier, 2006).

In Colorado, former University of Colorado system president Elizabeth Hoffman sought a similar deal, asking that the legislature and governor grant the three-campus system "enterprise status," a designation somewhat akin to a state-owned enterprise in which the institution would be exempt from constitutionally based revenue limitations and be freer to raise tuition and other revenues on its own. At the same time, though, the governor and his supporters in the legislature were advancing a proposal for higher education vouchers, which would have altered the way the state delivered its funding to public institutions. The Republican proposal was to create a flat subsidy amount for all public higher education institutions (and, in some cases, a reduced subsidy for in-state residents attending a private Colorado institution) in the state regardless of level.[3] Students who chose to attend a community college would receive the same amount as those who decided to attend the flagship institution at Boulder. Advocates argued that by extending a subsidy across all public institutions and some private ones, the state would provide schools with an incentive to be more responsive to families. They also claimed the highly publicized voucher amount would help the state address the low level of enrollment in higher education among the state's high school graduates. Although each proposal failed in 2003, in 2004 they were joined as a single legislative package after the governor struck a deal with higher education advocates and made the chance to get enterprise status available to all.

Other states sought similar reforms with less notable success. Wisconsin's president called for spinning off from the University of Wisconsin system into an independent authority, which is what the university's hospital had done. The change would have given the campuses and the main office greater autonomy in budget, personnel, and purchasing decisions. Wisconsin's governor, unlike his Colorado and Virginia counterparts, indicated little interest in the proposal. Three of South Carolina's research universities proposed separating themselves from the state coordinating board so they could enter into creative financial arrangements with private developers about the use of public lands (Selingo, 2003). Other states that saw significant changes in the state-institutional relationship included Ohio, Washington, Texas, and Massachusetts (AGB, 2005).

Thus far, the discussed changes in legal relationships have not involved the creation of a new legal status such as the conversion to a 501(c)3 nonprofit corporation. Whether designated as a charter university or an enterprise, the changes adopted thus far, and those likely in the near future, involve retaining the institution's state status, which provides certain legal protections. In some states, universities and colleges enjoy constitutional protections as well, so we are unlikely in the near term to see privatization take the drastic turn toward a conversion of the legal form, which has become common in the health care sector.

Essentially, for all involved privatization implies that the state relinquishes control over tuition setting in exchange for being let off the hook for funding institutions. For the institutions involved and for those who have pushed the privatization agenda, the key to reform has been an effort to arrange for a lighter hand from the public sector in setting and governing higher education policy. State officials have occasionally been sympathetic to these efforts. But overall, privatization is driven by exigency rather than ideology (McGuinness, 2005).

Still, ideology or at least discipline-based doctrine supports the privatization trend even if it does not motivate it. Although there are numerous political and theoretical justifications available to the privatization effort, there are various arguments for exercising greater caution and for attending to the serious governance challenges that these trends pose for higher education and for the attainment of public objectives. States have invested huge resources not just in the operation of these entities but in their infrastructure as well. Public higher education currently serves a number of public interests to which private higher education has traditionally not attended. The remainder of this chapter reflects on these considerations and looks at the empirical evidence gathered on the significance of governance and ownership.

The Role of Ownership and Governance: Theory

Whether privatization of public higher education represents a policy improvement or a step back depends not on which disciplinary perspectives are employed to review the question but on which tools from those different disciplines one employs to consider it. This section reviews contrasting perspectives on the appropriate ownership form and governing relationships that should exist in the public higher education sector. These theoretical perspectives underlie the arguments in favor of the privatization trend and suggest that policymakers can discover great promise in the trend.

Higher Education and the Invisible Hand (of the State)

For several reasons, higher education benefits from a light (if not invisible) hand from the state. From public policy comes the idea that higher education does not meet the requirements of a public good. It is certainly rival—there are more than

3,000 institutions of higher education in the United States. And it is certainly excludable—just ask the students who applied to Harvard. Typically, the public good argument support public provision and public subsidy of particular goods such as defense, law enforcement, or fire protection. And even goods that are not pure public goods can find justification from the field of public policy; consider a local park whose costs exceed what person is willing to pay but whose benefits exceed the cost of creating it. In the case of higher education, few of these rationales seem to apply. There are few of the typical market failures that would justify public ownership and provision that seem to apply to higher education. Particular outputs with a public good–like character, such as the production of knowledge, graduate education, or public service, can be purchased through a properly designed contract (see chapter 3 for a more complete discussion of contracts). Even the notion that lower-income individuals who might bypass college when society would benefit from their attendance can be addressed through public subsidy in a market dominated by private providers.

Ethics contributes to two more supporting ideas. First, if the state won't pay for higher education, by what right should it exercise control over it? Treating the public university as a private entity seems reasonable as the proportion of public money comprising the overall operating budget on some public campuses approaches that of private counterparts. Second, a privatized system that charges more for tuition can actually be a more socially equitable system. Critics of public higher education arrangements often single out the low flat-tuition and fee rates of the sector, remarking that this layout uses public funds to keep costs low for many who can afford to pay more. A more socially just organization of higher education would charge more to wealthy students and use much of this revenue to lower the costs of the less advantaged through financial aid. Since the privatization trend has thus far often exhibited this progression, those concerned with social justice can hail a transition away from the old system, in which significant amounts of public funds were tied up in subsidies for middle income and wealthy students when these resources could have been better used to assist more low-income students (Hauptman, and Merisotis, 1990; Rosovsky, 1990).

Such an arrangement, in which the public sector provides funds for students to attend higher education but steps back from articulating which decisions are appropriate, makes practical sense as well, for it is consistent with a fashionable trend in policy circles. The new public management employs the adage that "government should steer, not row" (Osborne and Gaebler, 1992). Public intervention in higher education through the heavy hand of ownership and interference in governance matters runs counter to this postulate. Adherents of this view argue that it is better for government to step back from day-to-day managerial matters and instead focus on goals and outcomes. Purchase arrangements and contract terms can better focus on the delivery of goal achievement than can interference in budget matters and tuition levels.

This approach is also in harmony with the higher education sector's philosophy of institutional autonomy and academic freedom. Both ideas rest on the premise that academics and academically trained managers know what is in the best interest of education and institutions. Such individuals are better suited to campus decision making than politically sensitive appointees or elected officials. The decline in public ownership elevates the role and status of on-campus leaders and potentially strengthens the bond between boards and employees as they work to achieve institutional objectives in concert. To the strictest advocates of academic self-government, the product's preservation can only be ensured through the principle of autonomy (Nelson, 1999).

Economics, in addition to supplying the market failure framework for the supporting the public policy arguments for privatization, also contributes the idea that privatization is further consistent with our society's faith in the powers and benefits of the free market. To let the market decide outcomes in higher education stands in contrast to a previous trend in state higher education policy to coordinate activities to produce rational policies that achieved state objectives. The coordination movement sought to minimize duplication and maximize the efficiency of public higher education's instructional scope (McGuinness, 1997). Coordinating bodies with program approval authority existed to prevent a state from having too many biomedical doctoral programs and not enough teacher education programs. Too much state control also opens the door to bureaucratic capture in which public employees drive institutional performance toward the achievement of their personal objectives rather that the public interest. Some research shows that public institutions with higher degrees of public control produce lower quality research and teaching outcomes (Toma, 1986). But the privatization trend offers a chance to move away from this approach and instead use the state's purchasing authority and contracts to secure the appropriate amount of educational services for that state.

A market-driven system of higher education puts its faith in individual preferences and consumer sovereignty. A properly designed market with sufficient information flows should free consumers to select the appropriate amount and kind of educational services. Such a market will provide educational providers with the proper signals to decide on educational content and program arrangements that are appropriate to state and national needs. Markets are supposed to render providers more efficient and responsive, improving consumer satisfaction and the proper use of national resources. A move away from public control and toward a freer market is aimed at bringing such benefits to higher education.

Higher Education and the Heavy Hand (of the State)

Clearly, there are numerous reasons to hope that a move away from public owner-ship and public provision of higher education represents a potential improvement in public policy. But there are also several theoretical reasons to think that a heavy hand from the state can better ensure the achievement of public objectives. Theories about the role of ownership, breakdowns in the higher education market, and questions about the discharge of state investments in higher education infrastructure challenge some of the broad hopes of privatization and suggest some necessary adjustments to the privatization trend.

The higher education market is actually a collection of input and output markets —a market for labor, a market for donors, a market for students, and a market for educational outputs. How these markets function in reality often departs signifi-cantly from the theories of neoclassical economics. A good deal of evidence sug-gests that competition drives up costs rather than improving quality or efficiency (Zemsky and Massy, 2005). Lee and Weisbrod (1977) have remarked that univer-sities are vehicles for cross-subsidization. Profitable activities generate income that subsidizes those that are less profitable or unprofitable altogether. Increasing compe-tition in this setting establishes a disincentive to invest in the unprofitable areas and to instead invest more resources in those areas that increase one's competitive advan-tage in the profitable areas. Cross-subsidization, like collaboration over financial aid, rests on an implicit agreement about the purposes of higher education and an environment akin to the lulls in trench warfare of World War I, when soldiers walked across no man's land to exchange gifts and partake in communal games. Elevating the competitive environment could actually lead to less socially optimal results. We would like to think that two competing institutions would carve up a market with one offering degrees in one field and the other seeking a competitive advantage in another. Instead, what we more often observe is competition over the same narrow set of aspects that figures prominently in social assessments of quality and institutional desirability. Already, this trend is apparent in health care, a field increasingly shaped by the actions of for-profit providers. Suddenly, every hospital is expanding profit centers like delivery units and cardiac care centers while closing or contracting less profitable areas such as burn units or level-three trauma centers (Mahar, 2006).

In health care, the ownership form is proving to be a significant predictor of hospital behavior (Bays, 1979; Frech and Ginsburg, 1981; Horwitz, 2002; Lee and Weisbrod, 1977; Patel, Needleman, and Zeckhauser, 1994; Shortell et al., 1986; Zeckhauser, Patel, and Needleman, 1995). Ownership does not figure prominently in neoclassical economic models of outcomes, but more modern approaches have taken account of the information asymmetries and misalignment of incentives that can plague an organization as a result of a particular ownership form (Fama and Jensen, 1983a, 1983b; Hansmann, 1996; Jensen and Meckling, 1976; Wilson, 1989). When economists look at the significance of ownership, they emphasize contractual obligations and aligning the incentives of managers with those who can be identified as the owners.[4]

Legal scholars, however, look to historical evidence when considering owner-ship's significance. Both public and private nonprofit institutions receive a public charter to serve public purposes. In fact, in the corporate governance world, there is a line of thinking that the charter argument supersedes the notion that a corporation exists to serve the shareholders (Blair, 1995). Whether public or private, for-profit or nonprofit, chartered entities exist to advance public interests.[5] So an argument could be made that we need to make both private and public institutions more account-able to the state, not less, even as public funding goes away.

How can we conceptualize the role of ownership in determining whose interests are served by the actions of a chartered entity, whether it is public or private, for-profit or nonprofit? The property rights tradition established by Coase (1937) points the way by reminding us that organizations produce multiple outputs, and the property rights over them often determine individual and collective behavior. In-stead of focusing on profits, which assumes that the residual benefit is obvious, securable, and apportionable, consider that every collective enterprise seeks to pro-duce benefits.

Rather than seeking to maximize the amount of value between revenues and costs, the objectives of the private for-profit, a more generalizable description of an organization is that it seeks to maximize the benefits created and to discover a way to distribute these among the different parties that lay claim to organizationally pro-duced value. The activities of the organization yield a benefit, B, and this benefit can be distributed among the cost factors or inputs, C; to the profit of the organization, π, which accrues to its legal owners; to price subsidies for consumers, P; and to the spillover effects of these benefits, S.

$$\text{Max benefits, } B, \text{ such that: } B - C - \pi - S - P = 0 \qquad (1)$$

This objective function can represent any organization. The spillover effects, S, represent the indirect benefit, which a broad number of parties can draw from the organization's activities without purchasing anything from the organization—what are typically called externalities in economics. The price subsidies, *P*, represent direct benefits that are granted to the consumer so that purchases can be made at prices that are below the cost of production. The net benefit then can be allocated among various organizational participants.

The following model expresses these relationships: The benefits, *B*, might be thought of as the total revenues that a profit-maximizing owner would gather if he could price discriminate perfectly and extract from customers' their true willingness to pay for all of the goods created by the organization.[6] Using this framework, one can consider the objectives of each ownership form and the effects on the various components of the objective function and in particular organizational costs.

1. The for-profit organization might seek to maximize the benefits and then capture them for the owners by minimizing spillover benefits and minimizing costs. If property rights were perfectly specified and owners exercised strict control, then spillover effects would be minimal, costs would be minimized, and subsidies would exist only as far as they advanced profit interests (Coase, 1937).

2. The public organization is usually uninterested in earning monetary profits. If the general public effectively monitored and tightly controlled the organization, it might seek to maximize benefits subject to a minimal expenditure of costs (and a lower tax burden) and a maximal production of spillover benefits and price subsidies for society. If the public's role were weakened by the bureaucratic structure, then managers and others might allow costs to rise as they distributed the surplus benefits to those who produced them.

3. The nonprofit organization cannot earn profits, if by profits we mean the residual distributed to controlling parties. But it can maximize the benefits created and then attempt to distribute those benefits to the members and nonmembers of the organization. It might choose to increase costs of production and transfer some of the residual benefit to employees without appearing to violate the legal ban on profit distribution.[7] It could distribute the residual as a spillover benefit to society or subsidize access to the good by reducing the costs of *B* for consumers.

Hence, the allocation of value / surplus within the organization should reflect the way ownership forms assign power and influence over such decisions, the interests of participating groups, and the size of the surplus. If large spillover benefits accrue from an entity's activities then, as Coase (1937) would say, the property rights are not perfect over the benefit stream emanating from the organization. If an organization is largely in the control of managers and employees, then much of the benefit will be allocated to them in the form of costs above what is minimally necessary to provide the benefit.[8] And if the organization rests in public hands, then, to the degree the benefits can be captured, public owners are likely to insist that the benefit be distributed through price subsidies and spillover benefits. In other words, ownership forms are likely to matter a great deal when production is joint and the parties' contributions are unclear, the outputs are diffuse and difficult to claim, and profits are not legally assigned or considered an organizational goal.

The Role of Ownership and Governance: Practice

What do we know about structural effects stemming from the ownership form and governance arrangements in higher education? How, for instance, do outcomes differ among private and public universities? Increasing evidence from the field suggests that ownership matters a good deal, that structural arrangements within public systems of higher education also influence outcomes, but that campus-level arrangements are of uncertain consequence. Public institutions behave, it turns out, quite differently from private ones.

Even a cursory look at data from the U.S. Department of Education suggests that public institutions educate students at a lower cost per full-time equivalent than private institutions. These differences persist once one controls for differences in institutional mission, region, endowment wealth, quality of the student body, composition of the faculty and of the student body, dependence on tuition, and having a medical school. All other things being equal, private institutions not only charge more in tuition, but they employ more resources to educate a student (Kaplan, 2002a). Additional evidence suggests that public institutions rely on lower levels of administrative and capital intensity (Kaplan, 1999).

Public and private institutional differences persist when the focus shifts to how professors spend their time and the outputs upon which they choose to focus. Departments in private colleges and universities are more likely to stress research over teaching and service while in public institutions they place more importance on teaching, public service, and outreach (Golden and Cartensen, 1992). Some evidence suggests that faculty in private institutions are more productive in research than their opposites in public institutions (Dundar and Lewis, 1998). Adams and Griliches (1996) suggest that private institutions have a comparative advantage at producing research that is more often cited than public universities and colleges. Modest evidence suggests that the ownership form of the institution has some effect on the research topics that scholars select, which explains differences in research productivity.

Governance arrangements at the state level can mirror private and public ownership distinctions in that different arrangements of authority can lead to different patterns of residual surplus distribution. Research on state governance systems indicates that significant differences in outcomes arise from the different methods of organizing state systems of higher education (Kaplan, 2002a, 2002b; Lowry, 1998; Toma, 1990). Scholars who look at state systems for organizing the relationships between the public institutions and the states typically categorize the approaches into three types. Centralized, or consolidated, governing systems use one governing board to oversee all public four-year higher education institutions in the state. Coordinating systems employ a coordinating board (which may or may not have budget setting authority) to oversee a system of autonomous institutions with their own governing boards. And planning systems employ relatively little centralized state control (Berdahl, 1971; McGuinness, 1997; Education Commission of the States, 1994, 1997).

State control, defined as the arrangement that best produces outcomes that seem consistent with the preferences of voters and legislators, appears to be best realized through coordinating bodies. Planning authorities appear to have little ability to direct policy toward particular state goals, and centralized governing boards often seem to identify with the institutional view of educational matters rather than the political views of elected officialdom. One investigation that looked at these matters examined the role of state-level institutions that govern and regulate public universities and found that greater political control—operationalized in the form of regulatory coordinating boards—led to lower university prices (Lowry, 2001). Toma (1990) looked at these same state-level institutions of system governance and assessed the degree to which they balanced the preferences of faculty and those of external stakeholders such as citizens and elected officials. She concluded that institutions in states with coordinating bodies were more likely to produce outcomes consistent with voter preferences while planning authority systems were most likely to produce institutional outcomes consistent with assumed faculty preferences. Kaplan also looked at state-system effects and found that after controlling for a variety of institutional differences, institutions in states that employed coordinating bodies spent significantly less per full-time equivalent than did institutions from states with only a planning authority or a consolidated governing board.[9] Knott and Payne (2004) found results consistent with these patterns. States with decentralized state governing systems encouraged university managers to pursue academic values such as research, external grants, and publication, while more centralized systems reflected the greater priorities of state policymakers to obtain lower tuition levels, greater access, and a higher emphasis on teaching. Hence, steps away from mechanisms of state control are likely to yield outcomes that are consistent with academics preferences but which may not be consistent with the preferences of state policymakers and voters.

The least-studied mechanisms of control and regulation in higher education are institutions of campus governance (Kaplan, 2006a). Although public university governance structures are often recorded by state level of national policy-oriented organizations, private institutions almost never get surveyed for their campus-based governance mechanisms. Two exceptions are surveys of campus-based governance conducted under the sponsorship of the American Association of University Professors (AAUP) in 1970 and in 2001 (Kaplan, 2004). The most recent survey comparing private and public institutions in their mechanisms of campus-based governance found relatively little difference in the way the institutions integrated faculty into the governance process and the means used to do this. One difference between the sectors observed in this data indicates that public institutions tend to have more formalized mechanisms for faculty participations—faculty senates comprising representatives rather than open campus-wide or division-wide faculty meetings. Public institutions are also more reliant on boards to do much of the decision making on strategic issues. On private campuses, governing boards more often fill a ceremonial purpose or are a tool of fundraising. Public institutions also employ smaller boards, are more likely to exclude the campus president from voting on matters before the board, and are more likely to include faculty or student stakeholders (Kaplan, 2002a, 2004). The differences in the size of the board and in the presidential role suggest that public boards are more usually tools of governing while private campus boards, because they are larger and therefore more likely to be unwieldy and are more likely to defer to the president, face a greater likelihood of capture by institutionally grounded interests. Although governing boards are the ultimate owners of the institution in that they have both the ultimate fiduciary responsibility and the obligation to ensure that the organization fulfills its publicly chartered purpose, in the private setting such boards appear to define this purpose in terms set by institutional actors—quality, research notoriety, and wealth.

Beyond the apparent differences at the board level, the similarity of governance approaches at the campus level and the research about the role of campus governance structures on outcomes suggests that the effects of campus governance are more muted than those of state-level coordination or ownership form. McCormick and Meiners's (1988) study of higher education governance structures and the role they play in shaping academic quality at both private and public universities used data from a 1971 AAUP survey of higher education governance. They found that schools with greater levels of faculty influence in governance were likely to have lower levels of faculty productivity and lower levels of student performance. McCormick and Meiners did not see this as a sign that faculty influence and power were associated with shirking as much as a result of self-selection in which faculty with lower teaching or research skills would gravitate to schools that required more participation in governance. Masten (1998) looked at similar survey data and concluded that the degree of centralized authority versus faculty participation in governance would be a function of the size and heterogeneity of the institution and its relationship to external interests. Masten argued that faculty participation served as a commitment mechanism and deterrence to appropriation when an institution needed to assure various parties of the credibility of decisions and promises. The homogeneity of the institution's population and its reliance on external patrons were shown to be predictors of autocratic decision modes.

States have not shown a great aptitude for strategic thinking within higher education systems, especially when it comes to the question of applying a shrunken amount of available resources (Kaplan, 2006b). Although state control appears to be associated with a greater likelihood of attaining some public-sector policy objectives, the record hardly suggests that state control assures the attainment of state objectives. Still, to the degree that state control is exercised, the evidence indicates that state goal achievement is enhanced.

Two problems seem endemic, even among the most coordinated and politically controlled state systems. First, few state officials or governing boards have claimed that state interests permit a strong role in strategic thinking about resource allocation within systems and on particular campuses. A recent study of budget retrenchment in eight states during the recessionary period between 2001 and 2004 showed that state officials encouraged campuses and systems to increase tuition in response to decreases in state aid rather than to engage in strategic thinking about reallocation among particular priorities (Kaplan, 2006b). In other words, even the most regulated and controlled systems of public higher education choose to shift burdens from states to students during the last recession. Few public institutions used the occasion as an opportunity to reexamine priorities or assign continued resource increases to areas of strength or state significance and away from lower performing and less crucial programs. State officials, bowing to precepts of institutional autonomy, have abdicated much of a role in resource allocation matters beyond the highest-level questions concerning overall amounts. Even when systems are designed to give the state influence in higher education input and output decisions, few states realize all of their opportunities to do so.

Second, we should be skeptical that state system boards and campus-level boards of public institutions can by themselves represent the public interest in policy matters. The evidence suggests that such boards are more likely to rubber-stamp decisions of campus administrators or to share the same sets of objectives for the campus as faculty, alumni, and administrators. This is understandable, for bureaucratic capture theory informs us that officials aligned with a department will quickly come to champion its perspective, regardless of their initial views on such topics. The theory suggests that even a small public board of a state institution will be likely to pursue institutional expansion and advancement and to contest efforts at reorganization or contraction.

Implications

The attainment of state policy objectives is extremely difficult in higher education because of the size of the systems, their entrenched and highly acculturated interests, the decentralized nature of such systems, and the bureaucratic challenges of information and control that face any centralized decision process. Still, the evidence confirms that to the degree that a state plays a role in ownership and control its chances of achieving public purposes are enhanced. To the degree that the state defers to the market and to the institutions to deliver on these objectives, the probability that costs will be contained, that resource efficiency will be maximized, and that access and public service will be promoted are reduced.

Does this suggest that central planning in higher education and state ownership is the preferred mechanism for policymaking? Not necessarily. It suggests that the advocates of decentralization, privatization, and deregulation in higher education might want to be careful about what they wish for. Privatization may get the state off the hook for direct budget obligations, but it may also reduce the state's influence over and ability to realize desired state higher education outcomes. The ratio of success in achieving policy goals per dollar invested could fall. Still, although private institutions and less regulated state institutions are not as likely to focus on the attainment of state objectives, they seek to maximize goods that benefit the state. Privatization, then, does not preclude the attainment of state objectives. But it suggests caution and attending to the design of deregulatory and privatization approaches so that the realization of such objectives can be enhanced for all rather than overlooked altogether. State policymakers considering the course of privatization might want to focus on several questions.

Does Central Planning Offer the Best Mechanism for Achieving State Goals in Higher Education?

Central planning hardly has a stellar record in policy circles. Nevertheless, some degree of a central planning philosophy underlies the design of state higher education systems. Results indicate that such planning can better succeed by holding down operating costs and tuition, promoting public service, and encouraging access. Still, Hayek's challenge for central planning remains (Hayek, 1960). For the evidence also suggests that institutional quality, research productivity and output, and attention to a broad array of student needs are enhanced by deregulation and privatized approaches. Central planners are unlikely to ever be able to gather sufficient amounts of information to ensure that systems of higher education can be managed to respond to rapid changes in labor market demand, social need, or policy challenge. And political systems will often become tied down with conflicts over reapportionment of resources and dealing with resource constraints. One challenge for state systems of higher education consists of navigating the limitations of central planning and the problems that arise from exercising a light hand over the entire system. Policy innovation must find a way to blend the best of both approaches to develop a system that is seamless, possesses minimal overlap, is focused on delivering value to the state for public and personal dollars expended, and produces both public service and high quality basic research.

What Is the Purpose of Enacting Privatization Policies?

Privatization-like policy responses have thus far manifested themselves as a default policy option. In the wake of decreasing public funding, institutions ask for and states grant greater flexibility in seeking revenues from alternative sources without an extensive conversation about alternatives such as institutional redesign. In response to this trend, the AGB issued a report on privatization, which sagely asked, What is the purpose of regulatory flexibility? Does it exist to achieve institutional purposes or public purposes (AGB, 2005)? The answer need not be mutually exclusive. The evidence suggests that without a close consideration of privatization's implications, it will serve institutional interests before those of the public.

How Will the State Address the Challenge of Writing Contracts with Providers, Especially Formerly Public Providers?

In both Colorado and Virginia, states at the forefront of the privatization movement (if it can be called this), policymakers have adopted a contractual approach to deregulation. The institutions involved have traded regulatory relief for greater flexibility as well as accountability through state contracts. Such contractual arrangements will be key if states shift from controlling inputs to seeking to shape outcomes. But the big question becomes how are states going to write these contracts? The same limitations that face a central planning regime also challenge state efforts to specify desired outcome ex ante through a contract. Even when states believe they have enumerated their policy goals, each side can disagree sharply over the terms of agreement. In the fall of 2005 in the first term of the new enterprise regime, conflict erupted between the governor and the University of Colorado over whether the institution had violated the understanding that it would keep tuition increases to a minimum. The university claimed it had honored the agreement by holding the average tuition increase tuition to what had been specified in the contract. The governor pointed out that the university had done so by keeping out-of-state tuition increases low and increasing in-state tuition significantly. Specifying all the necessary terms of the contract to achieve state objectives can be hard. Furthermore, many of the output measures necessary to assess the attainment of these objectives need further development or have yet to be properly identified. A contract's effectiveness is only as good as the ability one has to determine whether it realizes desired objectives.

Should the State Take Lessons from Its Approach to the Public Sector and Apply Them to the Private Sector?

The contrast in performance between public and private higher education and the legal arguments that charter law endows all corporate entities with existence to pursue a public purpose both remind us that implementing privatization policy also opens the door to greater state involvement with the private sector. Of course implementing privatization does not require greater state control or influence over private higher education. But if the state begins to negotiate outcomes with public institutions it might want to consider its ownership rights over nonprofit educational institutions as well. Engaging in contract development with private institutions may offer a chance for states to coordinate the full spectrum of four-year higher education. Although states typically have not done this, their attorneys general certainly have the legal authority to oversee their performance and monitor whether they are fulfilling the purposes for which they have been chartered.

Does Privatization Absolve the State of Any Responsibility for Controlling the Budgets and Expenditures of Higher Education Institutions?

Although contract design makes it possible for states to negotiate over certain outcomes, it makes it more difficult for them to oversee or participate in institutional and systemwide strategic planning—strategic downsizing when necessary, preventing program duplications and overlap, growing programs of strength or importance to the state. Most challenging for a state is to have influence over how budgets are pared when funding is lean. States do a poor job of this already (Kaplan, 2006b). If privatization limits their influence to negotiating over purchases, their abilities in this regard will move from mere potential to nonexistent. Most telling, states are already looking to privatization and decreased state funding without exploring other ways to reduce funding obligations such as requiring that states produce lists of areas of strength and areas of weakness. Ways exist to rig such a system so that schools are assisted in finding ways to cut while improving performance without the state involving itself in micro-level decisions that go to the question of institutional autonomy.

Conclusion

Privatization, deregulation, greater flexibility, even charter colleges and vouchers for public higher education have been on the minds of policy thinkers for some time before the budget crises engendered by the recessionary pull-back of 2001–4. The actual process of implementing such innovations has lagged until recently. Now that such reforms are not only on the minds of state policymakers but are actually occurring much thought needs to go into their implementation.

The AGB recently considered these challenges and came up with five policy recommendations (AGB, 2005):

1. Increase the size of public boards.
2. Reform the process of board appointment to yield better boards.
3. Conduct due diligence in assessing the trade-offs and benefits from shifting the legal status of state institutions.
4. Create some public oversight and input process to monitor tuition increases.

5. Ensure the policy infrastructure necessary to oversee the institutions and the negotiating process exists.

Clearly, the state will need to respond to the privatization trend by addressing the capacity of current systems to navigate the requirements of a more market dominated system. To prevent the wholesale transfer of what economists like to call consumer surplus (and what the model described in this chapter calls total benefits) from consumers to institutions, states will need to play an active role and consider how they will express their ownership interest and the public interest.

Increasing the size of state boards promises mixed benefits. Larger boards may have greater capacity to conduct board business, but they are also more unwieldy, more likely to be divided and conflict ridden, and the opposite trend from what has been urged from scholars of corporate governance. Improving the selection of board members so that boards better monitor their fiduciary responsibilities and the institution's obligations to the state would be welcome. However, in many states, this presents the serious obstacle of constitutional reform when such board members are elected by the public. It would be nice too if states proceeded through a process of due diligence in moving toward privatization, but thus far the trend suggests that states are looking to offload their financial and ownership responsibilities for some measure of fiscal relief. States will clearly have a continuing interest in the tuition setting decisions of institutions. But they will have to walk the thin line between instituting price controls and simply establishing bodies that record citizen commentary. States would benefit from an investment in an expanded policy infrastructure, which would develop their capabilities to monitor the sector and secure goal achievement for state systems. But this will cost money and represent a deeper investment in administrative overhead, something most state politicians are loath to do given the current economic situation.

States face numerous challenges in the wake of narrowing fiscal resources for public higher education. Privatization may offer some promises, but the challenges should not be minimized. Market segmentation is such that wealthy and prestigious public research institutions will probably face and pose the fewest challenges for state policymakers. For the less wealthy or influential institutions that often seek to hitch a ride on the privatization reform wagon, they, and the state politicians who encourage them, may find themselves striking a Faustian bargain. They may earn the flexibility to raise tuition revenues and dollars from other sources, but their character as teaching institutions, as repositories of public service energy, and as entryways into the middle class for state residents may fade.

NOTES

1. It is true, however, that public institutional faculty have seen their compensation levels deteriorate significantly relative to their counterparts in private institutions. If even only a fraction of what we know about economics and markets is true, then eventually, these shifts in relative compensation levels will have a significant effect on the composition of faculties and in the perceived quality of public institutions. But in the meantime, despite the failure of public-sector salaries to keep pace, there have not been marked changes in the makeup of public university faculties or a significant effect on college and university rankings (see COACHE, 2007; Smallwood, 2001).

2. Various terms have been employed to describe this trend—*privatization, deregulation, enhancing flexibility*—but this chapter uses privatization, to keep it consistent with the theme of this book.

3. While pro-market advocates had initially wanted to extend the voucher to all higher education organizations in the state to better stimulate the forces of market competition between schools, the final proposal, which passed and was signed, only extended the public voucher to students who enrolled at one of three private institutions in the state—Colorado College, University of Denver, and Regis University. Although this remained controversial, the last two institutions drew particular concern from observers since they are Roman Catholic–sponsored institutions.

4. In the case of the for-profit firm, the owners are the shareholders or proprietors. In the case of the public organization, the owner is the taxpayer or citizen. And in the case of the nonprofit organization, economists often point to the donor, although nonprofit scholars usually question this claim (Fama and Jensen, 1983a, 1983b).

5. Stakeholder theorists who study organizations argue that corporations should serve the interests of all parties with a stake in the organization (Freeman, 1984). Such an approach is more consistent with the legal view than the economic arguments of those like Jensen who argue that only a singular objective function like owing a sole obligation to shareholders can solve the problems of strategic choice in a collective setting.

6. Total surplus is generally represented as the combination of consumer and producer surplus and would be equal to the area under the demand curve and above the competitive supply curve formed at the equilibrium price. In this case, we ignore the supply curve because we consider that separately in the model and simply focus on the area of the surplus under the demand curve out to the equilibrium price. Although calculating the size of the surplus benefit presents complications because utility is typically seen as unmeasurable, we could use estimates of the demand curve to draw conclusions about the consumers' willingness to pay and to infer a quantitative value for the benefit. Whether a competitive supply curve can be ascertained in all markets is a problem for further consideration and analysis.

7. Recent changes by the Internal Revenue Service to the treatment of nonprofit costs are aimed at preventing employee or managerial inurement, but the enforcement problems are complex and actual IRS actions against nonprofits are rare. The IRS, for instance, cannot always know what the market wage for the CEO of a nonprofit would be and cannot always tell whether a portion of the compensation represents inurement.

8. Of course, such employees do not have to be as self-serving as economic models often imply. Rather, when employees control the firm, the benefits will be allocated according to their value function.

9. Volkwein looked extensively over a long period at the relationship between state systems of governing higher education and campus-level outcomes and found little effects in the areas of administrative expenditures, measures of quality, and productivity (Volkwein, 1986, 1987, 1989). But his assumptions and his models differed markedly from the political economy approaches employed by Lowry, Toma, and Kaplan (McLendon, 2004).

REFERENCES

Adams, James D., and Zvi Griliches. 2000. Research Productivity in a System of Universities. In *The Economics and Econometrics of Innovation*, ed. David Encaoua, Bronwyn H. Hall, Francois Laisney, and Jacques Mairesse. Norwell, MA: Kluwer Academic.

Association of Governing Boards. 2005. The New Interest in Charter Universities and State Performance Contracts. State Policy Brief No. 3. Association of Governing Boards, Washington, DC.

Bays, Carson W. 1979. Cost Comparisons of For-Profit and Nonprofit Hospitals. *Social Science and Medicine* 13C (4): 219–25.

Berdahl, Robert O. 1971. *Statewide Coordination of Higher Education.* Washington, DC: Association of Governing Boards.

Blair, Margaret. 1995. *Ownership and Control: Rethinking Corporate Governance for the Twenty-First Century.* Washington, DC: Brookings Institution.

Boyd, Don. 2002. State Spending for Higher Education in the Coming Decade. Paper prepared for the National Center for Higher Education Management Systems, Boulder, CO.

Coase, Ronald. 1937. The Nature of the Firm. *Economica* 4:386–405.

Collaborative on Academic Careers in Higher Education (COACHE). 2007. COACHE Highlights Report 2007. Cambridge, MA: COACHE.

Couturier, Lara. 2006. *Checks and Balances: The Restructuring of Virginia's Public Higher Education System.* San Jose, CA: National Center for Public Policy and Higher Education.

Donohue, John D. 1989. *The Privatization Decision: Public Ends, Private Means.* New York: Basic Books.

Dundar, Halil, and Darrell R. Lewis. 1998. Determinants of Research Productivity in Higher Education. *Research in Higher Education* 39 (6): 607–631.

Education Commission of the States. 1994. *State Postsecondary Education Structures Sourcebook.* Denver, CO: Education Commission of the States.

———. 1997. *State Postsecondary Education Structures Sourcebook.* Denver, CO: Education Commission of the States.

Fama, Eugene F., and Michael C. Jensen. 1983a. Agency Problems and Residual Claims. *Journal of Law and Economics* 26 (June): 327–48.

———. 1983b. Separation of Ownership and Control. *Journal of Law and Economics* 26 (June): 301–26.

Frech, H. E., and Paul B. Ginsburg. 1981. Property Rights and Competition in Health

Insurance: Multiple Objectives for Nonprofit Firms. *Research in Law and Economics* 3:155–72.

Freeman, R. Edward. 1984. *Strategic Management: A Stakeholder Approach.* Boston: Pitman.

Golden, John, and Fred V. Carstensen. 1992. Academic Research Productivity, Department Size and Organization: Further Results, Rejoinder. *Economics of Education Review* 11, no. 2 (June): 169–71.

Hansmann, Henry. 1996. *The Ownership of Enterprise.* Cambridge, MA: Belknap Press of Harvard University Press.

Hauptman, Arthur, and Jamie P. Merisotis. 1990. *The College Tuition Spiral: An Examination of Why Charges Are Increasing.* A Report to the College Board and the American Council on Education. Washington, DC: Macmillan.

Hayek, Friedrich A. 1960. *The Constitution of Liberty.* Chicago: University of Chicago Press.

Horwitz, Jill R. 2002. Corporate Form of Hospitals: Behavior and Obligations. Ph.D. diss., Faculty of Graduate School of Arts and Sciences, Harvard University.

Hovey, Harold A. 1999. *State Spending for Higher Education in the Next Decade: The Battle to Sustain Current Support.* San Jose, CA: National Center for Public Policy and Higher Education.

Jensen, Michael C., and William H. Meckling. 1976. Theory of the Firm. Managerial Behavior, Agency Costs, and Ownership Structure. *Journal of Financial Economics* 3:305–60.

Kaplan, Gabriel. 1999. Why Does College Cost So Much? An Assessment of the Factors Associated with Rising Costs as American Colleges and Universities. Malcolm Wiener Center for Social Policy. Working Paper. John F. Kennedy School of Government, Harvard University.

———. 2002a. Between Politics and Markets: The Institutional Allocation of Resources in Higher Education. PhD diss., Faculty of Graduate School of Arts and Sciences, Harvard University.

———. 2002b. When Agents Seem to Have No Principals: Resource and Benefit Allocation in Public and Nonprofit Institutions of Higher Education. Unpublished Paper, John F. Kennedy School of Government, Harvard University.

———. 2004. How Academic Ships Actually Navigate: A Report from the 2001 Survey on Higher Education Governance. In *Governing Academia,* ed. Ronald G. Ehrenberg. Ithaca, NY: Cornell University Press.

———. 2006a. Institutions of Academic Governance and Institutional Theory: A Framework for Further Research. In *Higher Education: Handbook of Theory and Research.* Vol. 11, ed. John Smart. New York: Springer.

———. 2006b. State Fiscal Crises and Cuts in Higher Education: The Implications for Access, Institutional Performance, and Strategic Reengineering. Working Paper. Boulder, CO: Western Interstate Commission on Higher Education.

Knott, Jack H., and A. Abigail Payne. 2004. The Impact of State Governance Structures on Management of Public Organizations: A Study of Higher Education Institutions. *Journal of Public Policy Analysis and Management* 23 (1): 13–30.

Lee, A. James, and Burton A. Weisbrod. 1977. Collective Goods and the Voluntary Sector:

The Case of the Hospital Industry. In *The Voluntary Nonprofit Sector: An Economic Analysis*, ed. Burton Weisbrod. Lexington, MA: D. C. Heath.

Lowry, Robert C. 1998. Mission, Governance Structure and Outcomes at Quasi-Autonomous Public Institutions: Evidence for American Universities. Paper presented at the Annual Meeting of the American Political Science Association, Boston.

———. 2001. Governmental Structure, Trustee Selection, and Public University Prices, and Spending: Multiple Means to Similar Ends. *American Journal of Political Science* 45 (4): 845–61.

Lyall, Katharine, and Kathleen Sell. 2006. *The True Genius of America at Risk: Are We Losing Our Public Universities to De Facto Privatization*. Westport, CT: Praeger.

Mahar, Maggie. 2006. *Money Driven Medicine: The Real Reason Health Care Costs So Much*. New York: HarperCollins.

Masten, Scott. 1998. Commitment and Political Governance: Why Universities, Like Legislatures, Are Not Organized as Markets. Paper Presented to the National Bureau of Economic Research (NBER). Higher Education Meeting, Cambridge, MA.

McCormick, Robert E., and Robert E. Meiners. 1998. University Governance: A Property Rights Perspective. *Journal of Law and Economics* 31:423–42.

McGuinness, Aims. 1997. The Functions and Evolution of State Coordination and Governance in Post-Secondary Education. In *State Postsecondary Education Structures Sourcebook*, 1–48. Denver, CO: Education Commission of the States.

———. 2005. Changes in Financing and State Policy Related to American Public Research Universities. Paper presented at the International Seminar on University Management and Higher Education Policies: Trends, Issues, and Prospects, Tokyo, Japan.

McLendon, Michael. 2004. State Governance Reform of Higher Education. In *Higher Education: Handbook of Theory and Research*. Vol. 18, ed. John Smart. The Netherlands: Springer.

Nelson, Cary. 1999. The War against the Faculty. *Chronicle of Higher Education* 45, no. 32 (April): B4.

Osborne, David, and Ted Gaebler. 1992. *Reinventing Government: How the Entrepreneurial Spirit Is Transforming the Public Sector*. Reading, MA: Addison-Wesley.

Patel, Jayendu, Jack Needleman, and Richard Zeckhauser. 1994. Changing Fortunes, Hospital Behaviors and Ownership Forms. Unpublished Paper, John F. Kennedy School of Government, Harvard University.

Rosovsky, Henry. 1990. *The University: An Owners Manual*. New York: W. W. Norton.

Selingo, Jeffery. 2003. The Disappearing State in Higher Education. *Chronicle of Higher Education* 49, no. 25 (February): A22.

Shortell, Stephen, Ellen Morrison, James Hughes, Bernard Friedman, James Coverdill, and Linda Berg. 1986. The Effects of Hospital Ownership on Nontraditional Services. *Health Affairs* 5 (4): 97–111.

Smallwood, Scott. 2001. The Price Professors Pay for Teaching at Public Universities. *Chronicle of Higher Education* 48, no. 32 (April): A18.

Toma, Eugenia Froedge. 1986. State University Boards of Trustees: A Principal-Agent Perspective. *Public Choice* 49:155–163.

——. 1990. Boards of Trustees, Agency Problems, and University Output. *Public Choice* 67:1–9.

Volkwein, J. Fredericks. 1987. State Regulation and Campus Autonomy. In *Education: Handbook of Theory and Research*, ed. J. C. Smart, 3:120–154. New York: Agathon Press.

Wilson, James Q. 1989. *Bureaucracy.* New York: Basic Books.

Zeckhauser, Richard, Jayendu Patel, and Jack Needleman. 1995. The Economic Behavior of For-profit and Nonprofit Hospitals: The Impact of Ownership Form on Responses to Changing Reimbursement and Market Environments. Working Paper (draft). Submitted to Robert Wood Johnson Foundation, Princeton, NJ.

Zemsky, Robert, Gregory R. Wegner, and William F. Massy. 2005. *Remaking the American University: Market-Smart and Mission-Centered.* Piscataway, NJ: Rutgers University Press.

CHAPTER SEVEN

Policy Lessons from the Privatization of Public Agencies

• ᘓᕋ •

MARK STATER

Many public institutions of higher education have been experiencing sharp reductions in state government funding over the past three decades (see chapters 2, 3, and 4). As a result, these institutions have been forced to rely on increased tuition and private donations to make up the revenue shortfall. As described in the chapter 6, institutions such as the University of Colorado and Penn State University now receive less than 10% of their overall funding from state appropriations for full-time enrollments. The phenomenon of reduced government support for higher education is referred to as the *privatization* of higher education. Privatization is increasingly gaining momentum as pressure on state budgets from rising health care, infrastructure, corrections, and pension costs reduce the amount of funding available for other state services. At the same time, reductions in the generosity of federal grant programs and shifts in the packaging of federal aid from grants to loans, have further placed the burden of financing for public higher education on students and their families.

Although public to private shifts in higher education finance have lately been rationalized on the grounds that the benefits to higher education are primarily private in the form of wage gains for the individual (Dennison, 2003), these developments raise serious concerns about how the fundamental missions of public institutions might be affected. Because a large fraction of the nation's college students are enrolled in public institutions, such changes have potentially widespread effects, especially for in-state students of limited income, who have traditionally been the beneficiaries of public institutions' access goals and for whom public institutions represent a relatively high-quality, low-cost educational alternative. Thus, state and institutional officials must have a clear understanding of the effects of privatization before taking irreversible steps in this direction.

This chapter examines privatization experiences with other formerly public agencies for lessons that can be applied to higher education. The evidence suggests that privatization is likely to improve the efficiency with which higher education services are delivered by reducing educational costs and providing incentives for investments in service quality. At the same time, however, the costs to in-state and financially needy students will increase and incentives for institutions to enroll these students will decrease. It follows that access to education among these groups will decrease, especially in the extreme case where the state fully divests from institutions. Thus, although privatization promises to save the state money in the near term, it could ultimately cost more in terms of political capital and future public assistance outlays to workers with less education and lower earnings than they might have otherwise enjoyed.

Two places offer guidance about the effects of privatization: currently, existing private institutions and past experiences with privatization in other formerly public agencies. Because the public institution would effectively become a private institution subsequent to privatization, the future of privatized public institutions is already to some extent embodied in private institutions of the present. The lessons drawn from private-public comparisons may be incomplete for several reasons. First are the significant size differences between public and private institutions, which may result in a relatively small comparison group of sufficiently large private universities on which to base predictions. Second, privatized public institutions would experience a period of significant transition that their private counterparts never experienced. An alternative source of lessons is from other formerly public agencies that have been privatized, some of which were very large enterprises and all of which experienced transition. Considering how public higher education compares with the services once provided by these agencies yields further insights into the effects of privatization.

This chapter is organized as follows: First, it draws a brief comparison between public and private institutions to develop a sense of what public institutions might look like after privatization and considers the empirical evidence on the effects of privatization in primary and secondary education. Then, it considers the empirical evidence on privatization experiences in noneducation services. It concludes with a series of broad observations and potential predictions about the implications of privatizing public higher education through this comparative lens.

Public and Private Higher Education

In an extreme case, after privatization of the public institution has been completed, which would entail zero state support for the institution and no state control over institutional governance, the public institution would effectively be a large private institution. Public and private institutions share important similarities. First, they are virtually all nonprofit organizations. Thus, they do not face the same pressures as private firms to place the goal of earning profits above all other objectives. Because of their nonprofit status, they have the opportunity to pursue other goals, such as hiring faculty capable of outstanding research or teaching, providing access to disadvantaged students, and providing cultural opportunities to their communities. As a result, it is unlikely that a privatized public institution will experience a drastic change in overall mission or focus.

However, as discussed in chapter 6, important differences exist between public and private institutions that are likely to be evident as privatization unfolds. The most obvious difference is that, because private institutions cannot rely on state subsidies, they tend to have much higher tuition than public institutions, although the higher price is partly a reflection of the greater value of resources used to educate students at private universities. Average aid awards are also higher at private institutions, so that the differences in net prices are not as large as differences in "sticker prices" might suggest. Despite this, and with notable exceptions in the case of institutions such as Emory University and other elite (and increasingly near-elite) private universities that provide very generous scholarship aid to needy students, private institutions are on average less affordable to low-income students than public institutions.

Another distinction is that, because private institutions do not have an obligation to prioritize the education of in-state students, private institutions have higher proportions of out-of-state residents than do public institutions. It is then reasonable to expect that, as public institutions are privatized, tuition will increase (indeed, this is what has been observed in many states and in Europe), financial aid will increase, and the percentages of low-income and in-state students in the student body will decline. Thus, it follows, that the traditional access goals of the public institution may be compromised under privatization. These conclusions are summarized in our first policy lesson:

PROPOSITION 1: Based on a comparison of public and private higher education institutions, privatization will likely lead to increased tuition, increased financial aid, and declining percentages of financially needy and in-state students at public institutions. Therefore, public institutions may move away from traditional access goals.

Other chapters in this book provide support for the statements in this first lesson. As chapter 8 illustrates, privatization in Europe has involved the introduction of tuition and fees into a system that has historically relied exclusively on public funding. However, as the European fees generally remain very low by American standards, the access effects of tuition increases might be difficult to assess from the European experience. Chapter 3 cites empirical studies about the United States that find public universities in less-centralized state systems generate more revenue per student and charge higher tuition than those in more centralized systems. Likewise, chapters 2 and 6 indicate that many states have allowed public institutions more flexibility to raise tuition in response to reductions in state support. Gabriel Kaplan also reports in chapter 6 that public institutions in states with more decentralized university governing systems are more likely to pursue academic values such as publication, while those in states with more centralized control tend to pursue state policy goals such as lower tuition, greater access and a greater emphasis on teaching.

Robert C. Lowry argues in chapter 3 that differences in the educational goals of academics and state politicians, coupled with the difficulty of writing enforceable contracts that align these interests, explains why we have publicly owned universities rather than state subsidization of privately controlled universities. The statutory codification of the relationship between the state government and the publicly owned university is a means of more closely aligning the interests of academics and university administrators with those of state government officials. Movements toward private control of the university should, therefore, result in an educational model that puts a higher priority on the interests of academics (e.g., prestige, selective admissions, and fundamental research) and a lower priority on the goals of state government (e.g., cost control, broad-based access, and applied research).

Lessons from Privatizing K–12 Education

Privatization is already widespread, and gaining momentum, in the primary and secondary sectors of education (Belfield and Wooten, 2003). Laitsch (1998) reports that in 1998, more than 400 bills related to public school privatization were introduced in state legislatures throughout the country. For obvious reasons, K–12 education is a natural policy laboratory in which to look for lessons that apply to the privatization of higher education. Moreover, some elements of the privatization movement in K–12 education are already visible in higher education, such as the ability to choose between public and private institutions and need-based financial aid grants that can be applied to tuition at any institution (i.e., school choice). However, an important caveat to this exercise is that the context and content of privatization are different in the two sectors. The impetus for privatization in higher education is not concern over instructional quality, student achievement, or the lack of educational choices open to students[1] but rather the desire of state governments to relieve mounting pressure on their budgets, by shifting the burden of financing from governments to private individuals. The details of privatization reforms also differ in higher versus K–12 education. Privatization in higher education involves a direct shift from public to private control of institutions, whereas privatization in K–12 often involves the creation of programs that avail families of educational options that are already under private control. Thus, it is important to realize that fundamental differences in the nature of privatization could lead some outcomes to differ between K–12 and higher education.

Privatization in K–12 education has taken many forms. They include publicly funded school vouchers that families can use to pay for tuition at private schools, autonomous charter and magnet schools that (while still functioning as public schools that do not charge tuition or practice selective admissions) are exempt from many state education regulations,[2] contracting out instructional services, and even ceding control over entire public schools to for-profit educational management organizations.

In K–12 education, privatization efforts are largely in response to common perceptions of poor and declining educational quality in public schools, which threatens to produce a workforce unprepared for the high-skilled jobs of the future, weakening the country's competitive position in the global economy. Critics of the public education system have argued that the reason for poor performance is that public schools are inefficient government-run monopolies. Confronting these schools with competitive pressures, such as would arise when families are allowed to choose from a menu of public and private school options, will create incentives for public schools to operate more efficiently and improve the quality of their instructional programs (Betts and Loveless, 2005). Critics of privatization contend that it will result in widening racial and socioeconomic gaps in student achievement, excessive specialization of schools in narrowly defined curriculums, increased racial and socioeconomic segregation, and a lower inclination on the part of schools to inculcate democratic values (Smith, 2003).

An important issue in discussing privatization is whether public or private schools do a better job of educating students. Most studies find that private school students have significantly higher test scores, higher high school graduation rates, higher likelihoods of earning college degrees, and higher labor market earnings than similar students in public schools (Coleman and Hoffer, 1987; Murnane, 1996; Neal, 1997, 1998). Thus, there is a basis for believing privatization improves the outputs of the educational process. If private schools were achieving these results at lower per student instructional costs, there would also be a basis for asserting efficiency gains from privatization. Nevertheless, the actual evidence on the effects of privatization in K–12 education is mixed and frequently controversial. Experiences with contracting out instructional services and the full privatization of schools generally have been disappointing (Ascher, 1996; Fitz and Beers, 2002). For-profit educational management organizations that have assumed control over public schools have experienced financial problems, met with limited success in producing achievement gains for students, and been accused of paying their executives exorbitant salaries (Maranto, 2005; Smith, 2003). These findings lend credibility to assertions that privatization is "not a panacea" for the difficulties of the public school system (Ascher, 1996).

In light of Lowry's arguments in chapter 3, it is important to understand the effects of school choice programs such as vouchers because direct support for students is among a menu of possible alternatives to the direct public ownership and control of higher education institutions. Furthermore, as Kaplan discusses in chapter 6, voucher proposals have already been on the higher education policy agenda in Colorado. The rapid growth of state-funded merit aid programs, such as the Georgia HOPE Scholarship discussed by Michael K. McLendon and Christine G. Mokher in chapter 2, also resemble voucher programs because students are able to apply the award toward tuition at the institution of their choice. However, unlike most K–12 voucher programs, merit aid programs in higher education are clearly not targeted based on student financial need.

Research findings on the effects of school choice programs in K–12 education are inconclusive. Some research finds that school vouchers produce test score gains for low-income students (Rouse, 1998) and that charter and private schools have a greater demand for highly skilled teachers than public schools (Hoxby, 2002). The latter result is important because of the strong link demonstrated between teaching quality and student achievement (Rivkin, Hanushek, and Kain, 2000). However, other studies question the reliability of observed achievement gains (Ladd, 2002), suggesting vouchers have insignificant effects on achievement (Levin, 1992) and produce lower gains for students with special circumstances such as a physical handicap (Underwood, 1991). Furthermore, vouchers may lead to increased inequality in achievement across races and income classes while failing to increase the quality of education offered by public schools (Carnoy, 1995). This is an important consideration in the debate over higher education privatization because providing access for disadvantaged groups has historically been a high priority for public institutions.

Other types of school choice programs, such as charter schools and magnet schools, have been positively linked to achievement (Gamoran, 1996), although in Texas pass rates on state standardized tests appear to be lower in charter schools than in traditional public schools (Smith, 2003). The latter finding may be due to relatively stringent charter school regulations in Texas or, alternatively, due to the disproportionate share of students from disadvantaged backgrounds that charter schools tend to attract in that state. Smith (2003) also finds that racial inequality in test scores is higher in charter schools than in traditional public schools. Thus, there is no clear research consensus on the effects of school choice programs on educational efficiency or equity.

A criticism of school choice programs is that they may lead to increased segregation on racial and ability lines in view of the positive correlations among socioeconomic status, achievement, and the propensity to participate in the programs (Levin, 1997). Accordingly, empirical evidence and simulation results suggest that universal voucher programs would increase the socioeconomic and racial stratification between public and private schools (Levin, 1992; Epple and Romano, 1998).[3] However, the segregating effects of vouchers may be reduced or eliminated by gearing them toward low-income students, which gives private schools an incentive to admit more low-income students, thereby increasing the level of integration in schools (Betts and Loveless, 2005; O'Sullivan, 2003). It appears, then, that the effects of voucher programs on school integration hinge crucially on the details of policy design.

In higher education, financial aid is targeted increasingly toward middle- and upper-income students, not to lower-income students. Federal aid is shifting from grants to loans, and many states have established programs that award aid solely based on academic merit. As McLendon and Mokher report in chapter 2, non-need-based aid is rising rapidly as a percentage of the total undergraduate aid awarded by state grant programs. These developments, together with the inconclusive evidence on the effects of school choice in K–12 education, provide grounds for concern that not all students will fare equally well under an increasingly privatized system of higher education. Indeed, a reasonable hypothesis is that, unless federal and state aid programs are targeted more aggressively to low-income students, privatization will result in reduced access to high-quality, low-cost education and increased race and income segregation across colleges. In summary, we have our second policy lesson:

PROPOSITION 2: Although private schools appear to produce student achievement gains relative to public schools, research has not reached a clear consensus that privatization programs in K–12 education (such as vouchers and charter schools) are associated with increased achievement. Furthermore, voucher programs likely increase segregation in schools by race, income and ability unless specifically targeted to low-income students. Therefore, because of recent reformulations of federal and state aid policies, the experiences with K–12 education suggest privatization in higher education will result in increased segregation across institutions, with minority and low-income students increasingly concentrated in lower-quality, lower-cost colleges.

Evidence from Privatization in Noneducation Sectors

The literature on privatization in other, noneducation industries is extensive. Privatization has taken place in many markets in many different developed and developing countries. In many cases, the experience with privatization has been positive, although there are some notable exceptions that are discussed shortly. The success of privatization appears critically linked to the specific nature and extent of reform policies. In particular, privatization policies that maintain strict government restrictions on firm behavior are associated with lower post-privatization performance.

In most industries under government control, privatization entails either contracting out, public divestiture, or deregulation. By contracting out, the government enters into a contract with a private provider who delivers the services to the public. In this case, the government maintains at least some indirect control over service delivery. Under divestiture, the government cedes ownership of the state-owned enterprise to a private for-profit firm or to a nonprofit organization. In this case, the government no longer has control over organizational structure or service delivery. Deregulation is where the government allows new firms to compete with a publicly franchised monopoly and may also involve the elimination of government subsidies to the incumbent firm and the relaxation of price-setting restrictions. This section examines the literature on contracting out, public divestiture and deregulation to uncover policy lessons pertinent to the privatization of higher education.

Contracting Out

According to Globerman and Vining (1996), contracting out is an efficient alternative to direct government production when it reduces the sum of production and transaction (or bargaining) costs. Contracting out generally leads to lower production costs but higher transaction costs than direct agency production; thus, contracting out is only efficient when the production cost savings exceed the increase in bargaining costs. Globerman and Vining identify three factors affecting the bargaining costs associated with contracting out: (1) task complexity, (2) market contestability, and (3) asset specificity.

Task complexity is the degree of difficulty in specifying and monitoring the terms of a contract (Weimer and Vining, 2005). In general, task complexity is low when the service has tangible, easily measured outputs, as with food service, garbage disposal, and highway construction. Market contestability is the ease with which capital is easily transferred into, and out of, the market. In a highly contestable market, a large number of firms are capable of entering the market in a relatively short time. Asset specificity is the degree to which assets used in production are specific to the market. When assets are highly specific to a market, they earn a significantly higher return in that market than in their next best alternative use. Bargaining costs are relatively low when task complexity is low, market contestability is high, and asset specificity is low. Thus, under these conditions, contracting out is likely to be the most efficient way to govern production.

Higher education does not come very close to satisfying any of these criteria. The outputs of higher education are not easily quantifiable, the capital requirements for entering the market are extremely high (Ehrenberg, 2002), and the assets needed to operate an institution, including the facilities, specialized equipment, and especially the human capital of the faculty, are highly specialized to academia. These conditions imply high bargaining costs associated with contracting out due to the potential for opportunistic behavior on the part of both parties to the contract, which makes this option unlikely to be an efficient privatization alternative for higher education.[4] Indeed, chapter 3 suggests that an important reason for the emergence of publicly owned higher educational institutions is the difficulty of writing enforceable contracts to perform complex tasks with objectives that are difficult to quantify.

The empirical literature on experiences with contracting out also underscores the inefficiency of this option in the case of higher education. Steel and Long (1996), in an analysis of contracting out for road maintenance and construction, found that contracting out appears to work better in urban areas while direct agency supply works better in rural areas. This is likely due to the greater contestability of road contracting markets in urban areas. Because contestability is low in higher education, contracting out would be relatively unsuccessful.

In a survey of two-thirds of the nation's 100 largest cities, Dilger, Moffett, and Struyk (1997) find that city officials believe that privatization reduces service costs and improves service quality. However, unlike higher education, most of the services analyzed are tasks where output is relatively easy to monitor, such as solid waste collection, building security, and street lighting and signals. Nevertheless, even for these relatively simple tasks, officials only report moderate satisfaction with their contracting out experiences. Among the top 10 privatized services in metropolitan areas, the two with the lowest satisfaction scores in the survey are drug and alcohol treatment and employment and training, which are the services most like education (all involve human capital transfers) among those examined.

Williams (1998) similarly finds that, although residential solid waste collection seems on the surface to be an activity ideally suited to contracting out, city leaders appear no more satisfied with contracting out than with direct municipal service delivery. This may be the result of the larger environmental concerns associated with this activity (i.e., the public health hazards from uncollected refuse). Because of the public health externality, losing direct control over the delivery of this service adds political costs to the local government that reduce the efficiency of contracting out. It follows that in markets where significant externalities are involved (such as solid waste collection, education, and health care), the merits of contracting out warrant reconsideration. Indeed, contracting out agreements for the delivery of health care services have also been criticized (Vining and Globerman, 1998).

Williams (1998) discusses another issue related to the privatization of refuse collection services that has a direct parallel in higher education: variation in service quality across customer groups. In particular, concerns have been raised that private waste collection firms fail to provide comparable service to both high- and low-income sections of the city. Likewise, in higher education an important concern is that privatization and the resulting increases in tuition (combined with reductions in the generosity of federal financial aid programs) will result in less service for financially needy students and more service for high-income students or those with high-ability. If privatization generally results in service quality that is positively correlated with income, it threatens to compromise the access mission of the public institution and reduce its role in promoting income mobility in society. Lowry, in chapter 3, explains this phenomenon based on a greater incentive for private rather than public officials to cut costs in ways that may decrease service quality, especially in settings where the incentives for product innovation are relatively small. In higher education, the basic production technology has remained highly stable for a long period.

Holcombe (1991) questions the ability of contracting out to even reduce production costs in the privatization of municipal wastewater treatment. The evidence in the study suggests that the costs of privatized treatment facilities are actually higher than those of publicly owned facilities. The finding is attributed to the details of the privatization contracts involved, which often contain provisions allowing the private firm to pass production cost increases onto municipalities. Such provisions eliminate the theoretical advantages of privatization by reducing incentives for firms to operate efficiently. Holcombe (1991) points out that unfavorable contract terms for the government are not particularly surprising in view of private firms having a greater incentive to strike profitable bargains, having more experience with privatization agreements, and having more production-specific knowledge than government officials. Furthermore, government officials may have political incentives that make them more willing to accept unfavorable agreements than to back out of privatization negotiations.

The Holcombe (1991) study clearly illustrates that contract details are essential in the privatization process. In markets where task complexity is high because of asymmetric information between the firm and the government concerning the production and bargaining processes, it is difficult to secure privatization agreements that increase efficiency even in production, where privatization is supposed to have the greatest advantage over direct government provision. This has a direct application to higher education, a market in which the education provider likely has a substantial information advantage over government officials concerning the details of the production process.

On the basis of analysis of the theory and empirical evidence on experiences with contracting out, we obtain the following policy lesson:

PROPOSITION 3: Contracting out higher education services to a private enterprise is a less efficient option than direct public production because of high transactions costs. Furthermore, the significant externalities involved in education raise the potential political costs to the state of loss of control over the institution. Empirical studies of contracting out agreements also raise the concerns that privatization will lead to uneven service quality across income groups and will fail to yield substantial production efficiency gains because of high information asymmetries between contract parties.

One important qualification to this lesson, however, is related to the status of universities as nonprofit organizations. The structure of the nonprofit dampens some of the incentives for opportunistic behavior that result in the high transactions costs of contracting out. Because by definition they cannot earn a profit, nonprofit organizations have less incentive to reduce investments in product quality and raise prices. They may also have a strong sense of mission that leads them to prioritize the production of high-quality education services and to pursue access goals (e.g., for low-income in-state students) that are also in the interests of the state. As a result, it is not clear that contracting out to a nonprofit is less efficient in terms of total production and transactions costs than direct agency production. However, because the nonprofit also lacks profit-making incentives, it is less likely that there will be significant production cost savings than if the contract were with a for-profit firm. Furthermore, the political costs to the state of losing control over the institution are not necessarily reduced simply because the new owner is a nonprofit. Thus, in the case of higher education, contracting out either with a for-profit or a nonprofit enterprise is likely less efficient than direct public production.[5]

Public Divestiture

Even though states are reducing their financial support for public institutions, they are not fully divesting themselves of ownership and control. As Kaplan points out in chapter 6, no states have yet auctioned off their public universities to the highest bidder or issued shares in these institutions on a major stock exchange. Instead, the states maintain ownership of the institutions' fixed assets and at least some jurisdiction over institutional policy decisions (e.g., tuition, personnel, salaries, and budgets). Nonetheless, in response to declining funding, many universities are demanding greater autonomy from state governments, which could be considered a small initial step on the way to a more complete separation between state governments and institutions. Consider, for example, the movements described in chapter 6 to designate public universities as enterprise or charter universities in the states of Virginia and Colorado. Similarly, chapter 8 describes how the move to a more market-oriented education model in Europe involves greater autonomy for public universities in operational decisions that have historically been the province of government education ministries.

In the extreme case of privatization, where the state subsidy is eliminated and the state cedes full ownership of the institution to a private enterprise, we have public divestiture. Consequently, in light of the greater autonomy pursued by institutions, it is useful in these discussions to understand the circumstances in which divestiture is the most efficient way to govern production (i.e., more efficient than contracting out or public production), under what circumstances divestiture has worked in practice, and whether higher education resembles any of these situations.

The theoretical arguments of Globerman and Vining (1996) imply that full divestiture privatization is the most efficient alternative, when the costs of public production and contracting are high, and the underlying market failure that justifies public production is small. It has already been argued in some detail in this chapter that contracting costs would be high if the government were to attempt to contract out higher education services. The contract costs of divestiture would be comparatively low because, although the state and the higher education enterprise would have to agree on a sale price for the institution's assets, the contract would not involve an ongoing monitoring role for the state. Furthermore, the costs of public production are likely higher than the costs of private production (for a given enrollment size and a given level of education quality) for two reasons. First, public institutions are insulated from competitive pressures to minimize costs because of the state subsidies they receive. Second, public institutions incur higher labor costs than private institutions because civil service protections for public employees make it difficult for public institutions to optimally adjust the capital-labor ratio. Therefore, these considerations weigh in favor of divestiture over either public production or contracting out.

The market failures commonly used to justify public intervention in higher education are productivity and tax revenue externalities for highly educated workers, credit market imperfections that limit the ability of individuals to obtain loans from private credit markets to finance their educations, and the external benefits of providing a vehicle for income mobility to low-income citizens (Gruber, 2005). Although these market failures are important to society, they are actually rationales for public subsidy, not necessarily for direct public production of higher education. Thus, the market failure rationale weighs in favor of divestiture, or contracting out, over public production. We see that, on a theoretical basis, divestiture seems to be the most efficient production arrangement in terms of reducing production and transactions costs. However, as Lowry mentions in chapter 3, one reason divestiture is seldom pursued is that changing the governance structure of the university from public to private is costly because such changes must not only receive the consent of state government officials but also must satisfy the conditions for a new institutional equilibrium. We now turn to an examination of the empirical evidence on divestiture.

Empirical studies of the full privatization of state-owned enterprises support a production cost savings associated with privatization (Megginson and Netter, 2001). Private firms generally produce goods and services in a more technically efficient manner than public agencies because they face explicit competitive incentives and have more flexibility in the use of inputs.[6] Likewise, Poole and Fixler (1987) surveyed evidence for the United States and found that privatization generally produces significant cost savings. Berkowitz and DeJong (2003) found that the extent of privatization reforms is positively correlated with economic growth in post–Soviet Russia, while Boardman and Vining (1989) found that large mixed- and state-owned enterprises perform worse in terms of profitability measures than similar private corporations. An implication of the Boardman and Vining (1989) study is that, for privatization to take place, it should be full privatization rather than the partial privatization we presently observe in higher education. This implies:

> PROPOSITION 4: Theoretical and empirical evidence on the privatization of state-owned enterprises suggests that full public divestiture of higher educa-tion institutions is more productively and contractually efficient than direct public production or contracting out. In particular, an arrangement with zero public subsidies and zero public control is more efficient than the partial privatization currently in place, in which the state offers a reduced but non-zero subsidy and maintains some institutional control.

The problem with the divestiture argument is that it ignores the importance of the state's ability to achieve access goals and possibly other political goals such as economic development through the activities of the institution. Promoting equality in access to educational opportunity (which is believed to have external social benefits) justifies subsidies to low-income students in the form of reduced tuition and need-based financial aid that are eroding under current policies. In view of these developments, it would be difficult for a state to commit to a credible, ongoing public subsidy sufficient to achieve access goals in the wake of divestiture. This means an important market failure will likely not be addressed unless private boards of trustees and administrators have the same access objectives as the government with regard to providing opportunities to low-income students. As chapter 3 points out, that we have public universities at all is evidence that this is unlikely to be the case. In fact, officials at private institutions have incentives to increase the quality of the institution on measures of student ability (Ehrenberg, 2002), which is an objec-tive that sometimes conflicts with access objectives (McPherson and Schapiro, 1998).

It follows that direct public production, that is, the arrangement in which the state subsidizes the institution and maintains ultimate control over its assets, may be optimal (proposition 4 notwithstanding) because the state can enforce access objec-tives directly. If so, then current movements toward privatization may represent an iterative process of finding the optimal levels of state support and control that balance the mandate to save revenue with the political expedience of promoting access objectives. There is little doubt that students, institutions, legislators, and the public would benefit from a more rapid convergence to the optimum, as it would reduce the uncertainty involved in private and public educational investment deci-sions. In summary, we have:

PROPOSITION 5: If the state cannot credibly commit to ongoing subsidies to low-income students sufficient for achieving society's access and income mobility goals after divesting ownership over the public institution, then the current arrangement of government subsidies and government control may be more efficient than divestiture. However, greater stability in the delineation of the state's financial commitments and degree of institutional control would benefit students, institutions, legislators, and the public by reducing the risk involved in educational investment decisions.

Deregulation

Privatization in higher education bears some resemblance to the deregulation of a natural monopoly. Deregulation is the form of privatization in which the government allows the entry of new firms to compete with a publicly franchised natural monopoly. It may also involve the elimination of government subsidies to the incumbent firm and the relaxation of price-setting restrictions. Although privatization in higher education lacks the entry of new firms into the market, it does feature the other two hallmarks of deregulation (i.e., reduced subsidies and the lifting of tuition controls).

Public higher education institutions are like natural monopolies in that fixed costs are extremely high (Ehrenberg, 2002), which implies declining average education costs over a wide range of enrollments, so that marginal cost is below average cost. To sustain efficient levels of enrollment, a public subsidy is required to cover the institution's losses. Privatization entails a smaller public subsidy, so that the institution must raise tuition closer to average cost to break even. Although states typically retain final authority over tuition charges even as the institution is privatized (particularly the tuition for in-state students, whose families are important constituents of state legislators), standard practice has been to allow relatively rapid tuition increases, especially for out-of-state students. Because of the similarity with certain aspects of deregulation, this section examines the deregulation literature for additional policy lessons.

Much of the deregulation literature points to the benefits to consumers of increased competition.[7] According to Winston (1998), firms in recently deregulated industries such as airlines, trucking, railroads, banking, and natural gas are "far more efficient" than under regulation. This results in cost savings that are passed onto consumers in the form of lower prices. Conversely, Moore (1978) contends that regulation of the trucking industry raises prices (freight rates) because the structure of regulation limits competition and fosters cooperative rate setting. He argues that the main beneficiaries of trucking regulation are organized labor and the owners of vehicle operating rights. Kim (1984) reports similar findings on the effects of trucking regulation in Canada, adding that regulation also appears to benefit fuel suppliers and that the inefficiencies of regulation arise from incentives for suboptimal capacity utilization. It follows, then, that deregulation in trucking should lead to lower prices and reduce the rents earned by labor, operating license holders, and fuel suppliers.

The lessons of trucking deregulation may not extend very well to higher education for several reasons. First and most important, whereas deregulation in the trucking industry (or most industries for that matter) involves the entry of new firms to compete with incumbents, privatization of higher education does not. Although the system of "regulation" in higher education serves to limit competition, this might be efficient because of the natural monopoly characteristics of a large public institution. In contrast, the economies of scale in trucking are likely to be very small. As a result, the trucking industry is much more contestable than higher education. Second, whereas regulators of the trucking industry may have exploited the lack of competition to set high prices, the regulators of higher education (i.e., state boards of regents) purposely set low tuitions (especially for in-state students) to promote access. Third, while truckers may have operated below capacity under regulation, it is doubtful that public universities do so. Because of low tuitions, enrollments at these institutions are high, such that many of them are probably operating at or near capacity. Thus, there is pressure on prices to move downward under trucking deregulation and pressure on them to move upward under higher education privatization.

Moore (1986) analyzes the effects of airline deregulation in the United States and finds that deregulation has helped in some respects by reducing fares and increasing the number of routes served. However, problems still remain in that prices are not fully competitive and along certain dimensions service quality is down. Increases in airline bankruptcies in recent years are also well documented. According to Moore (1986), the lack of complete success of deregulation is attributable to the lack of contestability in the airline industry, which certainly also pertains to higher education.

It has been suggested that prices have fallen and productivity has risen because of the privatization of the electricity and natural gas industries in the United Kingdom (Domah and Pollitt, 2001; Price and Weyman-Jones, 1996). However, in the case of electricity, prices initially rose, along with profits and production costs, before decreasing several years subsequent to privatization. Domah and Pollitt (2001) conclude that privatization yields significant social benefits but that these benefits are unevenly distributed across groups in society. Likewise, productivity gains differ across regions of the United Kingdom in the case of natural gas, which Price and

Weyman-Jones (1996) attribute to the government's failure to break up firms at the regional level. A lesson from the deregulation of the trucking, electricity, and natural gas industries can be stated as follows:

> PROPOSITION 6: Deregulation in the trucking, electricity, and natural gas industries is associated with lower prices and increased productivity. However, these gains appear largely due to increased competition among firms, which does not have a direct parallel in the case of higher education. Indeed, in cases in which deregulation is considered unsuccessful, the culprit appears to be a persistent lack of competition, even after deregulation. Evidence from electricity and natural gas also suggests that the benefits of privatization take time to be realized and may be unevenly distributed across different groups in society, which is a concern in higher education because of the access mission of public institutions. Therefore, even though privatization in higher education resembles the deregulation of a natural monopoly, the successes of deregulation in these other industries are unlikely to extend to higher education.

Observe that proposition 6 touches on concerns about the effects of higher education privatization on access to students from disadvantaged backgrounds, especially because tuitions are expected to rise rather than fall after privatization.

The literature on the deregulation of telecommunications industries throughout the world suggests reforms are associated with increased production efficiency in both long-distance and local markets (Oum and Zhang, 1996; Ying and Shin, 1993) and improvements in firm financial performance and technological capability (Bortolotti, 2002; Spiller and Cardilli 1997). However, a substantial amount of the improvement appears due to regulatory changes (such as the establishment of an independent regulator who sets and credibly enforces clear rules) rather than to privatization alone (Bortolotti, 2002; Spiller and Cardilli, 1997; Wallsten, 2001).[8]

In the United States, deregulation that allows firms greater pricing flexibility under a price cap is associated with lower long-distance telephone rates (Mathios and Rogers, 1989) and higher technical efficiency in the provision of local telephone service (Majumdar, 1997). However, price cap regulation (as opposed to the traditional rate-of-return regulation) weakens incentives for investments in service quality (Weisman, 2005) and increases incentives for opportunistic behavior on the part of state regulators (Weisman, 2002). The structure of regulation is once again important. Regulatory changes, such as the elimination of revenue-share penalties and the public dissemination of information regarding a firm's compliance with quality targets, are associated with higher investments in service quality (Weisman, 2005). In contrast, regulatory interference with the process of entry by new firms (where incumbents are required to sell connection access to new firms based on costs that would prevail in an ideally efficient market, rather than on actual costs) is associated with lower industry performance under deregulation (Harris and Kraft, 1997; Kahn, Tardiff, and Weisman, 1999). Thus, the evidence from the telecommunications industries in the United States and abroad suggests that privatization alone is not enough to achieve benefits for consumers. A less intrusive regulatory environment that allows more pricing flexibility, fosters more competition, creates less regulatory opportunism, and produces more transparent information is also required.

The findings on pricing flexibility in Weisman (2005) have potentially important implications for higher education, where the pre-privatization arrangement corresponds to price cap regulation and privatization corresponds to the lifting of a price cap. The prediction based on the telecommunications experience is that eliminating state-imposed tuition caps should lead to higher investments in service quality by higher education institutions. Hence, although students would face higher prices (Mathios and Rogers, 1989), they would also benefit from a higher-quality education. An important concern, however, is whether disadvantaged groups would have sufficient access to the higher quality but more costly education offered by large public institutions. A broad set of lessons drawn from telecommunications deregulation is, therefore, distilled here:

PROPOSITION 7: Evidence from the telecommunications industry suggests that deregulation results in increased production efficiency and improved firm financial performance. However, deregulation alone is not enough to achieve these benefits. A less intrusive regulatory environment that provides clear rules, allows more pricing flexibility, fosters more competition, creates less regulatory opportunism, and produces more transparent information is also required.

PROPOSITION 8: Evidence from telecommunications deregulation suggests that the elimination of price caps provides increased incentives for investment in service quality. If this is true for public universities as well, then we can expect students to receive a higher-quality education at a higher cost under privatization. However, the key policy question is whether low-income and minorities students will continue to have sufficient access to public universities under such an arrangement.

Although the consensus seems to be that deregulation results in greater productive efficiency, it does not always result in lower prices. Gomez-Ibanez and Meyer

(1990) and O'Sullivan (2003) examine the effects of the British Transport Act of 1985, which deregulated local transit services in Britain. This piece of legislation had a number of effects on the local transit industry. The overall quantity of service, measured by total mileage covered by transit carriers, increased. There were also changes in the style of service delivery (increased use of minibuses instead of full-size buses) and in cuts to unprofitable services (such as off-peak and low-density routes). Transit fares increased by about 35% in real terms over a two-year period, which resulted in a 14% decrease in total ridership. Because of lower labor costs, the increased use of minibuses, and the elimination of excess capacity, production costs fell by 15%–30%.

Extrapolating from the experience with the transit industry in Britain, one might predict that privatization in higher education will increase tuition, decrease enrollment, and promote efficiency by changing the manner in which institutions deliver education. This could entail more intensive use of information technology in classroom instruction or increased specialization by institutions in a narrower range of majors and course offerings. The analogue of unprofitable services that receives cuts may be low-demand courses, but a sobering possibility is that it could also be students. In particular, institutions without the cushion of a state subsidy might be less inclined to admit students who are relatively costly to educate, such as those with disabilities and those with high financial need. Clearly, this would be detrimental to diversity on campus as well as social access goals for low-income, minority, and disabled students. These points provide another privatization lesson for policymakers:

> PROPOSITION 9: The British experience with local transit deregulation suggests that, because of privatization, tuition at public universities will increase, enrollment will decrease, and the style of service delivery will change toward narrower, more specialized course offerings. In addition, it is possible that students who are relatively costly to educate, such as those with disabilities and high financial need, will experience reduced access to public institutions.

Another industry where deregulation is associated with higher prices is cable television. Rubinovitz (1993) finds that real basic cable prices increased 18% after deregulation and that this price increase is due to greater exercise of existing market power rather than an increase in market power. Thus, with respect to the effect of privatization on prices, it would seem that higher education resembles cable television and mass transit more than it does telecommunications. The reason may be that price caps were maintained after deregulation in the telecommunications industry but not the cable television or mass transit industries. In higher education, price regulation is maintained but states have been relatively permissive in allowing tuition increases requested by institutions.

Trebing (2001) critically examines the evidence on energy deregulation in the United States. He contends that, although the effects of deregulation appeared promising during most of the 1990s, recent events such as the bankruptcies of Enron and WorldCom, allegations of corporate fraud against deregulated utilities, and the California energy crisis portray a darker side to deregulation. Trebing (2001) contends that several specific features of energy markets in the United States serve to increase market power and make deregulation problematic, including the increase of market concentrations, the emergence of constrained supply as power plants are removed from service, and the lack of protections for customers in these markets. To the extent that these features apply to higher education suggests that privatization may have unintended side effects, such as sharp price increases and service reductions for students with few educational options.

Conclusion

This chapter examines the theoretical and empirical literature on privatization, public divestitures, and deregulation in a number of service areas and distills from these experiences nine policy lessons that pertain to the privatization of higher education. The lessons indicate that contracting out to a private enterprise would be an inefficient privatization alternative compared with either direct public production or full government divestiture of public higher education institutions. Indeed, among the top 10 privatized services in U.S. metropolitan areas, the two receiving the lowest satisfaction scores in customer surveys are drug and alcohol treatment and employment and training, which, among those examined, are the services most like education. Furthermore, in evaluating divestiture against direct public production, the empirical evidence suggests that divestiture is likely the more productively and contractually efficient alternative.

However, that important positive externalities are created by fulfillment of the access objectives of public institutions implies that the loss of state control over these institutions is costly to society. Therefore, direct public production may be superior to divestiture because it allows state governments to enforce access objectives directly. Nevertheless, the current system of privatization at best represents a costly convergence toward the social optimum and at worst an inefficient contract failure. Either way, society would likely benefit from greater stability in the relationship between states and their public universities.

Although privatization is taking place in another area of education, specifically

K–12, it is difficult to extend results on K–12 privatization to higher education. This is partly because privatization has a different impetus and a different form in these two sectors of education. Specifically, movements toward K–12 privatization are due to concerns about the ineffectiveness of public schools, while privatization in higher education is due to pressures on state budgets. Furthermore, privatization in higher education involves a reduction in state support and control of public institutions, where in K–12 education privatization equips families to choose options other than the traditional public school. Research on the effects of school choice programs in K–12 education is also inconclusive and controversial, except that researchers tend to agree that segregation in schools will increase if vouchers are not specifically targeted to low-income students.

Ultimately, questions about the desirability of privatization may be merely academic. Privatization appears to be an entrenched phenomenon with which society must contend. Pressure on state budgets from rapidly increasing costs in crucial service areas such as health care, infrastructure, corrections, and pensions leaves little room to doubt that higher education will receive less funding over time. It is, therefore, perhaps a more constructive exercise for analysts to focus on the likely effects of privatization. An especially pressing matter is to identify unintended effects and design policies to mitigate those that are the most socially undesirable.

Analysis of the privatization and deregulation experiences in a number of industries yields some consistent themes that can be used to predict the possible effects of higher education privatization. Evidence on student achievement in private K–12 schools and on the effects of deregulation in industries such as trucking, electricity, natural gas, and telecommunications suggests that privatization is likely to increase the output or production efficiency of the education sector. However, the efficiency gains from industry deregulation are primarily due to competitive pressures created by the entry of new firms, which lacks a direct parallel in the privatization of higher education because higher education is a market with very low contestability and one dominated by organizations without profit-making incentives.

Although the question of efficiency may presently stand unresolved, there is almost no question that tuition will increase under privatization, which is especially true for in-state residents, who currently pay tuition below educational costs. Enrollment, as a result, is likely to decrease. At the same time, those students who continue to enroll in public institutions may see an improvement in the quality of their education, albeit at a higher price. Of particular concern is the recurring pattern across a broad cross section of markets that privatization is associated with uneven service quality and frequency across different customer groups. Specifically, low-income customers and customers representing segments of the market deemed unprofitable tend to receive less service subsequent to privatization. While perhaps an acceptable outcome in the markets for many private goods, underserving low-income customers or others who are unprofitable may be unacceptable in higher education, which is regarded as an important vehicle of economic opportunity. With the typical access objectives concerning in-state, minority, low-income, and disabled students placed in jeopardy, the political and perhaps even financial costs to the state are potentially large.

Thus, state officials are cautioned to consider carefully the costs and benefits of full and partial privatization. The current system of declining state support and control may relieve pressure on the state budget in the near term but may also create a climate of uncertainty for students and institutions that may result in inefficient educational investment decisions. The option of full divestiture, while perhaps reducing production and transactions costs relative to direct public production or contracting out, has problems of its own. First, there are market failure rationales for public higher education subsidies even if the industry is privatized. Thus, the state is unlikely to avoid all of its financial obligations to higher education even in the event that it divests. Second, significant positive externalities are associated with the fulfillment of access objectives that may go unrealized once the state divests. After all, state lawmakers cannot necessarily be certain that fully privatized institutions will set tuition and enrollment policies in the interests of the state and its citizens. Maintaining ultimate jurisdiction over institutional policy, as in the current system, is one way to ensure this. Nevertheless, as the state continues to reduce its financial support, it cannot expect institutions to remain in a position to fulfill all of the traditional access goals. A reasonable and stable compromise needs to be reached concerning support and control to reflect the difficult fiscal realities states and their public institutions now face.

NOTES

1. These issues are sometimes raised in discussions of higher education accountability (Heller, 2001) but are not usually cited as important reasons for privatization in higher education.

2. Charter schools are public because they exist only with the approval of state governments and receive their funding from the state. Nevertheless, the charter school movement can be thought of as a form of "marketization" that offers families alternatives to traditional public schools and, therefore, provides public schools with market-like incentives to alter their instructional practices in ways that attract students.

3. This may not be a serious concern with voucher programs in practice because most proposals involve targeting the vouchers to low-income students rather than providing vouchers to everyone (i.e., a universal program). In California in 2000, the state legislature soundly

defeated a proposal that would have created a voucher program not based on demonstrated financial need.

4. The current relationship between states and public higher education institutions resembles contracting out with a nonprofit. Although the state owns all of the institution's capital, the institution is only partly state supported and is able to seek funding from external sources, unlike most government agencies. Also, while certain aspects of institutional policy are under government jurisdiction, the institution has considerable autonomy in its operations. It can then be argued that privatization (reductions in state support) is an example of opportunistic behavior on the part of the government that takes advantage of higher education–specific assets. Therefore, privatization may represent a contracting failure, which implies it is an inefficient outcome because at least one of the parties would have preferred not to enter into the contract had they known the eventual outcome.

5. Even if contracting out with a nonprofit is superior on efficiency grounds to direct public provision, it is still possible for the contract to fail, if incentives for opportunistic behavior change after the contract is written. For instance, greater pressure on the state budget due to increased costs of infrastructure, health care, and retirement benefits for state workers may give the state more incentive to renege on its financial commitments to higher education. Thus, privatization may also be interpreted as an ex post contract failure.

6. This argument does not imply that privatization will improve efficiency in higher education because the private organizations that operate institutions are nonprofit. They do not have the same incentives as private firms to operate at peak technical efficiency because they are not profit maximizers. However, institutions must compete with rivals to attract students or face the prospect of closing down. This may add to the efficiency incentives of colleges relative to those of the typical nonprofit organization.

7. Although privatization in higher education does not involve the entry of new firms into the education industry, it may promote increased competition because it reduces the artificial financial advantage that public institutions hold over their private competitors.

8. As Spiller and Cardilli (1997) note, in the telecommunications industry some regulation is still necessary after deregulation because the incumbent can maintain market power by exploiting network externalities. Thus, one continues to speak of certain types of regulation even after the industry has been deregulated.

REFERENCES

Ascher, Carol. 1996. Performance Contracting: A Forgotten Experiment in School Privatization. *Phi Delta Kappan* 77 (9): 615–21.

———. 1996. *Hard Lessons: Public Schools and Privatization.* New York: Twentieth Century Fund Press.

Belfield, Clive R., and Amy L. Wooten. 2003. Education Privatization: The Attitudes and Experiences of Superintendents. Occasional Paper, National Center for the Study of Privatization in Education, New York.

Berkowitz, Daniel, and David N. DeJong. 2003. Policy Reform and Growth in Post-Soviet Russia. *European Economic Review* 47 (2): 337–52.

Betts, Julian R., and Tom Loveless. 2005. School Choice, Equity, and Efficiency. In *Getting*

Choice Right, ed. Julian R. Betts and Tom Loveless, 1–13. Washington, DC: Brookings Institution.

Boardman, Anthony E., and Aidan R. Vining. 1989. Ownership and Performance in Competitive Environments: A Comparison of the Performance of Private, Mixed and State-Owned Enterprises. *Journal of Law and Economics* 32 (1): 1–33.

Bortolotti, Bernado. 2002. Privatization and the Sources of Performance Improvement in the Global Telecommunications Industry. *Telecommunications Policy* 26 (5–6): 243–68.

Carnoy, Martin. 1995. Is School Privatization the Answer? Data from Other Countries Help Burst the Voucher Bubble. *American Educator* 19 (3): 29–30.

Coleman, James S., and Thomas Hoffer. 1987. *Public and Private High Schools*. New York: Basic Books.

Dennison, George M. 2003. Privatization: An Unheralded Trend in Public Higher Education. *Innovative Higher Education* 28 (1): 7–20.

Dilger, Robert J., Randolph R. Moffett, and Linda Struyk. 1997. Privatization of Municipal Services in America's Largest Cities. *Public Administration Review* 57 (1): 21–26.

Domah, Preetum, and Michael G. Pollitt. 2001. The Restructuring and Privatisation of Electricity Distribution and Supply Businesses in England and Wales: A Social Cost-Benefit Analysis. *Fiscal Studies* 22 (1): 107–46.

Ehrenberg, Ronald G. 2002. *Tuition Rising*. Cambridge, MA: Harvard University Press.

Epple, Dennis, and Richard E. Romano. 1998. Competition between Private and Public Schools, Vouchers, and Peer-Group Effects. *American Economic Review* 88 (1): 33–62.

Fitz, John, and Bryan Beers. 2002. Education Management Organisations and the Privatization of Public Education: A Cross-National Comparison of the U.S.A. and Britain. *Comparative Education* 38 (2): 137–54.

Gamoran, Adam. 1996. Student Achievement in Public Magnet, Public Comprehensive, and Private City High Schools. *Educational Evaluation and Policy Analysis* 18 (1): 1–18.

Globerman, Steven, and Aidan R. Vining. 1996. A Framework for Evaluating the Government Contracting-Out Decision with an Application to Information Technology. *Public Administration Review* 56 (6): 577–86.

Gomez-Ibanez, Jose, and John R. Meyer. 1990. Privatizing and Deregulating Local Public Services: Lessons from Britain's Buses. *Journal of the American Planning Association* 56 (1): 9–28.

Gruber, Jonothan. 2005. *Public Finance and Public Policy*. New York: Worth.

Harris, Robert G., and C. Jeffery Kraft. 1997. Meddling Through: Regulating Local Telephone Competition in the United States. *Journal of Economic Perspectives* 11 (4): 93–112.

Heller, Donald E., ed. 2001. *The States and Public Higher Education Policy*. Baltimore: Johns Hopkins University Press.

Holcombe, Randall G. 1991. Privatization of Municipal Wastewater Treatment. *Public Budgeting and Finance* 11 (3): 28–42.

Hoxby, Caroline M. 2002. Would School Choice Change the Teaching Profession? *Journal of Human Resources* 37 (4): 846–91.

Kahn, Alfred E., Timothy J. Tardiff, and Dennis L. Weisman. 1999. The Telecommunications Act at Three Years: An Economic Evaluation of Its Implementation by the Federal Communications Commission. *Information Economics and Policy* 11 (4): 319–65.

Kim, Moshe. 1984. The Beneficiaries of Trucking Regulation, Revisited. *Journal of Law and Economics* 27 (1): 227–41.

Ladd, Helen F. 2002. School Vouchers: A Critical View. *Journal of Economic Perspectives* 16 (4): 3–24.

Laitsch, Dan. 1998. *School Choice and Privatization Efforts: A Legislative Survey.* Research/Technical Report. Washington, DC: American Association of Colleges for Teacher Education.

Levin, Henry M. 1992. Market Approaches to Education: Vouchers and School Choice. *Economics of Education Review* 11 (4): 279–85.

———. 1997. Educational Vouchers: Effectiveness, Choice and Costs. *Journal of Policy Analysis and Management* 17 (3): 373–92.

Majumdar, Sumit K. 1997. Incentive Regulation and Productive Efficiency in the U.S. Telecommunications Industry. *Journal of Business* 70 (4): 547–76.

Maranto, Robert. 2005. A Tale of Two Cities: School Privatization in Philadelphia and Chester. *American Journal of Education* 111 (2): 151–90.

Mathios, Alan D., and Robert P. Rogers. 1989. The Impact of Alternative Forms of State Regulation of AT&T on Direct-Dial, Long-Distance Telephone Rates. *RAND Journal of Economics* 20 (3): 437–53.

McPherson, Michael S., and Morton Owen Schapiro. 1998. *The Student Aid Game.* Princeton, NJ: Princeton University Press.

Megginson, William L., and Jeffery M. Netter. 2001. From State to Market: A Survey of Empirical Studies on Privatization. *Journal of Economic Literature* 39 (2): 321–89.

Moore, Thomas Gale. 1978. The Beneficiaries of Trucking Regulation. *Journal of Law and Economics* 21 (2): 327–43.

———. 1986. U.S. Airline Deregulation: Its Effects on Passengers, Capital, and Labor. *Journal of Law and Economics* 29 (1): 1–28.

Murnane, R. J. 1996. Comparisons of Private and Public Schools: What Can We Learn? In *Private Education: Studies in Choice and Public Policy.* ed. D. C. Levy, 138–52. Oxford: Oxford University Press.

Neal, Derek. 1997. The Effect of Catholic Secondary Schooling on Educational Attainment. *Journal of Labor Economics* 15: 98–123.

———. 1998. What Have We Learned about the Benefits of Private Schooling? *Economic Policy Review* 4 (1): 3.

O'Sullivan, Arthur. 2003. *Urban Economics.* Boston, MA: McGraw-Hill/Irwin.

Oum, Tae Hoon, and Yimin Zhang. 1996. Competition and Allocative Efficiency: The Case of the U.S. Telephone Industry. *Review of Economics and Statistics* 77 (1): 82–96.

Poole, Robert W., and Philip E. Fixler. 1987. Privatization of Public-Sector Services in Practice: Experience and Potential. *Journal of Policy Analysis and Management* 6 (4): 612–25.

Price, Catherine W., and Thomas G. Weyman-Jones. 1996. Malmquist Indices of Productivity Change in the UK Gas Industry before and after Privatization. *Applied Economics* 28 (1): 29–39.

Rivkin, Steven G., Eric A. Hanushek, and John F. Kain. 2000. Teachers, Schools, and Academic Achievement. NBER Working Paper 6691. Cambridge, MA: National Bureau of Economic Research.

Rouse, Cecelia. 1998. Private School Vouchers and Student Achievement: An Evaluation of the Milwaukee Parental Choice Program. *Quarterly Journal of Economics* 113 (2): 553–602.

Rubinovitz, Robert N. 1993. Market Power and Price Increases for Basic Cable Service since Deregulation. *RAND Journal of Economics* 24 (1): 1–18.

Smith, Kevin B. 2003. *The Ideology of Education.* Albany: State University of New York Press.

Spiller, Pablo T., and Carlo G. Cardilli. 1997. The Frontier of Telecommunications Deregulation: Small Countries Leading the Pack. *Journal of Economic Perspectives* 11 (4): 127–38.

Steel, Brent S., and Carolyn Long. 1996. The Use of Agency Forces Versus Contracting Out: Learning the Limits of Privatization. *Public Administration Quarterly* 22 (2): 229–51.

Trebing, Harry M. 2001. New Dimensions of Market Failure in Electricity and Natural Gas Supply. *Journal of Economic Issues* 35 (2): 395–403.

Underwood, Julie K. 1991. The Financial Toll of Choice. *School Administrator* 48 (8):18–19.

Vining, Aidan R., and Steven Globerman. 1998. Contracting-Out Health Care Services: A Conceptual Framework. *Health Policy* 46 (2): 77–96.

Wallsten, Scott J. 2001. An Econometric Analysis of Telecom Competition, Privatization and Regulation in Africa and Latin America. *Journal of Industrial Economics* 49 (1): 1–19.

Weimer, David L., and Aidan R. Vining. 2005. *Policy Analysis: Concepts and Practice.* 4th ed. Upper Saddle River, NJ: Pearson Prentice Hall.

Weisman, Dennis L. 2002. Is There "Hope" for Price Cap Regulation? *Information Economics and Policy* 14 (3): 349–70.

———. 2005. Price Regulation and Quality. *Information Economics and Policy* 17 (2): 165–74.

Williams, Russell L. 1998. Economic Theory and Contracting out for Residential Waste Collection: How "Satisfying" Is It? *Public Productivity and Management Review* 21 (3): 259–71.

Winston, Clifford. 1998. U.S. Industry Adjustment to Economic Deregulation. *Journal of Economic Perspectives* 12 (3): 89–110.

Ying, John S., and Richard T. Shin. 1993. Costly Gains to Breaking Up: LECs and the Baby Bells. *Review of Economics and Statistics* 75 (2): 357–61.

CHAPTER EIGHT

Privatizing the Public European University

• ℰℛ •

CARLO SALERNO

Since the late 1990s, European ministers and policymakers have given considerable attention to how a more unified higher education and research strategy could be constructed to facilitate and strengthen the region's economic stability. The development and maturation of the European Higher Education and Research Areas, the result of a process that has been evolving since the beginning of the Common Market (van der Wende and Huisman, 2004), stands to link thousands of institutions, hundreds of thousands of academic scientists, and millions of students into a more market-like framework that will encourage mobility as well as facilitate the discovery, dissemination, and application of new knowledge.

Yet the path is challenging. On a continent known for its strong public financial support of higher education institutions, exhausted public coffers can no longer provide the funding increases needed to quell the public's growing thirst for advanced education and the economy's dependency on new knowledge. The unique yet disparate academic program structures and internal labor markets that have successfully served European countries' needs for so long are now perceived as serious shortcomings in the more unified European Union (EU). And while universities have long taken pride in their pursuit of basic research, that reputation is now making it frustratingly difficult for the same institutions to seek out and obtain much-needed income from private industry's lucrative, yet largely unexploited markets for application-based research. The consensus is that becoming the "most competitive knowledge-based economy in the world" will require a serious infusion of financial resources to stem the exodus of talented scientists and students to resource-laden and structurally flexible higher education markets such as the United States (European Commission, 2003).

Alarmed by such factors and concerned that the gap between American and European investment in research and development (R&D) is both massive and growing (Conraths and Smidt, 2005), member states find themselves being uneasily pushed into reshaping the traditional European public research university. The widespread introduction of tuition fees on the continent and top-up fees in the United Kingdom have received the bulk of the press coverage, but shifts toward providing higher education institutions with greater fiscal autonomy through block-grant funding or performance-based contracts are also evident (Salerno, 2004). In a sign that the era of generous public subsidies for research are coming to an end, institutions increasingly find themselves under pressure to restructure internally or to form international and interinstitutional "networks of excellence" to increase their likelihood of securing new revenue streams and to compete more effectively for scarce European-wide funding.

The extent that such changes have been driven by competition or fiscal pressures on public budgets obscures the fact that the public European research university has undergone a remarkable degree of privatization over the past 25 years. Although the structures in place, or those in the process of being implemented, can still be regarded as "state-heavy" by American standards it is nevertheless worth exploring how this shift across Europe overlaps with what is occurring in the United States. One can observe similar trends in both "systems"; yet, the academic, social, and cultural fabric supporting the structures in each are remarkably different. This chapter explores the European perspective, with a focus on understanding the parallel happenings in the United States. The public/private distinction can be considered in numerous ways. I will only consider two rather narrow perspectives that are most widely observable: (1) funding and (2) operating autonomy. In documenting the change and exploring the consequences of policymakers' actions, this chapter provides a basis for considering the extent to which Europe's experiences have practical implications for public research universities in the United States.

Changing Modes

European higher education has long been a public undertaking marked by a dual system of state-established classical universities and professional education institutions coupled with a good amount of governmental oversight.[1] The contemporary structure of the German higher education system probably offers the most illustrative example of the historical mode. Higher education providers are subdivided into universities, which, among other things, are the providers of doctoral education and primary conductors of academic research, and professional/technical institutions (*fachhochschulen*), that often provide education in fields similar to the universities but with a more applied and pragmatic focus. Nearly all institutions are public and most facets of their operations are directed by the individual states (*Länder*). Public higher education providers do not own their own buildings nor do they make scientific appointments[2] and funding comes almost exclusively from the state, primarily through detailed line-item budgets based strongly on historical funding levels. That said, Robert C. Lowry's discussion in chapter 3 nicely differentiates between American public and private universities, showing this fundamental structure of the public higher education institution is certainly not a uniquely European characteristic.

Private higher education providers are a relatively new addition to the European landscape. Though a small number boast significant histories (e.g., the private *Grandes Ecoles* in France), most have been established over the past two decades. In general, this wave of European private providers can be characterized by their strong emphasis on offering a select number of professional and postbaccalaureate programs (e.g., MBAs or MScs in computer science). They are more prominent features of the Central and Eastern European countries, especially Poland or the Czech Republic, than of Western Europe—a geographic coincidence of post-Soviet market fervor in the 1990s.

The adoption and implementation of pan-European initiatives such as the Bologna Declaration has contributed greatly to the homogenization of European higher education; yet, an impressive amount of program, governance, and funding variation remains.[3] This variation can be viewed in many ways. A convenient yet illustrative approach to characterizing such system diversity has been to simultaneously position countries along two general dimensions (Jongbloed and Koelman, 2000):

1. The extent to which governments seek to directly manage higher education institutions' operations
2. The extent to which funding is predicated on meeting different objectives

The first is simply a more formal way of clarifying the extent to which authority in the system is centralized or decentralized. In cases marked by low government oversight, institutions maintain the freedom and responsibility to organize and manage their ongoing operations (e.g., universities are more likely to receive unrestricted block-grant appropriations from the state for both research and education activities as well as have the flexibility to reorganize internally, to hire faculty members at market wages, or to set their own tuition fee schedules). As one moves toward centralization, government oversight and regulation intensify—first toward government steering and eventually toward government control. At the extreme, faculty members are civil servants and governments line-item appropriations from large and small capital purchases to individual institution's staff allocations and salaries. Surpluses in any given line item do not usually carry over to other categories; instead, excess funding goes back to the state.

The second dimension considers the criteria on which appropriated funds (or resources in general) are allocated for meeting various goals and objectives. At one extreme, input-based criteria are the norm and their justification is warranted by a perceived need for higher-level planning or the view that output quality is a function of the resources devoted to it. At the other end lie the more recently adopted output- or performance-based criteria, whose rise has paralleled many societies' eagerness to impose more accountability on higher education institutions as prices continue to rise while public budgets shrink. Of course, no institutions really lie at the extremes of either axis, but this provides a useful way to capture graphically broad-based system characteristics in a positional framework. Indeed, as chapter 2 shows, privatization by way of governance decentralization has not been the exclusive domain of European countries' higher education systems nor has the shift from input- to output-based performance measurement.

A visual representation is presented in Figure 8.1. Quadrant one (Q_1) is characterized by systems that generally allocate funding based on annual requests (activity plans or budget proposals) submitted to budgetary authorities. Separate budget items are negotiated between representatives of educational institutions and the relevant funding authorities (i.e., education ministries or national funding councils). Annual changes for any given line item are treated on an institution-by-institution basis and often rely on cost projections, or norms, with respect to unit costs or student places.[4] Typical appropriation categories include staff salaries, material requirements, building maintenance costs, and investment. The German and French systems still retain many of these characteristics.

Quadrant two (Q_2) still captures centralized systems, but the criteria on which resources are allocated are more performance, or "output" oriented and can include measures such as graduation rates or the number of credits (i.e., weighted number of passed courses) accumulated by institutions' students in different academic fields. A good example for this quadrant is Denmark's model or Sweden's funding scheme, which both allocate funds to institutions on the basis of a mix of enrollment numbers and credits earned. The Netherlands also straddles this region as annual appropriations are based, in part, on both the number of first-year students and the number of master's degrees conferred (see Jongbloed and Vossensteyn, 2002). The Research Assessment Exercise conducted in the United Kingdom would also fit here.

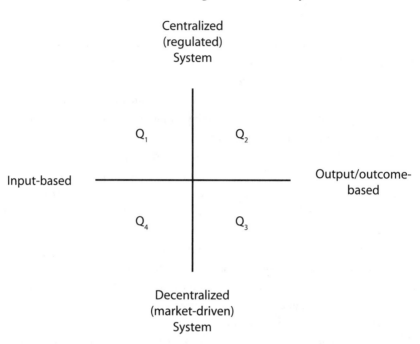

Centralized
(regulated)
System

Q_1 Q_2

Input-based   Output/outcome-
                                                          based

Q_4 Q_3

Decentralized
(market-driven)
System

Figure 8.1. Mapping public funding regimes

Quadrant three (Q_3) characterizes market-oriented systems whose key feature is higher education institutions that essentially compete on price by way of tendering bids to national funding agencies (for public funding) or marketing themselves to consumers on the basis of their past performance (of students and faculty). Competition is encouraged and applies to education and research activities, the latter usually occurring through industry-based applied research. Contracts are established between agencies and higher education institutions who agree to deliver graduates for targeted labor market needs or research outputs targeted at strengthening the innovative capacity of the country. Importantly, institutions do not receive all of the funding in these cases until after they have met the agreed upon criteria. Most European higher education institutions today operate in this quadrant.

The last quadrant (Q_4) is probably the most progressive and characterized by voucher-style funding schemes. Resource allocation is dictated heavily by consumers' preferences, thus institutions have strong incentives to protect the quality of their teaching and course supply because unattractive programs will not receive sufficient funding. Tuition levels may be regulated, but flexible pricing is encouraged to make students pay attention to the quality of the service they get from the higher education institution. The only real difference between research here and in

Q_3 is the greater emphasis on basic research. Where education activities are concerned, no European higher education systems currently fit squarely in this quadrant, although the growing importance of national research councils means that all of the systems probably operate here when it comes to basic research.

As a rule, the general trend in Europe over the past 25 years has been for systems' education activities to move in a clockwise fashion from Q_1 to Q_3 and research activities to move in a counterclockwise motion from Q_1 to Q_4. In the early 1980s, for example, the Dutch collapsed more than 300 vocational schools into 85 *hogescholen*, partly to infuse greater competition into the system by offering students a practical alternative to enrolling in one of the traditional universities. The United Kingdom took a different route in 1992 when it granted all of its polytechnic institutions (the former second tier) university status, partly to increase competition, while the Higher Education Funding Council for England funding formula gradually came to include more performance-based criterion. More recently, a number of German *länder* have begun shifting to a lump-sum funding model and the use of performance criterion. In 2006, Estonia completed a new systemwide strategy proposal that encourages more private funding and changes the current mode of input-oriented financing into one based on multiyear performance contracts. In terms of research, most systems have pulled a significant portion of basic research funding out of the institutions' annual appropriations and instead increased national research councils' annual budgets so that funding is more competitively allocated. Moreover, public calls for "socially relevant" research coupled with reduced public funding have driven a continent-wide push to embrace the industry-oriented research that is typical of Q_3 (more on this later).

The balance between public and private funding is a useful if crude barometer for the extent to which universities privatize; yet, reliable comparative statistics are rather difficult to come by. The limited data available from the Organization for Economic Cooperation and Development (OECD, 2005) probably offers the best quantitative information to highlight this balance and the changes that have occurred in recent years. The trend among European OECD countries is that private financing (as a percentage of expenditures for tertiary education) has become more important for both the more prominent countries such as Germany, the Netherlands, Italy, and the United Kingdom, and for less prominent ones as well (i.e., Denmark, Hungary, Portugal, and Austria). That said, the OECD reports that private outlays still represent less than a third of systemwide expenditures.[5] Furthermore, some countries, such as the Czech Republic and Ireland, have sizable amounts of public funding that runs counter to this general trend.

European higher education still has a public character. Indeed, as a percentage of gross domestic product, U.S. private expenditures alone exceed the private expenditures of Belgium, the Czech Republic, France, Germany, Hungary, Ireland, Italy, the Netherlands, Norway, Poland, the Slovak Republic, Spain, Sweden, and the United Kingdom combined. Such a discrepancy has prompted the European Commission to support ambitious EU-wide research investment objectives.[6]

Aggregate American figures of this nature are deceptively simplistic. Desire for prestige coupled with institutions' abilities to leverage their existing wealth (Geiger, 2004) has allowed a small group of about 250 private liberal arts colleges, private research universities, and public state flagship universities to command the bulk of the impressively large private resource pool and successfully exploit it. The thousands of remaining American public higher education institutions rely almost exclusively on limited state support, homegrown student populations, and small-scale, regionally financed research: a model not so different from the typical European university. This more balanced picture of the "typical" American public research university would suggest it is not unreasonable to build a claim that American and European providers are more similar in the makeup of their resource pools and the competitive arenas in which they operate than most generally believe.

The Face of Privatization

Most scholars agree that European countries' adoption of policies to promote greater competition and their willingness to grant their public universities broader operating autonomy have worked to create a more responsive and less state-dependent higher education structure. Next, I look in greater detail at three particular facets of funding and the changes that, for better or for worse, have come to symbolize the new face of the public European research university.

Tuition Fees

Arguably, the most visible example of privatization has been the introduction of tuition fees. Historically, European higher education has been free with the exception of students paying token union or activity fees. This has changed dramatically in the past 15 years. As a rule, most countries now maintain elaborately structured tuition schedules that differentiate between undergraduate, graduate, foreign, and part-time students as well as those who study beyond their program's nominal time period. On the whole, undergraduate fees remain low by American standards: usually around €200 to €600 per year and only in rare instances do they exceed €1,000. The main exceptions are the United Kingdom, which at one extreme has recently introduced top-up fees that can push the cost up to €4,000 per year, and at the other extreme, the Scandinavian countries, which charge no tuition to either domestic or foreign students. EU countries are required by law to charge students from other EU countries resident tuition rates, but all are essentially free to set their own fee schedules for postgraduate education programs, which can exceed €10,000 per year for MBA courses in particular. In some countries, such as Estonia, government-subsidized students pay no tuition, but those enrolling in remaining slots at public universities pay at levels consistent with non-EU citizens or graduate students.

Although the introduction of tuition has increased private contributions to higher education, its implementation has drawn serious criticism from institutional leaders. Charging flat tuition fees across all programs (and in some cases even across institution types) has been the preferred solution to date, but on balance, it is inequitable and provides a classic example of a government failure (Wolf, 1993). Generous subsidies students in costly programs receive over other students provide no readily apparent economic benefit, nor do they help redress socioeconomic inequities or market imbalances. They are simply a benefit allotted to those students who happen to enroll in more costly courses.[7]

If one abides by the mantra that "he who benefits, pays," then the equitable solution is to charge students in costlier programs some premium so that the ratio of public to private contributions more accurately reflects the distribution of public and private benefits to higher education. In practical terms, this means introducing top-up fees, which is what Nicholas Barr (1993, 2003) has long argued for in the case of the United Kingdom. Allowing fees to vary encourages competition and efficiency by forcing education providers to offer the best education for the lowest cost. And given how difficult it is to value a good whose benefits do not accrue until long after it is consumed, differential pricing also provides prospective students with valuable information about the quality of what is being purchased. Provided that (1) the financial aid is there to make education consumption costless at the point of use and (2) loan recovery schemes spread repayments out both over time and under differing financial circumstances, two things Barr rightfully argues are also necessary, then top-up fees have many advantages, not the least of which is that they ensure that detrimental cross-subsidization practices do not occur.

On the one hand, the public backlash from introducing top-up fees in the United Kingdom, the one system in Europe well accustomed to substantive tuition fees, is a sobering reminder of how Europeans' economic and political views of equity still clash. On the other hand, it also demonstrates how well-intentioned policies can fall short when economic and political concerns conflict in a zero-sum game. When all was said and done, the economic solution in the United Kingdom debate prevailed, but instead of giving universities free rein to set their own fees, the political solution, built on ill-founded fears about harming access, drove the government to cap the increases. Critics expressed worry that, while revenue may increase, competition and efficiency would be stifled because all institutions would simply raise the fees to the capped level. As it turned out, the fears proved to be warranted: all but three United Kingdom universities raised their fees up to the caps. Had institutions been given a free hand to set their own fees, the more tiered structure that was originally envisaged would have emerged. If tuition fees buy access rights and opportunities, then lower-quality institutions (based on resources) would not have been able to successfully match the price increases put in place by the more internationally prestigious universities.[8] Raising tuition always engenders concerns about access but as stated, provided that the funding for anyone seeking an education is available and repayment is not overly burdensome, the cost of an education is remarkably cheap.[9] Although the available evidence shows enrollment declines in the first year following a tuition hike, research also consistently shows that over time higher education enrollments eventually surpass the pre-increase levels (Vossensteyn, 2005).

On a more abstract level, growing interinstitutional competition coupled with the greater reliance on tuition as a revenue source runs the risk of compromising public mission in favor of securing greater institutional prestige. If, as many believe, tuition is an important market signal of institutional quality and prospective students are willing to pay for obtaining a degree from (what they believe to be) a more prestigious institution, the effect will be for institutions to both raise prices and to seek out applicants from a much larger market (Hoxby, 1997). As growing competition induces greater prestige differentiation and possibly greater admissions selectivity, one can expect that taxpayers in some countries will increasingly find themselves publicly subsidizing institutions that they cannot attend.

Privatization through greater private household investment in higher education would appear to offer a logical short-run solution to European universities' fiscal problems. The absence of tuition, or very low rates coupled with generous public subsidies, has long been characteristic of many European countries' higher education systems. Yet the desire to maintain this vestige of the past while aggressively pursuing the development of a more market-oriented system is at odds with the growing volume of research on how tuition policies shape the market for higher education students (Winston, 1999). Arguments about education as a public good or rising costs harming access have lost much of their luster in the wake of research that shows the inelastic demand for higher education (see Vossensteyn, 2005, or

Salerno, 2004, for literature surveys) or the successful adoption and implementation of tuition fees in highly reputable systems such as the United Kingdom or the Netherlands.

Of course, culture and tradition concerns must be accounted for, but arguments along this line fail to account for the unprecedented growth in demand for higher education. Europe's traditional model of a public higher education system financed entirely by the public purse has long fitted nicely with its views on social welfare; yet, perversely, recent history has shown that it was only tenable when it served an elite few. The fiscal crisis facing many European systems today is ironically linked to the rise of mass higher education, the progressive march toward universal higher education, and the general unwillingness to adopt policies with politically adverse consequences.

Private Philanthropy

Procuring private funding through fundraising is a strategy that has only really begun to take hold in the United Kingdom and in a scattered group of recently established private higher education institutions (across Europe) that have been founded on the American model. Unfortunately, data on European universities' endowments is not systematically collected so much of what is available is anecdotal.

It is not surprising that public European universities have gradually migrated to this kind of revenue stream. In light of continued fiscal belt tightening in many EU countries, such gifts possess at least three desirable qualities: (1) they do not require further contributions from taxpayers or education and research consumers; (2) endowment income (and even in drastic cases the principal) can be used as a buffer against declines in public funding; and (3) targeted gifts can strengthen individual programs when internal allocations are neither feasible nor incremental. The establishment of development offices is a nascent, albeit rapidly expanding facet of the public European university's periphery (Labi, 2004). Yet of all the different ways in which Europe can feasibly reach out for private support, this is probably the one that will require the longest investment period and lowest payoff, at least in the short to medium term.

The difficulties Europe faces in securing such private revenue streams are embodied in Bruce Johnstone's (2004) four pillars on which the Americans' success with philanthropy lies: (1) donative wealth, (2) favorable tax regulations, (3) strong internal university support, and (4) a culture of giving. First, American capitalism has done much to create the wealth imbalance that produces the superrich from which many of the world's most famous foundations have been formed: from Ford,

Rockefeller, Carnegie, Kellogg, and Mellon at the turn of the twentieth century, to Hewlett, Packard, Ellison, and Gates at the turn of the twenty-first century. Though Europe has its own stock of such individuals, the pool is much smaller because of the stronger social welfare system in most European countries. Second, as Johnstone points out, "the income tax deductibility of philanthropic contributions, the full deductibility of appreciated capital gains, and other features of the United States tax code as it affects philanthropy provides, in effect, a substantial governmental contribution—almost a *match*—to philanthropic giving" (Johnstone, 2004, 4). Europe, however, is constrained, particularly in terms of cross-border philanthropy, by complicated laws and regulations that make giving a costly undertaking (King Baudouin Foundation, 2005). For example, from a tax perspective, it is difficult for an Italian philanthropist to realize tax benefits from making a contribution to a Belgian university. Third, social traditions that are simply not present in European higher education institutions have played a strong role in American universities' abilities to secure alumni contributions, the largest percentage of voluntary support (Koning, 2006). Intercollegiate athletics and on-campus living at American universities, two facets that until recently have been absent from the European institutional structure, have done much to create institutional "sagas" (Clark, 1970) that tie students to their institutions long after they graduate and which alumni foundations or development offices exploit when encouraging charitable giving.

The growing emphasis on philanthropy is changing the internal structure of the European research university.[10] Many universities have begun establishing honors colleges where students live on-campus in close-knit communities that encourage both academic and social bonding. Development offices have expanded, and there has been a growing push to both "brand" universities as well as foster alumni networks. At the same time, branding has not only become formalized and centralized in key support structures but integrated with other areas. One recently completed study of members of the European Consortium of Innovative Universities found that development offices were coordinating closely with patent and licensing offices to exploit the advertising benefits of commercial research. In the end, the dedication to establishing and strengthening university fundraising is probably best exemplified in the Council for the Advancement and Support of Education's decision to open a European office in London.

In some instances, it is possible to identify excellent examples of fostering what can be termed "smart" periphery growth. Linköping University in Sweden staffs its university grants office with doctoral students as a way to jointly provide capacity and on-the-job training. Strathclyde University in Scotland finances its development office by ensuring that it receives a core appropriation but forces the unit to rely in part on its own income generation. This works to mitigate "administrative bloat" by tying any expansion to the office's work volume. Aalborg University in Denmark has consolidated its development, technology transfer, and information transfer into one unit: basically, in recognition of the high degree of overlap between each unit's prospective target groups and the synergies between each one's operations (i.e., local industry as both philanthropic investors and potential partners in technology transfer activities). These approaches and changes indicate how European universities' support offices are expanding in the face of declining public financial support, but the consensus is that efforts are still in the most preliminary stages. The idea that one must spend money to bring in money is a fundamental tenet of development, one that is, for the most part, against European cultural instinct and thus still largely overlooked.

Basic and Applied Research

On a pan-European level, little disagreement about the perceived shortcomings in the way European basic science is funded remains. Access to project funding from national research councils is often closed to foreign scientists, and academics' mobility is still largely restricted (Musselin, 2004). There is also little coherence between national and pan-European research programs, and thus macro-inefficiencies exist in the form of program duplication. The current mode of EU funding (Framework Programs) has a lengthy process, which makes it difficult to adjust research priorities to changing needs in the short run (European Science Foundation, 2003), but it also requires multicountry research teams. European concerns about the imbalance these factors create are warranted as they have larger economic consequences, particularly when one considers the boost university research has on local and regional economies.[11] It also obscures the possibility that the best science may be done within a single nation (even institution) or with possibly just one partnering country.

It is not off the mark to suggest that some type of pan-European identity and common goals will be necessary for Europe to successfully establish its grand Research Area. The recent establishment of the European Research Council (ERC) and the support for such a body from trans-European organizations such as the European University Association and European Science Foundation is a step in the right direction toward fostering common goals. But the ERC's form is a step backward for fostering a pan-European identity, mainly because it seeks to make the organization's funding role *complementary* to the problematic existing structure of national research councils (European Science Foundation, 2003). The exclusion of foreign scientists from applying for research monies hurts the quality of the science conducted, and while there is greater coordination today between national councils' funding priorities, as long as the money is considered Dutch, Italian, or Lithuanian, then national priorities will always win out and mediocre academic units will persist. Keeping national research councils, and thus national funding streams, intact will continue to hinder macro-efficiency because no country wants to subsidize pan-European competition that turns their most prestigious universities into second-class institutions, even if long-run gains exceed short-run losses.

Competition may produce hierarchies and wealth imbalances, two aspects that Europe would much like to avoid (European University Association, 2003), but as the American experience shows, it also works to ensure that resources are allocated efficiently and that the most capable scientists are doing the research. Though the system in the United States is noted for its institutional hierarchy, institutions' exhaustion of scale economies (Geiger and Feller, 1995), preferences for engaging in different types of research, consolidation and specialization, and the development of new research areas have all worked to flatten the structure somewhat, even in the face of competitively allocated federal funding.[12] It remains to be seen whether a system of national science councils can be maintained in a larger European framework or whether European science in general will suffer.

Universities have long enjoyed generous basic subsidies but are now finding such a source to be a dwindling supply of steady income. A key aspect of refinancing the public European research university has been this shift toward more funding distributed competitively through national research councils rather than as direct appropriations. The outlier is the United Kingdom's long-running Research Assessment Exercise (the next and last round is scheduled for 2008), which was originally intended to allocate more efficiently block research funding to the academic units in the best position to do the highest-quality research.

One major consequence of greater competition for research funding in general has been widespread restructuring, particularly through the consolidation of academic units or the establishment of "centers for excellence." Many European universities have come to believe that this route is necessary if they are to strongly compete not only for the expanding share of EU funding distributed through the Framework Programs but also for the lucrative market for industry-based contract research. One recent set of studies, which examined more than 100 European higher education institutions' research income portfolios (Lepori et al., 2005; Salerno et al., 2005), found that most institutions believed that their private revenue streams, at the least, had not declined in the past 10 years. In fact, many suggested they had increased substantially and given rise to a host of now familiar terms: commercialization of research, sale of educational activities, regional development, venture capital invest-ment, and the establishment of separate institutes. These trends are summarized by country in table 8.1.

In the face of declining public funding, European policymakers have increasingly encouraged such activities (Mowery and Sampat, 2005) because they foster innova-tion and regional economic development. Universities, however, have found that greater international competition for such funding also demands new incentive structures that encourage private income generation, such as allowing units to keep part of their own income, creating performance-based funding structures that re-ward research productivity, and offering funding premiums for income generation.

Interestingly, although most respondents in the study believed that government funding had declined and had been supplanted by new income sources, an analysis of the available financial data showed government funding as a percentage of total institutional revenues to be remarkably stable between 1995 and 2004 (in real terms). When asked about international funding, most respondents indicated that EU-funding had increased substantially, while funding from other international sources had increased only slightly or remained stable. An overwhelming majority of the survey respondents also indicated that their primary motivation for pursuing struc-tural changes was the implementation of national and state government policies as opposed to factors such as changes in disciplinary structures, the importance of EU policies, or private industry concerns. Although royalty income has not yet become an important component to a more diversified funding base, institutions identified that such activities are, for the moment, still critical if only for the purpose of fostering networks and institutional reputation.

Europe's industry stakeholders still remain reluctant participants in light of high tax rates and a longstanding public perception of European universities as bastions of basic research. What is more, the diverse modes of higher education financing in different EU countries do little to provide institutions in some systems with the incentives to seek out such forms of financial support. In large European countries, where the older social model of classical universities receiving a significant amount of basic research funding from the state still prevails (e.g., France, Portugal, or Italy), there are few incentives for universities to seek out links with private industry. ‑

Calls for further investment highlight the problem but do not offer solutions. If we accept industry's longstanding reluctance to exploit university research in favor of other sources (Cohen et al., 2002), and the polarized expectations of both partners,[13] then developing such linkages will require considerable effort, not from industry but from the universities and, more specifically, their faculty members.[14] This is not to

TABLE 8.1.
Key Changes Made to European Universities' Research Infrastructure

Czech Republic
- New research centers/labs consultation centers
- Introducing responsibility-centered budgeting
- Establishing an internal grant agency
- Creating support units for (contract) research

Denmark
- Merging and restructuring departments
- Creating focus areas
- Creating research centers and cross-disciplinary research teams
- Creating support units to aid grant applications
- Implementing research evaluations

France
- Closing/merging departments/units
- Establishing new research units, e.g., in transdisciplinary areas
- Implementing research evaluations
- Thematic priorities selected (institutes established)
- Grouping together researchers

Hungary
- Establishing new faculties and multidisciplinary research centers
- Creating alliances with industrial partners
- Creating support offices for research grant applications
- Strengthening Ph.D. training

Italy
- Establishing support units/research offices for income generation
- Establishing an industrial liaison office
- Establishing new research units, excellence centers
- Multidisciplinary and multithematic research
- Merging departments

Netherlands
- Merging faculties
- New research institutes and knowledge centers (often interdisciplinary)
- New planning and control cycle (steering approach)
- Cooperation with regional partners
- Introduction of research schools
- Introduction of performance-based funding (internally)

Norway
- Introducing contract research support agency
- Establishing research schools
- Identifying thematic areas for research (in research centers)
- Creating interdisciplinary research units
- Simplifying organizational structure
- Increase of research activity in Hogescholen

TABLE 8.1.
Continued

Spain
- Introducing new research centers/institutes
- Interdisciplinary research
- Support research services
- Merging research groups
- Science Park; center for technology transfer created
- Introduction of performance-based funding

Switzerland
- New research centers (interfaculty centers, interdisciplinary centers)
- Tech transfer office; research support unit
- Identifying research priorities; research competence centers
- Introducing position of a pro-rector for research
- Decentralization
- Reorganization; merger
- Collaboration with external partners

United Kingdom
- Reorganization (into larger schools/faculties)
- Technology transfer
- Research centers established (in areas of research strength)
- Central research administrative support unit (research enterprise services)
- Devolvement of responsibility to faculties
- Appointing deans of research in faculties
- Incentives for researchers

Note: The notion that such an incentive structure would not work in Europe would have to explain why so many European scientists train and then choose to find employment in the American system.

say that European industry-university partnerships are in dire straits. Germany, for example, has largely retained its model of providing universities with large amounts of state funding for research while at the same time its percentage of industry-financed higher education R&D (HERD), at 10%, exceeds that in the United States and the rest of Europe. Small, relatively wealthy countries such as the Netherlands, Finland, and Slovenia, which could feasibly support their universities with state-allocated research funding, maintain higher percentages of HERD than the United States (Conraths and Smidt, 2005). The problem is how Europe as a whole can procure the greater investment it seeks. In the United States, low levels of state-allocated basic research funding, the ostracizing effect of tenure denial, and the extremely competitive nature of securing competitively allocated federal research funding have all worked in tandem to provide the incentives or pressures on faculty members and their universities (particularly in engineering and the biosciences) to consciously seek out private revenue sources.

Conclusion

The analysis and presentation here is purposefully crude. Issues such as financial aid, which I have skirted over, and the many nuanced aspects of each funding source that are addressed in the vast literature on the topic are left unaddressed in favor of considering the more general questions of how European experience can better inform American research and policymaking. As the European Higher Education and Research Areas continue to develop, more detailed comparisons and analyses will surely follow.

In many ways, Europe and the United States represent two ends of a spectrum based on market versus state coordination, and it would seem that the two are gradually converging on each other. Although the intense competition, consumerism, and high tuition of the American system may not be desirable from a European perspective, it does much to explain the reputation it has for producing world-class education and research. Indeed, it is the path that Europe is gradually adopting. At the same time, one can see that the hierarchies in the American system have gradually flattened; policies at both the state and federal level are increasingly focusing the university's role as an engine for regional economic growth. Therefore, the effect over time has been to distribute wealth and capacity far more evenly than before.

What the European case highlights is the implications of moving beyond the ill-defined threshold that separates higher education systems governed by markets and by states. The problem is a mismatch between structures and goals, which, when viewed in the abstract, lends added support to Lowry's points in his chapter about how feasible solutions arise to incomplete contracts that are based on divergent preferences. Efforts to maintain a high degree of social equity while simultaneously incorporating more market-like features into the higher education structure are, as the examples in this chapter highlight, not necessarily doomed to failure but are certainly difficult to achieve. At some point, public universities under the auspices of a state in a larger federal framework must accept the implicit trade-off that comes with having a state-mandated public purpose and internal ambitions that can only be satisfied through market competition. Privatization efforts are, in effect, embracing the latter but, ironically, at the behest of state-level policies.

In the end, the American public research university has enjoyed the historical good fortune of originating and growing up in a federal system where tuition fees have long been the norm, and citizens are eager to support public missions through philanthropy. From both a fiscal and institutional autonomy perspective, practice makes perfect, and time has given American public universities the opportunity to not only adapt but also to change continuously in the face of political, economic, and social shocks. This flexibility has served American higher education rather well in the past as a crucial component to building the country's economic infrastructure, and today endows American universities with a competitive advantage as global integration stands poised to reshape higher education in the coming years. If imitation is indeed the sincerest form of flattery, then casual observation would suggest that developing, transitional, and modern economies have more to learn from the American experience than the other way around.

That said, it is a long-held belief that the scale and scope of private higher education in the United States has done much to shape the behavior of its public peers. Although this may be true, the European experience provides much evidence to support the idea that the fiscal privatization of a public higher education sector can be, and is, fostered in the absence of direct competition from elite private providers. From a theoretical perspective, if there is a more general explanation behind growing privatization of public research universities, it may lie in the confluence of a rising-cost industry, products/services that are difficult to characterize but increasingly more valuable to an ever-expanding audience, and the delicate balance between what society would like to support and what it can feasibly afford.

NOTES

1. The two technical exceptions to this "public undertaking" notion are the cases of the United Kingdom and the Netherlands. In the United Kingdom, institutions are privately owned corporations, but their relationship with and dependency on the state effectively drives them to behave like publics. In the Netherlands, alongside the public institutions are a small number of church-established universities and a large number of private *hogescholen.* However, Dutch law mandates that the state treat both public and private providers equally. As such, over time the Dutch have taken instead to distinguishing between the "publicly funded system" and the nonfunded system (the latter essentially including small trade schools).

2. An institution can identify potential candidates, but these must then be forwarded to the state where the education ministry makes the final hiring decision.

3. Higher education providers in most countries have continued to offer their traditional degree courses alongside the new bachelor's/master's structure.

4. In practice, the various line-item budgets are often based on the previous year's allocation.

5. OECD statistics distinguish between private household and commercial expenditures, but disaggregated figures are only available for a limited set of countries.

6. See, for example, (1) *Investing Efficiently in Education and Training: An Imperative for Europe*, Communication from the European Commission, COM (2002), 779 of 10.1.2003a. (2) *The Role of the Universities in the Europe of Knowledge*, Communication from the European Commission, COM (2003b), 58 of 5.2.2003. (3) *More Research for Europe: Towards 3% of GDP*, Communication from the European Commission, 2002.

7. If anything, these subsidies are counterproductive from an access standpoint because the available research shows that students from disadvantaged backgrounds are less likely to enroll in math- and science-intensive courses. In addition, private returns to education in the physical and biological sciences are often higher than from courses in the humanities and social sciences, which means that not only do students in these fields pay less toward their education in relative terms, but they also get a better return on their investment in the long run. Where tuition fees represent a marginal contribution to a system's gross education resources such a practice may be tolerated, but when tuition fees rise and start to involve a larger percentage of the overall resource pie, the profit skimmed off low-cost programs comes more and more from the students' pockets and not the state's.

8. World-class institutions such as Oxford and Cambridge would have raised their prices to levels consistent with places like Harvard and Yale, their international peers. While most students accepted to these institutions would pay such a rate, it is highly unlikely that former polytechnics could charge students such a fee without a serious decline in enrollments.

9. The reluctance to take up student loans for a higher education is a curious one. Researchers estimate that individuals with a bachelor's degree earn roughly €800,000 or more over their working careers that individuals with just a secondary education. Even at a price tag of €25,000 for a bachelor's education, spreading the payments out over 30 years would make for an annual payment of €1,000, which comes to about €84 per month or €21 per week: basically the same amount that an individual spends on a week's worth of lunches. Most of us will at some point in our lives purchase a new automobile for the same price, yet pay it off in four or five years and maybe drive it for up to 10 years before having to replace it.

10. I recently completed an internal study for the European Consortium of Innovative Universities in which I looked at the changing role of centralized support services as they relate to advancing universities innovative capacities. The discussion that follows is based on that unpublished work.

11. The gap between the resource-rich countries in northwestern Europe and Scandinavia and the rest of the EU as well as greater competition for research funding will eventually drive academic scientists in the eastern and southeastern parts of Europe west, dampening the economic prosperity that many Central, Eastern, and Southern European states expected to enjoy from EU membership.

12. One can look to the EPSCoR program, which was first implemented by the National Science Foundation in the early 1980s and rapidly adopted by other federal departments, as an example of policies designed to promote distributional equity.

13. As Hall (2001) points out, in a survey of some 400 industry-university partnerships conducted by Lee (1996), industry participants indicated their top reasons for collaborating with universities were (1) access to new research, (2) development of new products, (3) maintaining a relationship with the university, (4) obtaining new patents, and (5) solving technical problems. In stark contrast, the top two priorities for university participants were (1) obtaining funds for research assistance, laboratory equipment, and their personal research agendas and (2) being able to field test theory and empirical research.

14. In the American case, relatively low levels of basic research funding from the states (embedded in annual appropriations) provides one incentive for universities to seek out and

maintain industry-university partnerships. Another is more rigid tenure and promotion standards. The notion of "publish" or perish is certainly important, but in practice, securing external funding is probably more important to successful tenure bids, even at the least-selective public universities.

REFERENCES

Barr, Nicholas. 1993. Alternative Funding Resources for Higher Education. *Economic Journal* 103 (418): 718–28.

———. 2003. Financing Higher Education in the UK: The 2003 White Paper. Post-16 Student Support Sessional Paper, 2002–3. House of Commons Education and Skills Committee, March.

Clark, Burton R. 1970. *The Distinctive College: Antioch, Reed, and Swarthmore.* Chicago: Aldine Publishing.

Cohen, Wesley M., Richard R. Nelson, and John P. Walsh. 2002. Links and Impacts: The Influence of Public Research on Industrial R&D. *Management Science* 48 (1): 1–23.

Commission of the European Communities. 2003. *The Role of the Universities in the Europe of Knowledge.* Brussels: Communication from the Commission.

———. 2002a. *Investing Efficiently in Education and Training: An Imperative for Europe.* Brussels: Communication from the Commission.

———. 2002b. *More Research for Europe: Towards 3% of GDP.* Brussels: Communication from the Commission.

———. 2000. *Towards a European Research Area.* Brussels: Communication from the Commission.

Conraths, Bernadette, and Hanne Smidt. 2005. *The Funding of University-Based Research and Innovation in Europe.* Brussels: European University Association.

European Science Foundation. 2003. New Structures for the Support of High-Quality Research in Europe. April, www.esf.org/publication/159/ercpositionpaper.pdf.

European University Association. 2003. EUA Policy Paper Concerning the Establishment of a European Research Council. July, www.eua.be.

Geiger, Roger L. 2004. *Knowledge and Money: Research Universities and the Paradox of the Marketplace.* Stanford, CA: Stanford University Press.

Geiger, Roger L., and Irwin Feller. 1995. The Dispersion of Academic Research in the 1980s. *Journal of Higher Education* 66:336–60.

Hall, Bronwyn H. 2001. University-Industry Research Partnerships and Intellectual Property. Paper presented at the National Science Foundation—CISTP Workshop, Washington DC, October.

Hoxby, Caroline M. 1997. How the Changing Market Structure of U.S. Higher Education Explains College Tuition. Working Paper 6326. National Bureau of Economic Research, Cambridge, MA.

Johnstone, D. B. 2004. University Revenue Diversification through Philanthropy: International Perspectives. Keynote Address Given at the 17th International Conference on Higher Education, Luxembourg, August 27.

Jongbloed, Ben, and Jos Koelman. 2000. *Vouchers for Higher Education? A Survey of the Litera-*

ture. Study Commissioned by the Hong Kong University Grants Committee, CHEPS, Enschede.

Jongbloed, Ben, and Hans Vossensteyn. 2002. Financiering Masters: Argumenten en Arrangementen [Funding Masters: Arguments and Arrangement]. Studie in opdracht van de Werkgroep Financiering Masters. Ministerie van OC&W.

King Baudouin Foundation. 2005. Current State of Cross-Border Philanthropy in Europe, www.givingineurope.org.

Koning, W. K. B. 2006. The Case of the University of Amsterdam: First Friendraising Then Fundraising; Involving Alumni in the Fundraising Strategy. Presentation given at the EAU Workshop on Fundraising for European Universities: Exploring Options. Istanbul Technical University, February 17–18.

Labi, Aisha. 2004. Chasing the Money: As Government Purse Strings Tighten, Universities Embark on American-Style Fund-Raising Campaigns. *Chronicle of Higher Education* (April 30): A29.

Lee, Yong S. 1996. Technology Transfer and the Research University: A Search for the Boundaries of University-Industry Collaboration. *Research Policy* 25: 843–63.

Lepori, Benedetto, Martin Benninghoff, Ben W. A. Jongbloed, Calro S. Salerno, and Stig Slipsaeter. 2005. *Changing Patterns of Higher Education Funding: Evidence from CHINC Countries.* Report for IPTS-funded *Changes in University Incomes* study. Lugano: Servizio ricerca USI-SUPSI, Università della Svizzera italiana.

Mowery, David C., and Bhaven N. Sampat. 2005. The Bayh-Dole Act of 1980 and University-Industry Technology Transfer: A Model for Other OECD Governments? *Journal of Technology Transfer* 30 (1/2): 115–27.

Musselin, Christine. 2004. Towards a European Academic Labour Market? Some Lessons Drawn from Empirical Studies on Academic Mobility. *Higher Education* 48 (1): 55–78.

OECD. 2005. *Education at a Glance 2005.* OECD: Paris.

Salerno, Carol S. 2004. Rapid Expansion and Extensive Deregulation: The Development of Markets for Higher Education in the Netherlands. In *Markets in Higher Education: Rhetoric or Reality?* ed. Pedro Teixera, Ben Jongbloed, David Dill, and Alberto Amaral, 271–90. Kluwer: Dordrecht.

Salerno, Carol S., Ben W. A. Jongbloed, Stig Slipsaeter, and Benedetto Lepori. 2005. *Changes in European Higher Education Institutions' Research Income, Structures, and Strategies.* Report for IPTS-funded *Changes in University Incomes* study. Enschede: Center for Higher Education Policy Studies (CHEPS), University of Twente.

Vossensteyn, J. J. (Hans). 2005. *Perceptions of Student Price-Responsiveness.* Enschede: Center for Higher Education Policy Studies (CHEPS), University of Twente.

Wende, Marijk van der, and Jeroen Huisman. 2004. "Europe." In *On Cooperation and Competition: National and European Policies for the Internationalization of Higher Education,* ed. Anneke Luijten-Lun, Marijk van der Wende, and Jeroen Huisman, 19–49. Bonn: Lemmens.

Winston, Gordon C. 1999. Subsidies, Hierarchy, and Peers: The Awkward Economics of Higher Education. *Journal of Economic Perspectives* 13:13–36.

Wolf, Charles. 1993. *Markets or Governments: Choosing between Imperfect Alternatives.* Cambridge, MA: MIT Press.

CHAPTER NINE

Toward a Clearer Understanding
of Privatization

• ∽ •

PETER D. ECKEL AND CHRISTOPHER C. MORPHEW

The trend toward privatization in higher education is clearly accelerating, as evidenced in both the scholarly and popular presses. It remains unclear whether governments cannot, or choose not to, provide sufficient resources to public postsecondary education, but intelligence points to a myriad of possible points of contention. For instance, the subprime mortgage crisis, downturns on Wall Street, declining state tax bases, and other recently emerging trends suggest little relief is in sight. Furthermore, higher education and the states most likely won't be relieved by other long-term fiscal pressures. K–12 education and Medicare are frequently factors behind funding shortages. State policy continues to encourage competition not only with private institutions but also with other public institutions on a mounting set of issues. For example, Ohio created a program in which its public institutions compete for a $150 million pot of research funding (Richards, 2007). Institutions continue to compete for students and their tuition dollars, particularly those students who have the means to pay or to use their state-based merit dollars. The competition for students will be especially acute in states, such as Colorado, that have adopted a voucher-style funding structure. Tuition and vouchers, not state block grants, have become an increasingly important source of revenue for some public research universities. States too are recognizing the funding problem and realize that if they cannot provide the resources for their institutions, they should allow them the autonomy and flexibility to set and keep their tuition and to compete for students, investments, and faculty with little state intervention.

What seemed like science fiction only a few years ago is now a familiar (albeit not well-accepted) part of the higher education landscape. Consider the following examples:

- A member of a statewide commission in Virginia suggests inviting a private institution from another state to set up a branch campus to meet the state's projected high-tech needs. This proposed campus would be a neighbor to a growing public, four-year university, competing directly with it for students, faculty, and research support.
- Miami University in Ohio doubles the price of its in-state tuition to "allow it the same pricing flexibility as its private university competitors."
- The most prestigious universities in Virginia seek legislation to become "state-assisted charter universities" under which they would accept limited state aid and, in exchange, receive freedom from many state policies and regulations.
- The governor of South Carolina offers to let any public institution become private because, "given the unusually high number of colleges and . . . and the scarce dollars with which we've got to fund all of them, this is a way to give certain schools the flexibility they want, while saving the state money at the same time" (Eckel, Couturier, and Luu, 2005).

While these examples are a limited set within a highly complex and differentiated higher education system, they nonetheless are remarkable in their demonstration of how the rules governing higher education are being rewritten. They are the real-life examples that the models, propositions, and arguments in the preceding chapters address. What they have in common is the element of the market: each example demonstrates a state's willingness to allow (or some might say push) its universities into the competitive marketplace.

The footprints of privatization are clearly recognizable, not only in the chapters here but also throughout the landscape of higher education in the United States and elsewhere. Its contours are consistent: (1) increased reliance on private dollars to supplement insufficient public investment, (2) changes in oversight to alleviate cumbersome regulation, and (3) an increasing reliance on market mechanisms. Even though the authors in this volume adopted definitions that closely reflected these dimensions, their approaches, and, interestingly enough, the questions they pursued varied greatly. This was intentional. The book sought multiple lenses through which to understand privatization because, while not overly complex by definition, it is conceptually ambiguous and highly involved. Only through multiple perspectives can we begin to understand why, how, and with what potential effects privatization has and may have on public higher education.

A Collective Understanding

As the book demonstrates, privatization is a nuanced phenomenon, and one that can and must be understood from a variety of vantage points. Key insights into privatization readily appear when the chapters are taken as a whole. They surface from commonalities across the different approaches, divergences that distinct frameworks naturally suggest, and, interesting enough, from points not said.

Points of Convergence

Some important intersections exist throughout the chapters. First, positive externalities need to be factored into discussions of privatizing public higher education. The consistent message by the various authors that addressed it, regardless of framework, was that understanding the effect of privatization on higher education required more than acknowledging its primary effect on individual or sets of students. Broader societal, economic, cultural, social, and civic benefits must be factored into any equations that attempt to measure or to define the value of postsecondary education and its institutions. Although higher education is very much a value proposition to students and their families, it offers much more to the larger communities and society. This point cannot be lost or even downplayed in public policy discussions.

Second, access and affordability are primary factors in discussing privatization. Closely linked to these ideas are the questions of who pays, how much, and why. As states consider where and how to make their investments, what will the effect be on low-income students? How can states best meet their public policy objectives of expanding access, particularly for disadvantaged students? A serious consideration of privatization cannot take place without considering its effects on the growing numbers of potential students for whom cost is often a primary hurdle to access.

Third, potential trade-offs for decision makers exist in discussions of privatization, particularly for those leaders responsible for formulating policy and trying to lead their campuses in this dynamic, if not confusing, age. The trade-offs examined throughout this book not only focus on who pays, but the elasticity of demand given funding approaches and policy constraints, the values and detriments of increased competition, and the degree of influence and control states may have (or lose) over institutional strategy and direction. Privatization has direct and indirect consequences that must be factored into discussions about it.

Finally, trends in privatization may make it more difficult for states to meet traditional public policy objectives. More precisely, the loosening of state control and substantially fewer public dollars mean that public higher education most likely will have more masters rather than fewer, and public officials will be one of many constituents seeking to exert influence over what were once very public universities. Existing steering mechanisms have less influence and instead of a single source (public policy/funding), institutions are responding to numerous drivers, political, social, and particularly economic that may pull higher education in competing directions. Ultimately, privatization may be about exchanging one set of controls for another, and institutions and policymakers may not like the direction in which public higher education is steered.

Different Starting Points

Consistency and consensus were not the objective of this book. Instead, the differences surfaced by the approaches in this book may be more illuminating than the similarities. The different starting points of each inquiry are insightful and point to key issues that demand further attention from higher education scholars, campus leaders, and policymakers. Authors identified a striking range of entries into the privatization conversation. Although we asked authors to write from a different conceptual framework, we didn't anticipate the variety of the questions they would pursue. For instance, Michael K. McLendon, Christine G. Mohker, and Carlo Salerno asked context-based questions:

- Chapter 2: What are the drivers shaping state-policy privatization, and what are the sources of these drivers? What trends in allocating resources and proposing new policy initiatives do these drivers create? What do we know empirically about the trends?
- Chapter 8: How are the fiscal pressures on public budgets shifting across Europe and what effects is this having on European universities? What is changing and with what consequences, with a particular emphasis on funding and operating autonomy? What are the practical implications of trends in Europe for public research universities in the United States?

Robert Toutkoushian; Peter D. Eckel and Christopher C. Morphew; Gabriel Kaplan; and Mark Stater ask questions relevant to particular (and different) actors in the privatization debate.

- Chapter 4: How have decision makers justified public subsidies for higher education, and what factors might account for the decline in state funding over time? What options can states use to support higher education, and what are the costs and benefits of these alternatives? What are the costs and benefits of state support for higher education from the perspective of taxpayers? Why are institutions concerned with their mix of revenues, holding constant the level of total revenues?

- Chapter 6: What should the public role in governance, be given trends in decreased funding? What are the appropriate ownership forms and governing relationships that should exist in the public higher education sector? What are the benefits of privatization (as predicted by theory)? What are the drawbacks (as predicted by theory)?
- Chapter 7: What lessons about privatizing higher education can be learned from the experiences of other formerly public agencies and from existing private institutions?
- Chapter 5: What are the predicted effects of privatization on the decision-making processes of public research universities? How might the organized anarchy and garbage can decision making familiar to these types of institutions be altered by privatization?

In chapter 3, Robert C. Lowry poses deeply fundamental questions about the very purpose and nature of public higher education:

- Why do all 50 states and the District of Columbia have universities that are publicly owned and subsidized universities rather than some alternative arrangement supporting higher education? What are the advantages of the prevailing arrangements, and what concerns would state government officials have when considering proposed changes to the status quo? What are the advantages of public ownership of universities over a system where the state purchases research and other public services from private universities and supports students through vouchers or scholarships?

Because the questions start at different points, the discussions followed different trajectories. Thus, the richness of this book is not a convergence but a divergence that mirrors the complexity of the issue. No simple solution or easy understanding exists. Together, the insights and conclusions help paint a broad picture of privatizing public higher education.

The Unspoken Agreements

What is unsaid across these chapters is also powerful. First, none of the authors questioned privatization as a phenomenon affecting higher education. Wide consensus emerged that public higher education was facing the trilogy of decreased public support, increased market forces, and a distancing from public control. Together, these create a powerful force with the potential to reshape higher education in the United States and elsewhere. Second, no one makes a case that privatization is the consciously made policy answer to the nation's postsecondary concerns (in response to Ikenberry's query in the opening chapter). Rather, it is the seeming result of actions addressing other concerns and in response to limitations—a type of possible policy drift—rather than intentional strategy or objective. Third, the diversity of institutional types and missions important to American higher education (and increasingly important to European higher education) may be increasingly under threat. Privatization may undermine this strength by pushing public institutions to be much more like their private brethren or force institutions with different missions and strengths to pursue similar strategies in pursuit of revenue as institutions follow the lead of the successful ones (Frank and Cook, 1995). The diversity of U.S. higher education has served the nation well. Will this be lost, given the issues addressed throughout this book? Last, no expectations exist for recapturing the earlier glory days of a well-funded public higher education system. Public universities most likely will not see the favoritism and resources (and growth) that followed World War II and continued through the 1960s—we simply live in a different world.

Pieces of the Privatization Puzzle

Taken as a set, these chapters provide the foundation on which to make inferences about higher education's future. They contain the pieces of an emerging puzzle about the privatization of public higher education that can begin to be assembled. When fully constructed, that puzzle may reveal the answers to a number of key policy concerns, several of which are discussed next.

Competition, Potentially Unchecked

Privatization means that it may be increasingly important for larger numbers of institutions to compete vigorously for funding, and they will have both the incentive and the political freedom to do so. On their own, institutions may pursue strategies that best advantage themselves: the recruitment of students with merit aid; the agreements they enter into with corporations regarding research and intellectual property; the types of degree programs they offer; the amenities they build; or the faculty they recruit. The potential danger exists at a collective level. For example, recruiting talented students through merit aid helps an institution compete, but when most institutions are leveraging their aid dollars this way, it does little to expand access. The arms race in amenities provides further negative examples.

Institutions may invest in ways that do not advance their public purposes but instead are driven by a sense of competition. Columbia University spent an estimated $18 million on its failed online effort Fathom that tried to capture the distance learning market (Arone, 2002). That investment represents money that may have gone a long way to support other more socially relevant efforts. Another extreme is the way Texas institutions are competing for students with one another through amenities:

> The competition for students and recognition is fierce in Texas. . . . The new distinction [of the tallest climbing wall at the student recreation center] will help separate [the University of Texas at San Antonio] from the rest of the pack. The wall . . . beats out [the University of] Houston's wall by one measly foot. That should sound familiar to Houston officials. Two years ago they built their climbing wall to be exactly one foot taller than the one at Baylor University. (McComack, 2005)

Furthermore, competition unchecked has the potential to put new drivers behind the institutional steering wheel. Students and their families (as consumers wielding large tuition checks) may gain significant influence over institutional priorities. The degree programs students want, the curriculum they think they need, the amenities they seek (including higher and higher climbing walls), and the convenience they demand may be hard to deny, particularly given the potential threat to enroll elsewhere. Some institution somewhere will be willing to meet their demands regardless of how far afield they may be. Concurrently, corporations willing to support institutional ambitions may demand (or be allowed) greater influence over institutional agendas, relating directly to their investments and potentially more broadly. For example, BP has awarded the University of California at Berkeley, the University of Illinois at Urbana-Champaign, and the Lawrence Berkeley National Laboratory a $500 million grant for research on alternative energy sources that would give BP the ability to capitalize on research breakthroughs. Berkeley is the same institution that entered into the controversial five-year, $25 million deal with Novartis that involved most of the plant sciences department and allowed the company first rights to negotiate licenses on inventions by faculty members who participated in the agreement, even if the work had been supported by other funds.

Growing Disparities and Increased Homogenization

Not all institutions are the same. This differentiation has long been a comparative strength of American higher education. Different types of institutions serve different populations of students in different ways (and at different price points). No other nation has the diversity of institutions as the United States; however, this diversity means that some institutions are better equipped to play by the new rules of privatization than others. Those institutions best positioned to benefit will likely be the diversified, entrepreneurial universities that already have a reputation and track record of financial success. These institutions will have a range of available revenue streams to tap and offer a variety of degrees across the spectrum of fields and disciplines to respond to changing market needs of students and employers. In addition, they have well-developed auxiliary services and the means to commercialize research. A small subset of institutions with specialized missions or niche reputations may buck this trend, but they will most likely be few in number. The flip side of this argument, of course, is that not all public institutions fit into one of these two descriptions, particularly tuition-dependent, undergraduate-focused regional colleges. They too must play by the same rules regarding financial self-sufficiency and policy autonomy as new public policies emerge and the role of the state declines. The higher education sector may well see a further stratification of institutions by wealth. In turn, institutions on the losing end may not have the resources or the protection of well-meaning public policy to maintain their quality. Since these colleges and universities tend to enroll larger proportions of students who may benefit most from a higher education (i.e., underrepresented students), downturns in quality at these institutions has potential tremendous social consequences.

Concurrently, and conversely, more institutions may work feverishly to become more like one another. They will see what the successful institutions, which often are more prestigious and already wealthy institutions, are doing and try to imitate them. Because organizational success in higher education is complex and difficult to understand, institutions will look to mimic others regardless of their own strengths, capacities, and starting points (Meyer, Deal, and Scott 1981; Morphew, 2002). U.S. higher education may witness a common organizational model begin to emerge as institutions learn what works (and what is rewarded) in the new privatized environment. At risk is differentiation as well as waste in a system as institutions pursue the same strategies, which in turn simply cancel out the various investments. Does American higher education (or society) really need another executive MBA program?

Limiting Access

Privatization has the clear potential to undermine access and affordability. For example, between 1995–96 and 2005–6, tuition and fees increased in constant dollars at public four-year universities from $3,564 to $5,491 (College Board, 2007). Given the discussion throughout the book, trends toward privatization seem to suggest that such increases will only grow more rapidly. Students from disadvantaged backgrounds will continue to struggle to afford college. Furthermore, potential students in the pipeline may begin to think that college, or any postsecondary education, is financially out of their reach and thus may not lay the foundation of success in high school. Simultaneously, privatization may push more colleges and universities to compete for those best able to pay for the full cost of their higher education (see chapter 7, for example).

Tensions in Quality

Privatization elevates a different type of quality than historically advanced through public policy, which creates tension. Quality in the public policy arena has notably focused on outputs: how well students learn or the extent to which they contribute as informed citizens after graduation. From this perspective, quality often focuses on undergraduate education and the preparation for civic, vocational, and intellectual participation. It also encompasses the service activities institutions in addressing pressing social needs, such as K–12 education, poverty, or health care. However, the notion of quality in a privatized (and competitive) environment is different. For example, quality is measured as input, for example, on SAT scores, class rank, the number of National Merit Scholars, and, even, the number of volumes in the library.[1] In addition, quality becomes associated with graduate and professional education (although it may not leave undergraduate education behind). It is about the number of graduate students and the range of graduate degree programs— advanced and specialized learning—not foundational education or deliberative democracy. Furthermore, privatized quality stresses the research dimensions of higher education. It is about the status and credentials of "star" faculty, who may or may not teach undergraduates or the ability of an institution to attract external support— government and corporate—for research. Finally, it is about regional economic development: that is, how well and to what extent has higher education applied its strengths to solve economic problems or to make the region more competitive? Although these two notions of quality are not complete opposites they have some important inconsistencies that may have significant social impact as institutions choose where to spend their scare resources and time.

Conclusion: Where Next?

This book has covered much ground. It has explored, dissected, and explained many aspects of privatization from numerous vantage points. However, the ideas suggest many questions. In fact, many of the authors pose important questions that need to be addressed. For instance:

- Is privatization simply a shorthand description of the diminished will and capacity of state government, or does the concept suggest a broader, deeper transformation?

- How do the shifting political contexts of the states and the political process by which public policy for higher education is formulated shape privatization trends?

- How might researchers empirically show decision makers why they should reallocate funds for public higher education? (Simply listing potential externalities is a poor substitute for empirically based estimates of the social benefits.)

- What empirical research might support or challenge the idea that privatization will lead to more anarchy and less organization for campus decision makers?

- How will market segmentation and mission differentiation effect and be effected by privatization?

- How do states develop fiscal and governance approaches that, as Kaplan asked in chapter 6, "walk the thin line between instituting price controls and simply establishing bodies that record citizen commentary"?

- If privatization is going to be a long-term reality for public higher education, what are the likely effects of privatization, particularly the unintended consequences?

- What are the trade-offs of efficiency / effectiveness / public purpose in privatization? What tools might be helpful for decision makers to understand the potential effect of their approaches?

Privatization is a topic growing in importance and supported by an expanding research and theoretical underpinning. The debate is far from over, however, and must be informed by theories from many disciplinary perspectives. Too many complex discussions on the surface are about funding and oversight, but in reality, they get to the heart of public higher education and need to be treated as such. Privatization is truly about higher education's ability to provide access and to ensure social mobility, its ability to deliver on unmet state needs, its growing role in the exploding knowledge economy, and its ability to be a social conservator. These discussions need to be treated with the weight they deserve.

NOTE

1. Ironically, measuring the quality of higher educations using these inputs is exactly what many critics of higher education, including those in government agencies, have been arguing against.

REFERENCES

Arone, M. 2002. Columbia Senate Questions Spending on Fathom. *Chronicle of Higher Education.* A41, http://chronicle.com/weekly/v48/i35/35a04102.htm.

College Board. 2006. *Trends in Student Aid.* Washington, DC: College Board.

Eckel, Peter D., Lara Couturier, and Dao T. Luu. 2005. Peering around the Bend: The Leadership Challenges of Privatization, Accountability, and Market-Based State Policy. Paper 4 in The Changing Relationship between States and Their Institutions Series. Washington, DC: American Council on Education.

Frank, Robert H., and Phillip J. Cook. 1995. *The Winner-Take-All Society.* New York: Penguin Books, 1995.

McCormick, E. 2005. A Battle of Inches. *Chronicle of Higher Education* 51 (33): A6.

Meyer, J. W., W. R. Scott, and T. E. Deal. 1981. Institutional and Technical Sources of Organizational Structure: Explaining the Structure of Educational Organizations. In *Organization and the Human Services*, ed. H. D. Stein, 151–78. Philadelphia: Temple University Press.

Morphew, Christopher C. 2002. "A Rose by Any Other Name": Which Colleges Become Universities. *Review of Higher Education* 25 (2): 207–23.

Richards, Jennifer Smith. 2007. Schools Drool over $150 Million in Grants. *Columbus Dispatch*, www.dispatch.com/live/content/local_news/stories/2007/12/02/stem_schools .ART_ART_12-02-07_B1_7H8L7D0.html?sid=101.

PETER D. ECKEL is director, Programs and Initiatives in the American Council on Education's Center for Effective Leadership. His portfolio includes programs that focus on leadership and governance, including the ACE Institute for New Chief Academic Officers and the presidential roundtable series. His latest book is *The Shifting Frontiers of Academic Decision Making* and his research appears in many of the leading peer-reviewed higher education journals and ACE occasional paper series. He received his Ph.D. in Education Policy, Planning, and Administration from the University of Maryland, College Park.

STANLEY O. IKENBERRY is regent professor at the University of Illinois and former president from 1979 to 1995. He holds appointments in the College of Education, the Institute for Government and Public Affairs, and co-directs the Forum on the Future of Public Education. From 1996 to 2001, he led the American Council on Education as president and chief executive officer. A fellow of the American Academy of Arts and Sciences, he is past chairman of the board of the Carnegie Foundation for the Advancement of Teaching and currently serves as president of the Board of Overseers of TIAA-CREF. Ikenberry earned a B.A. degree from Shepherd University and an M.A. and Ph.D. from Michigan State University.

GABRIEL KAPLAN has been director of the Epidemiology, Planning, and Evaluation Branch in the Prevention Services Division at the Colorado Department of Public Health and Environment and a research associate at the Center for Education Policy Analysis at the University of Colorado, Denver since October of 2007. From 2002 to 2007, he was assistant professor of public policy at the School of Public Affairs at the University of Colorado. His research focuses on higher education policy, health policy, and K–12 education policy, with a particular focus on the role of governance and organizational form on policy outcomes and performance.

ROBERT C. LOWRY is professor of political science in the School of Economic, Political, and Policy Sciences at the University of Texas at Dallas. He earned his Ph.D. in political economy and government from Harvard University. His scholarly work has appeared in numerous peer-reviewed journals, including *American Political Science Review, American Journal of Political Science*, the *Journal of Politics, Economics of Education Review, Economics of Governance*, and *State Politics and Policy Quarterly*. In addition to the political economy of higher education, his other research interests include state fiscal policy, interest groups and civil society, and campaign finance and political parties.

MICHAEL K. MCLENDON is associate professor of Public Policy and Higher Education at Peabody College, Vanderbilt University, where he chairs the Program in Higher Education Leadership and Policy. He studies state governance, finance, and politics of higher education. McLendon serves as an associate editor of *Higher Education: Handbook of Theory and Research*, as consulting editor to *Research in Higher Education*, and as a member of the editorial board of *Review of Higher Education*. He holds a Ph.D. in Higher Education Policy from the University of Michigan.

CHRISTINE G. MOKHER is a research analyst with CNA Corporation, Alexandria, Virginia. Mokher holds a Ph.D. in higher education from Vanderbilt University and a master's degree in education administration and policy from Harvard University. Her research focuses on P–20 education policy and on postsecondary policy and finance.

CHRISTOPHER C. MORPHEW is associate professor at the Institute for Higher Education at the University of Georgia. He studies state higher education systems and issues related to institutional diversity. His work has appeared in many journals, including *The Review of Higher Education*, the *Journal of Higher Education*, and *Higher Education*. He earned his Ph.D. from Stanford University.

CARLO SALERNO is a senior analyst with the U.S. Government Accountability Office where he conducts research related to general higher education finance, federal student aid, and university cost/productivity issues. Before GAO, he was a senior associate with the Center for Higher Education Policy Studies in the Netherlands, where he worked on a range of education finance projects for international education organizations, including the Organization for Economic Co-operation and Development and Council of Europe and consulted for various European and African higher education ministries. He earned his Ph.D. in higher education, with a concentration in economics, from the Pennsylvania State University and holds a bachelor's degree in economics from Eastern Michigan University. He currently resides in the Washington, DC, area.

MARK STATER is assistant professor of economics at Trinity College in Hartford, Connecticut. His research interests include labor economics, public economics, and urban and regional economics. He has previously published articles in *Economic Inquiry and Policy Sciences*. Other articles are forthcoming in the *Review of Regional Studies* and the *Economics of Education Review*.

ROBERT TOUTKOUSHIAN is associate professor of Educational Leadership and Policy Studies and coordinator of the Educational Leadership program at Indiana University. He received his Ph.D. in economics, with a specialization in econometrics from Indiana University and teaches courses in education finance, economic dimensions of education, and quantitative methods. Toutkoushian currently serves as the editor-in-chief for the journal *New Directions for Institutional Research* and is on the editorial board for *Research in Higher Education*. He has published over 40 studies in peer-reviewed journals and edited volumes, with most of these publications relying on quantitative analyses of education data. He currently directs a research team that provides analyses for the state of Indiana on its school funding formula and consults with legislators and representatives from state agencies on a wide range of school funding issues.

Page numbers in italics indicate figures and tables.